www.united-pc.eu

A Tramp for all Oceans

Anecdotes of the Far East and beyond sailing under the Red Duster from Apprentice to Captain

By
Geoffrey Walker

Author's Synopsis

The author arrived in Hong Kong at a very early age and spent the majority of his life living and working there. Childhood recollections of the early years growing up in Hong Kong, friends and experiences mentioned in this book are as accurate as memory permits. The content is generally correct throughout and is a mere snapshot based on the writer's lifelong and seagoing experiences. Some terms used are of a bygone era but common during the period depicted in the book.

"A Tramp for all Oceans" is in two parts. Part one covers the early years the author spent in Hong Kong then as an Indentured Apprentice Navigating Officer in the British Merchant Navy, whilst part two "East of Pulau Weh" describes the years spent as a Captain, loosely based on his real life experiences.

The Book focuses on the Author's anecdotes in Africa, India, Asia and Oceania, where he spent many adventurous years tramping the various sea routes whilst serving as Apprentice through to Master, calling at small and large ports alike. Some of the ports were little more than clearings in the jungle, up rivers that were only just navigable or not even marked on an Admiralty Chart.

The book captivates the last of an era, when ships all possessed their own particular "heart and character" and were crewed by what may be affectionately referred to as a "different breed" of seafarer. Light reading is the objective so technical terms used in the shipping industry have been avoided or kept to a minimum wherever possible.

The author has now retired from an active seagoing occupation and resides in Australia. He maintains a close personal and cultural association with his beloved Asia, in particular Hong Kong.

The painting illustrated on the cover of this book is from his private collection of original paintings by the renowned British Maritime Artist, Tony Westmore to whom acknowledgement is made.

Sincere appreciation to fellow Mariner and former Hong Kong resident, Karsten Petersen, for permission to include a number of his stunning photographs in this book. He like me was fortunate enough to witness the end of a shipping era in the Far East. For the very best in photography, I suggest a visit to his site (www.global-mariner.com)

Other Photography contained within, some of which dates back more than 50 years, are from various unknown or long forgotten sources. Notwithstanding long hours of research, any copyrights that may exist and that have been omitted or overlooked are hereby respectfully acknowledged, with no infringement intended.

Disclaimer

I have attempted to recreate events, locations and conversations as best my memory permits. In order to maintain privacy and anonymity in some cases I have changed the names of individuals and places, I also changed some identifying characteristics and details such as physical properties, occupations and places of residence whilst I have attempted to maintain authenticity throughout.

Geoffrey Walker
Melbourne,
December, 2018

A Tramp for all Oceans

By Geoffrey Walker
Copyright © 2018 Geoffrey Walker

In memory of my time spent at

King George V School – Hong Kong

Honestas Ante Honores

and

HMS Conway Merchant Navy Cadet School

Llanfairpwllgwyngyllgogerychwyrndrobwllllantysiliogogogoch

Commonly abbreviated to:- Llanfair PG

Index

Part One

Part Two

East of Pulau Weh
(Approximately 5 50.2 N   95 17.7 E)

This book is dedicated to "Tin Hau" – an ancient Chinese Goddess of the Sea

Worth remembering:-

"Any man who would be fully employed should procure a ship or woman, for no two things on this earth produce more trouble if not handled properly".

Plautus: ca 254-184 BCE

1 The Beginning – China Bound

Born in England towards the end of WW2, growing up and life thereafter has been one continuous adventure for me. Although having achieved no major accolades in life, I do, nevertheless believe I have been fortunate enough to have seen more than most in my lifetime thus far, for which I am eternally grateful.

At a very young age, I along with my family left Liverpool and relocated to Hong Kong – my father being a Telecommunications Engineer and my mother an English teacher.

My recollection of all my adventures stem from one cold, rainy January morning when a taxi rolled up at our home in Liverpool to take us to the city bus depot and the comfort of a quite luxurious motor coach which would take us on the long ride to Southampton. There we were to join the P and O liner "Canton" that would be our home for the next month during our passage to Hong Kong.

Most of the trip by road is vague but once having arrived at Southampton I am blessed with absolute clarity. My young eyes feasted upon the majestic gleaming white steamer sporting a creamy yellow funnel and masts, which would be my playground for the next 30 days.

My father, being a senior executive, was privileged to first class travel so we all boarded the "Canton" and settled into our accommodations. My parents occupied an impressive suite on one of the upper decks, complete with large seaward facing window, quality fittings and facilities and of course ensuite. The décor was very tasteful and on a par with at least a five star hotel. My younger brother and I occupied an adjoining double cabin, also very luxurious, well appointed and complete with two tier bunk beds. Being the elder I insisted on the upper bunk, naturally.

The interior of the First Class decks was very plush. Teak veneered bulkheads, highly buffed linoleum tiles on the decks, numerous brass fittings all polished to perfection and everywhere lingered that sweet odor reminiscent of a mix of disinfectant and furniture polish. The public rooms and dining areas were equally impressive. Spotless white linen tablecloths spread upon round tables, silver service and stewards immaculately turned out to cater for ones every wish. Food was endless with enormous choices which included a never ending buffet in addition to a la carte menus. Everything down to the last detail was very well presented.

Outside, the wooden decks were holystoned white, paintwork in the passenger areas was kept like new and the wooden and brass hand rails varnished and gleaming.

The entire ship was an absolute picture and although not new by any means was obviously well maintained.

Eventually we cast off amid crowds of well wishers and as the passenger liner gained headway I recall watching the other ships tied up at the various wharves slip past, as we headed serenely down Southampton water towards the Solent (waterway between the Isle of Wight and UK mainland). The weather was very cold, overcast with drizzle and I remember wondering to myself when I would return. I must admit at that impressionable young age it was all a bit bewildering for me and at the time I didn't realize the significance this departure from English shores would play in my future life. Nevertheless, we soon settled in on board.

For the first few days at sea life was miserable, until we cleared the Bay of Biscay. Continuous seasickness affected most passengers and was very unpleasant but lifted as soon as we approached the coast of Portugal at which time the sea lost most of its vengeance resulting in the ship's motion becoming more stable. The sky turned from overcast to blue and the sun shone brilliantly. At this point life on board quickly took a turn for the better. The only one of us that had been unaffected by seasickness was my father, he being ex RN with exploits on the "Kelly", "Dido", "Zest", "Cowslip", etc., during the fateful war years. I hold vivid memories of Mom and Dad dressing formally for dinner every evening, long hours in the swimming pool, movies, deck games and most importantly endless ice creams, served on the boat deck, morning and afternoon. It was just like a huge holiday camp with ship's staff doing all they could to make life as pleasurable as possible. For the adults and those with an inclination towards gambling there was even a ship's tote, whereby the passenger who came closest to selecting the exact distance the vessel had steamed during the previous 24 hour period received a cash prize. My parents won it once.

One of my most interesting memories early in the voyage goes back to when we had just passed Gibraltar, by this time I guess we had been on board about a week. One evening, I was asleep in my upper bunk, whilst my mother and father were at dinner. Suddenly something startled me and I awoke abruptly. The cabin adjoining ours was a single and occupied by an attractive young lady schoolteacher bound for Singapore. Being in the upper bunk I could hear faint voices and giggles coming from a ventilator outlet close to the deck head. By standing on the bunk I could just reach it with my ear. Naturally, I did so being an inquisitive youngster. I immediately recognized the voice of the female lady passenger and that of "Danny" our cabin steward. Danny must have been in his early twenties and an amiable young man. Having satisfied my curiosity, I thought no more of this and just went back to sleep.

The next morning, I innocently said to Danny "What were you doing in that lady's cabin last night". His face went a paler shade of pink and I earned a stern glare, but I did receive his immediate response – "if you and your brother don't mention this to anyone, you can come to the pantry every afternoon at 3 pm and have as many cakes and as much ice cream as you like"! This was the proverbial carrot and my brother and I exploited this invitation to the maximum for the duration of the voyage, despite my mother's objections. It was not until years later that I realized Danny's motives for such generosity!

Captured during the 1950s, **RMS "Canton"** berthed at Kowloon Wharf. She was always a picture of elegance right up to her demise. For her day she was sleek and serene ocean liner and operated a monthly service between Southampton and Hong Kong. She was a very popular vessel amongst the expats on which to travel, more so than other P&O vessels plying the route around that time such as "Corfu" and "Carthage" which were a tad older and smaller.

As a young student at KJS, we had a day excursion to the **"Canton"** which was berthed at Kowloon Wharf as usual. I was allocated the task of hoisting the school flag up the foremast to signify our presence on board and then retrieving it once our visit was over. The afternoon tea provided to us pupils and accompanying teachers was memorable – needless to say we made absolute gluttons of ourselves and the ice cream was still just as good as ever.

She was sold for demolition at Hong Kong in October 1962 following some 24 years service and a sorrowful farewell to a fine ship. Her memories linger on with me.

Photograph courtesy of P&O Lines Postcard Collection

RMS Canton - Ship's postcard showing various aspects of the ship's handsome interior.

Typical First Class Cabin with adjoining Bath Room, similar to that of my parents' beautifully appointed and oozing comfort. The double berth cabin used by my brother and I was immediately adjacent through a connecting door, family friendly arrangement.

The First Class, Verandah Café. This was great meeting place and the source of my numerous daily ice cream(s).

Once **"Canton"** was scrapped in 1962, the **"Chusan"** assumed the role as most popular ship on the Far East route. By the mid1970s air travel had taken over and the beautiful white passenger liners became less frequent more engaged in cruising rather than regular passenger services to the Far East.

Suez Canal and Indian Ocean

We transited the Mediterranean Sea heading eastward. Our first stop was at Port Said in Egypt, and transit through the Suez Canal. It was a one day adventure because this was my first experience of being in a foreign country. Hitherto, my only exposure to foreigners had been the occasional Asian salesman who came to our front door peddling household items from a suitcase – whenever they came I would run and hide under the kitchen table, absolutely petrified.

We tied up to a jetty somewhere, I guess for bunkers and stores, and to wait the designated time for the southbound convoy to transit the canal. We stayed there most of the day and of course there were the usual 'Bum Boats', alongside with their occupants peddling their wares. Bartering with hawkers hoping to sell those terrible stuffed camels, leather stools and turquoise trinkets of various assortments made time pass quickly. One excitement for me was the young urchins that dived to recover coins thrown overboard into the water by passengers. The kids would dive then break surface with the coin firmly gripped between their teeth. For a youngster like me, never having been further than the Mersey Docks, this was marvelous entertainment, as was the "Gili Gili" man with his tricks. However, I was still very cautious of the natives and it took me some time to really feel at ease even though I stuck to my parents like wool on a sheep's back.

I saw my first camel during the canal transit, several of them in fact, all gaping aimlessly at our ship as we passed by. Even at that young age they struck me as being rather dumb looking creatures.

Our passage through to the Gulf of Aqaba was otherwise uneventful except I recall, everyone by now had changed into tropical rig, namely, tropical evening dress for passengers and crispy white uniforms for the officers and crew. By this point in time the voyage had taken on a different perspective. People had forged friendships and life was much more informal, with most being on first name terms at least. Drinking sessions at the Verandah Café or Lido Bar, cards, deck games and competitions were commonplace within the various groups.

Not to be outdone, I met my first girl friend – puppy love I guess. Her name was Alison, and she was on her way to India with her family. She had a terrible younger brother named Simon who delighted in teasing us! We went everywhere together and I was very sad when she eventually left the ship. I missed her pig tails.

Obviously, by this time the vessel had its fair share of somewhat more serious romances and affairs. There were the usual twosomes who never separated or parted company until disembarkation. They were very conspicuous, morning, noon and night. One evening, my brother and I were wandering the boat deck under the watchful guidance of the folks. I received a serious reprimand from my father for annoying a young romancing couple who were really quite oblivious to happenings around them, they being very preoccupied. I do not recall seeing this couple thereafter; I think we frightened them off and they may have sought a more private venue. I believe they disembarked at Bombay. However, other couples were like beacons, being in the same old fixed position, night after night. This activity and presence seemed to dwindle as the voyage progressed, perhaps because flourishing romances had taken a more serious turn which demanded more discrete surroundings.

The climate was, by this juncture starting to change quite dramatically. Long hot and quite humid days, passing squalls and the odd rough patch – seasick again! The passage between Suez and Bombay was the longest stretch of the voyage. The days did not drag because there was always enough to keep one occupied, however it did start to wear a bit thin. The same cannot be said for the ongoing supply of ice cream and chocolate cakes, éclairs and other delights we received from the pantry with daily regularity….even my mother was starting to become suspicious of the amounts being consumed and went to pay a visit to Danny the cabin steward, to investigate from where we were getting all the goodies. She must have received adequate assurances because it did not have any impact on our daily consumption.

Gateway to India

At long last Bombay and the gateway to India. First impression was dusty, dirty and smelly with a sort of heat haze that was so thick it lingered above like an umbrella, most of the day. The crowding was immediately imprinted on my brain and was only rivaled by what I encountered in China, years later. The ship was alongside the wharf at some dock complex, still there were hundreds of urchins milling about and begging. Security guards clad in khaki uniforms each with a long cane had little success in keeping them at bay and the wharf had its share of mangy "Pani Dogs" all scavenging about in packs, yelping and annoying passersby. The air one breathed seemed heavy, rather like taking a gulp of steam from a steam engine as it passes by when standing on a station platform as one is momentarily engulfed in steam or funnel fumes!

My father had been in India during his seagoing years and did venture to alert us two boys as to what we may expect, prior to our arrival. Nevertheless being so young we were not prepared for our encounters. At that age I was shocked to see the level of 'undress" by many of the local workers called "coolies", milling about wharf side. Just clad in a simple loin cloth in most cases. Needless to say we did not take the opportunity to go ashore whilst in Bombay but instead spent most of the day looking at the hawkers and their wares, who had been allowed on to one of the promenade decks, to set up small stalls, obviously under the close scrutiny of the ship's staff. We bought and bartered and bargained, well at least my parents did. I can't remember what they purchased but figure it was more a case of buying for the sake of it, mainly to pass the time and belay the boredom.

I have to say, at a very young age my parents always tried to educate we brothers as to the "outside" world and how it ticked! For this I am eternally grateful as it prepared me for later life, especially when I embarked on a seagoing career myself.

We sailed from Bombay early evening with cheering crowds and a large brass band which could not resist playing "Rule Britannia" and other classic marching tunes – all very nostalgic and so much for my first snapshot of India, still coming to grips with nationhood following its recently acquired independence from Great Britain. During my subsequent sea going ventures in later life I had occasion to visit India on numerous occasions and discovered what a wonderful country India really is once past the crowds and squalled exterior. What diverse cultures the Indian people enjoy within their democracy.

The ship headed on a southerly course along the west coast of India but the pungent aromas and odors of the sub-continent still drifted seaward– even though we were miles offshore. These heady airs remained with us for several days at least, until we approached what was then called Ceylon (modern day Sri Lanka). Our Port call at Colombo was very brief, only about 6 or 8 hours, I assume for fuel and other consumables. Having departed Colombo, it was back to the usual shipboard routine until arrival at our next destination, Penang.

The sector from Bombay to Penang interrupted only by our short call of only a few hours at Colombo was particularly depressing for me, since I no longer had my "friend" Alison on board as she had disembarked at Bombay. She had been my constant companion. I did not even establish her family name, but I sure missed her company. In retrospect I do feel she was of perhaps mixed blood as she was a little dusky in appearance, very pretty, eyes like chocolate drops and spoke with a definite "plumb" reminiscent of most colonials of that era. In addition to which, she was very sophisticated for her age and always ultra polite to my parents

South East Asia

Penang is a small island laying a short distance off the Malayan peninsular in the Andaman Sea. It is in sharp contrast to the sub continent, very different indeed – far more lush, tranquil and extremely beautiful and picturesque; a true tropical delight. Our family went ashore for sightseeing and a long walk through its bustling and historic township, which took up most of the day during which I discovered the delight of drinking chilled coconut milk straight from the coconut husk, ideal for quenching ones thirst in the heat of the tropical day. My father let my brother and I try some local dishes, amongst which were Satays on wooden skewers which was very novel to us, but enjoying them immensely nevertheless, along with a mild curry served delicately on Banana leaves. This was a new experience to us both.

I was struck by the island's outstanding scenic beauty, very friendly people and I clearly recall seeing many wonderful colonial style villas set in exquisitely landscaped and manicured gardens (still my envy of today), palm groves, Kampongs and the odd Monkey, mostly kept as pets on long chains. Our stay was all too short and soon after our return on board ship it quickly became time for our departure. We sailed early evening and as we all stood on deck the sun was dipping over the horizon, making for one of those wonderful sunsets for which the Andaman Sea is so renowned. We were southbound for Singapore.

The passage from Penang to Singapore through the Malacca Straits was relatively short and I believe we arrived in Singapore sometime late the following day.

Singapore, what a marvel – initial impression of arriving there was so exciting for a young kid. This was my first real inkling of the Orient. The hustle and bustle of Singapore Island instantly aroused my interest, even being so young at the time. Looking back I now realize what a lasting impression my first trip to Asia on the majestic "Canton" was registering upon me. It endorses the significance of how much one's overall education is gained from outside the class room.

My dear parents had some distant friends who resided in Singapore so next day we joined them for lunch at the Raffles Hotel, even then a splendid Singapore icon. Following luncheon we took a conducted tour of the island (approximately the same size of the Isle of Wight). How different it was then compared to the Singapore of today. Most local residents usually lived in two story shop houses above their place of work and I clearly recall all the wide storm water drains and Nullahs that paralleled the streets. At that time I could not envisage living and working in the Far East as was to be the case later in life.

The place itself has expanded rapidly and is in fact remains one of the jewels of the Orient. Under the inspired leadership and guidance of modern Singapore's late founding father and mentor, Mr. Lee Kuan Yew, the people of Singapore have managed to maintain their own style of culture and sophistication, having achieved a level of development which is the envy of many regional countries. At the time of my first visit however, Singapore was still part of the fledgling Malayan Federation. It was a wonderful place and a real eye opener. The town and surrounds consisting of the two or three story shop houses, narrow streets (save for the main roads) was mostly one big China Town with a lesser number of Kampongs. It had its share of beautiful colonial residences discreetly situated amongst the most beautiful and scenic surrounds. The few high rise buildings were concentrated on the waterfront and central business areas. There remained a significant British military presence at this time and soldiers and sailors seemed to be everywhere. Orchard Road at that time consisted chiefly of Bars catering mainly for the military, nothing like the Orchard Road of nowadays with its classy shops and Malls.

Canton cast off from Keppel Harbor jetty and headed eastbound into the Singapore Strait. The outer anchorages as well as inside the stone breakwater were crowded with a variety of ships, large and small. Amongst all this mingled the odd sailing junk with sails flapping grasping for what they could get from the light airs. Everything was so placid and what struck me most was that the sea was literally like glass – absolutely flat calm, not even a ripple. The now familiar sweet scents of Asia were everywhere but nevertheless much sweeter and pleasant on the nose than those of India. We now sped on our way towards the Horsburgh Lighthouse which marks the eastern end of the famous Singapore Strait, which eventually opens out into the South China Sea.

The following morning we passed the mountainous Anambas Islands (distant to port) as we continued north easterly towards our final destination – Hong Kong. The trip from Singapore to Hong Kong only lasted some 4 days or so but nothing could prepare my young mind for what I was about to encounter and the significant role it would play on me for the rest of my life.

Photo KP ©

Above, a panoramic view of Hong Kong Harbor photographed from the Peak in early 1970s. It bears little resemblance to the Hong Kong of 20 years later, as seen below. Sea and Land reclamation was always an ongoing activity in Hong Kong.

Photo KP ©

Final Destination – Hong Kong

Hong Kong, sometimes dubbed "The Pearl of the Orient" was first settled by the Portuguese in 1513, which they used as a staging post for their trade with China. Hong Kong is an enclave completely surrounded by Communist China.

The Hong Kong of today originated from its colonization by the British towards the end of the Opium Wars which ended in about 1841 and Hong Kong became a fully fledged Colony in 1842. Hong Kong was founded and developed by several iconic British shipping and trading merchants who became known as the "Hongs" (defined as warehouse or commercial establishment) with their respective bosses bearing the esteemed title of "Taipan" – meaning boss or big shot.

The Island of Hong Kong, together with Lantau and Stonecutters Islands was ceded to the British in perpetuity. However, in 1898 the colonizers realized they needed to expand their territory in order to make their acquisition more viable, so they negotiated an agreement with the Chinese to lease part of the Kowloon Peninsula (subsequently known as the New Territories) together with numerous other outlying Islands, for a set period of 99 years. All was encompassed within the Colony of Hong Kong, which remained intact until 1997 when sovereignty of the Colony was relinquished to China under the treaty.

Arrival in Hong Kong had been during the night. I awoke early, enjoyed breakfast then went out on deck. The ship was secured alongside Kowloon Wharves, just next to the Star Ferry terminal at Tsim Tsa Tsui on the Kowloon peninsula. It is an understatement to say that I was awed by the panoramic surrounds. Most of all the busy port, consisting every conceivable size and type of vessel, dominated by Victoria Peak on the other side of the harbor, shrouded in mist with its majestic presence complete with impressive array of buildings which encroached up the mountain's lower slopes.

The Hong Kong of the 1950s bears little resemblance to the modern Hong Kong. At that time I believe the tallest building was the original "Bank of China" closely followed by the "Hong Kong and Shanghai Bank" located in what is commonly referred to today as the "Central District" of Hong Kong Island, quite close to the Supreme Court and Hong Kong Club building. Nevertheless, this was still an outstanding spectacle for that point of time in the Colony's development. The main mode of transport between Hong Kong Island and Kowloon Peninsula was either the strictly passenger "Star Ferry" or "HYF" - Hong Kong Ya Ma Tei Ferry which carried both passengers and vehicles across the harbor, in addition to the outlying islands.

Nothing I had seen this far during our voyage could even come close to the excitement I now experienced. I do believe, even as a youngster, seeing Hong Kong for the first time stimulated something inside of me and triggering the onset of my everlasting love affair with Asia.

In so many ways I was sad to leave the Canton lying serenely at Kowloon Wharf, making ready for her return voyage to England. She had been our home for over a month. However, we were to maintain our relationship with the famous white Peninsula and Orient liners that plied the oceans between the UK and Hong Kong. Over the ensuing years we did one further round trip on another of their superb passenger ships, when along with my family, we returned to Britain for home leave. Airlines offering services from Hong Kong to Europe did not become common place until a good number of years later, about 1958 onwards. Even when available the early air passage was almost 2 days from Hong Kong to London, courtesy of four prop piston types and later turboprops such as the comfortable Bristol Britannia or "Whispering Giant" as it was to become affectionately known.

We eventually said our goodbyes and disembarked from the great white liner and headed straight for another well-known Hong Kong icon, the Peninsula Hotel where we were fortunate enough to be allocated rooms with a superb and unimpaired harbor view with Hong Kong Island as a back drop. These magnificent vistas have remained with me since childhood, in particular the "Junks" wallowing in the harbor, seeking a breeze, numerous cargo ships secured to the typhoon mooring buoys and at night the awesome display of lights on Hong Kong Island and Kowloon Peninsula.

2 The Early Years

There are so many memories of my early years spent in Hong Kong, far too numerous to record in this short narrative. Nevertheless, most were pleasant by virtue of their nature, remembering that this was the era of the Cheungsam, Cashmere beaded Cardigans, afternoon Tea Dances, Transistor Radios, Street Letter Writers, Rickshaws, Pigtails, elderly Chinese ladies with bound feet and European males being widely referred to as "Gweilos". Not to mention Dai Pai Dongs on every street corner. The 1950's ushered in the start of the defining period of Hong Kong's development and identity which spanned through to the late 1970's. This era shaped Hong Kong into the international icon it is today.

It was a cultural shock to me but it all had an electrifying kind of addiction and I always had a real sense of belonging in Hong Kong during all my many years living there. I think Hong Kong was then, and still is a unique environment in which to live, work and play. One is spellbound, excited by something new every day. There exists a great sense of adventure about the place. Hong Kong has a certain something that other major cities within the Orient lack and try to rival but are unsuccessful in their attempts to equal Hong Kong's unique qualities.

At that time, in the backstreets of Hong Kong lined with dingy shop houses with their pillars festooned all over with shop signs and ornate Chinese characters, one could still see the odd Mandarin in traditional Chinese robes complete with skull cap, pigtail, stringy beard and excessively long finger nails. Females in the main wore their drab pants suits, (mostly black or grey) straw hats and wooden clogs. Teenage Chinese girls carried their younger siblings in a hammock like arrangement on their back. Even the Amahs were adorned with their hair buns or pigtails, white apron tops and black pants. The better to do Chinese ladies wore their delightful Cheungsam dresses with high collars and splits up the side. It was said, the higher the neck and longer the splits, the more affluent the wearer – true or not?

It was not uncommon to see coolies with long bamboo poles slung across their shoulders carrying over loaded baskets of goods, or indeed to get a momentary whiff of Nga Pin (Opium) as one passed by an illegal den hidden in some narrow dark side street or back alley. Crowding was prevalent, especially in the squatter areas or Kowloon Walled City but for expats they could escape to the classier residential areas. Street markets and hawker stalls were abundant selling everything imaginable. In short the influence of mainland China imposed very dominantly despite British Colonial Administration. Nonetheless, the Colony fostered a unique quality in so many ways and grasped most of whom visited Hong Kong with a magnetism influencing their desire or wish to stay or soon return. Sailing junks of all sizes frequented the harbor, many of which at that time were still active in the China coastal trades, as well as remaining the main stay of the local Hong Kong fishing fleets well into the late 1960's until replaced by purpose built wooden trawlers.

Kowloon Walled City was located close to Kai Tak Airport, mostly consisting of illegal structures – said to be a lawless Mainland China enclave from which many Triad gangs, drugs, prostitution and other organized crime syndicates operated. It was reputed to be the most crowded place on earth. No doubt the Royal Hong Kong Police knew full well of all the lawlessness but preferred to have it more or less confined to one place where it could be more easily monitored and "controlled". It was demolished under the direction of the Hong Kong Government in 1993 and a Park is now situated on the original site.

The 50s and 60s was a period for the making of popular Hollywood movies that prominently featured Hong Kong as their main theme. Soldier of Fortune, Ferry to Hong Kong, World of Suzie Wong, and Love is a Many Splendored Thing, to name but a few. My brother was engaged as an "Extra" in one of them but I can't remember which one.

Life style for expats living in Hong Kong was very comfortable and sociable and one of privilege by any standard. Of course there was the downside, the crowding, great squatter hut fire at Shek Kip Mei on Christmas Day 1953, which cleaned out the homes of 50 thousand Mainland Chinese refugees literally overnight, which in turn triggered a massive Government Resettlement Housing scheme for small low cost apartments – a huge effort. Other noteworthy occurrences during those years was several bad Typhoons which caused significant damage including the grounding and wrecking of many ships, and the serious water shortages and rationing during 1963 caused by periods of prolonged drought. This required the Hong Kong Government to charter tanker ships to import fresh water purchased from mainland China.

Riots during 1956 between Pro Communist and Chinese Nationalist supporters at time of double "10" celebrations marred Hong Kong, whilst again in 1966 and 1967 rioting was repeated – increasing dissatisfaction amongst the working population over low wages coupled with Police corruption and substandard Policing were the main causes. However, in 1966 the reported collusion by the Hong Kong Government with the Star Ferry and HYF concerning applications for substantial increases in ferry fares was the final straw which triggered the unrest. These events got somewhat out of hand over ensuing days   Communist Chinese agitators took advantage to try to cause escalation and destabilize Colonial Rule. The Red Guards and so called Cultural Revolution prevalent in Communist China during the late 60s caused overspill into Hong Kong and Macau. These riots were eventually quelled by the Royal Hong Kong Police supported by the British Military and life quickly returned to normal. On the whole however, life was good for the foreign resident the majority of whom respected the local Chinese with great affection and reverence.

After about a week in the Peninsula Hotel, complete with its ornate lobby ceiling, magnificent central staircase and…. the first tiny sales kiosk for Cathay Pacific Airways situated in the main lobby, we were relocated to larger accommodations at the Miramar Hotel on the corner of Nathan Road and Kimberley Road, adjacent to the Princess Theatre. Legend has it that The Miramar is said to have been built on the site of the initial staging post for Catholic Missionaries traveling between Europe and China in a bygone era around the time of the opium wars and very early years of the Colony, it being established by the Vatican for this sole purpose. Similarly, Macau (Portuguese enclave about 40 miles to west of Hong Kong) is steeped in history also claiming Vatican connections for pilgrim Catholic Monks and Priests en-route to the Inner Kingdom during the dynasties of imperial rule.

During our ensuing years in Hong Kong the family would occasionally take a trip to Macau, either for the annual Grand Prix (very amateurish affair in those early years) or so my folks could visit the Casinos. During these visits I recall seeing herds of goats and buffalo in the main streets of Macau and when we were allowed into the Gambling Hotels with my parents, I remember standing on an upper balcony watching the gambling tables below. Unlike modern day Casinos, at that time bets were placed in wicker baskets and lowered to the staff attending the gaming tables situated on the floor below in a sort of inside court yard. Primitive security I suppose! Fan Tan seemed to be the most popular mode of betting which was a long established form of gambling in China. The Ferry that took us to and from Macau was something almost straight out of "Ferry to Hong Kong", save it was a propeller driven vessel rather than by paddle wheels and of course missing Orson Wells as the Captain. The one way trip in those days took about 4 hours, on a good day!

Photo KP ©

Above - Hong Kong to Macau Ferry **"Tung Shan"** taken at Macau old harbor mid 1970s. It was preceded by the **"Fat Shan"** which sank off Lantau Island in 1971 during Typhoon Rose. Fast Ferries, Hydrofoils and Jetfoils were used on the service from the mid 1970s onwards.

By comparison, highlighted below is a fast Hydrofoil "Cerco" pictured at speed in the East Lamma Channel, taken about 1974. These fast craft substantially reduced the transit time between Hong Kong and Macau for passengers to just over 1 hour each way, offering a service speed of around 40 knots.

Photo KP ©

About a month after we arrived in Hong Kong we shifted to a wonderful colonial villa, in Kowloon Tong, located in Somerset Road at the top end of Waterloo Road (with its central water drainage Nullah running the entire length of the road). More or less in the shadow of "Lion Rock" the foothills of which still housed thousands of squatters in their sprawling shanties. Waterloo Army camp was just across the road. The house was huge with wonderfully large shady verandahs, tall French style windows and well manicured gardens with graceful "Flame Trees" which bloomed profusely with their crimson flowers during the summer months. Kowloon Tong was a lovely quiet leafy suburb in which to reside. It was all together delightful and holds very fond memories.

We spent several memorable years in that house, and soon after we took up residence our two new family members joined us, "Ah Kwan" and "Ah Wong". The former was the cook Amah and the latter was the wash Amah and cleaner. They were to remain with our household for 15 years, until their retirement, and were both to become most revered and respected extended family members. It was a very sad day when we all said goodbye and they returned to their original homes in Canton for a well earned retirement. In fact my brother and I owe much to them for our upbringing and guidance during those former years in Hong Kong. They taught us to speak Cantonese amongst other things and rescued me from numerous indiscretions that would have undoubtedly rattled my father's saber and wrath if discovered.

At dinner parties they were very gifted and excelled by turning out the most wonderful spreads with ornate decorative carvings made from carrots, turnips and the like. My parents were always busy with their work and social calendars so my brother and I spent much time with the two "A's". Sadly, the wonderful old house was later demolished sometime in the 1970s to make way for a short time hotel, what sacrilege. I went back to visit it in later years expecting to see the elegant building but I was frankly shocked at the replacement.

After two happy summers, we moved to a very comfortable and modern ground floor apartment in Oxford Road, where we remained for a further two years. This was in the same residential area, known as Kowloon Tong in the Waterloo Road area. In actuality, leading off Lancashire Road, and just up the street from Christ Church. This area, together with Kadoorie Avenue and close by Ho Man Tin, was a favored residential area for Cathay Pacific and Pan American expatriate Pilots, (due to its ease of access to Kai Tak airport). Many friendships were forged with the aircrew and their families. I guess this was the beginning of my becoming enamored with flying. I was often taken on visits to Kai Tak Airport by the Pilots to see the planes and occasionally hitch a ride on a test flight or some such event. I enjoyed every minute of it and naturally never had to be asked twice.

In those days the Hong Kong Airport's runway did not extend to seaward but was purely a land bound affair. One of the runways crossed the Clearwater Bay Road, which required stopping traffic when the runway was active. I recall this happening when I was returning to London for holidays with the family, on a BOAC Bristol Britannia "Whispering Giant" via all points west – Bangkok, Rangoon, Karachi, Tehran, Beirut, Zurich, Frankfurt and London. A journey of almost 2 days but with an aircraft configured to all one class, relaxed and comfortable without the stress of airline security and with cabin crew who actually smiled occasionally. A far cry from today's air travel chaos and misery. In those times the airport terminal at Kai Tak consisted of a small building which was little more than a "Dairy Farm" soda fountain and when embarking or disembarking aircraft one strolled casually across the tarmac, Airport security as it is today was unknown (and unnecessary to a large part) in those days. The presence of a few Royal Hong Kong Police in the area was an adequate deterrent to those of ill intent.

There were two approaches to Kai Tak, it being operational only during daylight hours, one hugging the hills under Lion Rock and the other very low over Boundary Road. Both were every much as nerve racking as the notorious "Checker Board" approach over Kowloon City into Kai Tak's single seaward runway used from about 1960 until the mid 90's. I remember well the original Kai Tak as I spent much time there with my binoculars, Brownie camera and notebook. Equally, vivid images remain of the construction and opening of the seaward runway, the first ever night flight being made by a DC3 and if memory serves me, under the command of one of our Pilot neighbors. I believe the aircraft was operated by CPA. Night flights into Hong Kong only officially commenced in July 1959. This was a much talked about event in the colony and really kick started tourism to Hong Kong in a big way.

Whilst living in Kowloon we spent a lot of our leisure time at the USRC (United Services Recreation Club) located in Gascoigne Road, just across the road from Club de Recreo, relatively close to the Jordan area. Needless to say I spent a lot of time at the USRC. Mostly lounging around the beautiful swimming pool or eating the best lemon sponge cakes.

Our long lasting abode in Hong Kong was to be on the Peak, in actuality Mount Kellet, very close to the British Military Hospital. This remained our residence for the majority of my remaining years in Hong Kong until the late 1970s when I purchased an apartment at Taikoo Sing and later at Academic Terrace in Pok Fu Lam Road. The views from "Kellet Grove" were superlative, overlooking the Pok Fu Lam reservoir, across towards Repulse Bay and East Lamma Channel (southern approaches to Hong Kong to and from the South China Sea, passing Ap Lei Chau and Aberdeen). Access was either by car up the winding Peak Road that originated from Garden Road in the vicinity of the Botanic Gardens, close to Government House, or via Stubbs Road from the Happy Valley area via Wong Nai Chung Gap. Of course for the tourist there is always the he Peak Tramway. The Peak Tram was then, and still is, one of Hong Kong's icons and is an absolute marvel of engineering. I think the views offered from the tram are without doubt some of the most spectacular in the world. Similarly, the Peak Café was a charming spot to sit and have a beer whilst looking over the Island scapes towards Mount Kellet.

During this period in Hong Kong my brother and I sought our entertainment mainly from the "Rediffusion" radio with ears keenly tuned to daily and weekly episodes of "Riders of the Range" and "Journey into Space". TV was in its infancy at this time in Hong Kong, only a few hours vision per day until fulltime programming was introduced in 1956; so the term Couch Potato had yet to evolve. We also regularly visited "Diamond Music Store" to buy gramophone discs – mostly 45s, which we swopped with our friends.

We made plastic airplanes and ships bought from Eastern Model Supplies in Nathan Road or the Radar Company Model Shop situated in Austin Avenue. Both were very interesting shops with lots to see, so many memorable hours were spent in these establishments. On the other hand our worst nightmare was long shopping outings with my Mother, which we did our best to avoid, wandering around Lane Crawfords, Whiteaways or Wing On department stores.

Our weekends were mainly family affairs with trips to the beach or launch picnics, extravagant boring Sunday lunches with friends of my parents, going to the cinema or a car ride around Hong Kong Island followed by a slap up afternoon tea at the Repulse Bay Hotel. My favorite was a Sunday morning visit to the Luk Kwok hotel for "Yum Cha" where the food was excellent. It was situated next to the "China Fleet Club" building on Gloucester Road. At that time the Luk Kwok Hotel had the reputation of being the best place on Hong Kong Island for "Yum Cha" – hence it was always totally crowded, on Sundays in particular.

Now and then perhaps we would be taken on a day trip to Rocky Bay or Silver Strand Beach or occasionally we would be entertained by a drive to the New Territories (crossing the harbor from Hong Kong Central to Jordan Road area in Yau Ma Tei via the HYF vehicular ferry). We sometimes ventured close to the border at Lo Wu and peered across into communist China, or went to Castle Peak visiting the Dragon Inn at the 19.5 mile stone.

The New Territories were a step backwards in time from the rest of crowded Hong Kong and Kowloon. The traditional Chinese way of life was still evident, old Chinese ladies with their black outfits and straw hats, sometimes smoking long pipes. These elderly Chinese people could still be seen quite regularly throughout the 1960s, especially about the old walled villages and hamlets, working in the paddy fields or tending their water buffalo. Their faces looked so kind and were like weatherworn road maps, full of wrinkles, depicting a life of hardship and poverty. Many of these folks had come across the border from Communist China when the United Kingdom leased the New Territories.

These rural activities were in sharp contrast to the sophisticated lifestyles of Kowloon Peninsula or Hong Kong Island. On the way home we generally stopped off at the Sha Tin Heights Hotel for refreshments or so my Mom and Dad could attend the afternoon tea dance.

My parents became members of various clubs which offered tennis, swimming and a variety of other sporting and social activities, so my brother and I spent much time at these venues as junior members. The LRC (Ladies Recreation Club) in mid-levels Hong Kong Island being our most frequented. We both learned to swim at the LRC under the tutorage of the well known BillyTingle. The late Mr. BillyTingle was both a legend and celebrity in Hong Kong and he used to conduct swimming classes on a Saturday morning at the LRC.

He was very popular with the parents and adored by the kids. Tingle was an Australian and started his career as a Boxer but was interned in Shanghai during WW2. He relocated to Hong Kong in the late 1940s where he soon became renowned for his Physical Fitness and Swimming classes. I seem to recall he also used the Hong Kong Cricket Club as a venue for his other classes, but I never attended.

Soon after we arrived in Hong Kong I was enrolled in Kowloon Junior School, close to Boundary Road and co-incidentally conveniently situated right on the flight path for aircraft on approach to one of the Kai Tak runways. I enjoyed super views of the landing aircraft right from the class room desk! It was a major but enjoyable distraction from class activities.

There was not much choice in those days in respect of schooling, there basically being only a couple of "International" elementary and senior schools and a couple of others reserved for the military kids as there still remained a substantial garrison in Hong Kong. It later changed in the mid to late 1960s but in those early days of Hong Kong's development education options were, it must be said, somewhat limited. Junior school was a breeze for me, I did exceedingly well in most subjects and regularly ranked in the top places at exam time during those early years. By the time I had progressed to 11 plus exams I was losing my edge as school was taking a very secondary place to my other interests and activities – planes, ships and sports. I managed to scrape through the exams to grammar school and went up to King George V School at Ho Man Tin in Kowloon, where I admit to becoming a very average and unproductive student but rather an enthusiastic sportsman.

KGV was a good school with excellent facilities for its time, the only real alternative to KGV was to attending Boarding School overseas, but like most schools is only as good as the willingness of its pupils to learn. The majority of students were the offspring of British or European expats but also with a few American and a handful of overseas Chinese. Oh and a few offspring of military types (mostly Admiralty or Royal Flcct Auxiliary based in Hong Kong). The teaching staff was all expatriate and of a very high standard. I struggled academically, mainly because of my lack of application, not through lack of personal ability. I excelled at sports and at the age of 14 became Captain of 1st X1 Cricket. I believe my name is still to this day on the role of honor in the lobby of the school's main entrance. Many former pupils went on to establish distinguished careers in business, literature and the sciences. The School motto was - "Honestas Ante Honures" (honesty before glory). KGV is now a truly international school and still going strong.

My mother being a school teacher seemed to have little if any influence over my studies. Between the years of 11 and 14, I was never out of trouble with my father over my poor scholastic results. Typically, school reports used to feature comments such as "It's impossible to help this student as he is seldom here" or "This pupil knows more about the rigging of a Four Mast Sailing Ship than he does about French verbs". The sort of personal comment a teacher would not even contemplate making today. Nevertheless it was all absolutely true, I would regularly skip school and instead sit the day out at Kai Tak plane spotting or indeed by HMS Tamar Naval Dockyard, right on the Hong Kong waterfront, watching the ships sailing in and out of the harbor.

I well remember my favorite ship; she was a classical small vintage tramp that had certainly seen better days. Her cigar like funnel (usually casting out volumes of dense black smoke from her coal fired furnaces), rigid lines and counter stern with propeller blades often awash as she slowly steamed through the Harbor, captured my imagination. She was named "Juno". From later research I learned that she was lost with all hands during 1964 in the South China Sea whilst on passage from Hong Kong to Brunei. 1964 was a notoriously bad year for devastating Typhoons. Sadly she just disappeared without trace after radioing she was engulfed in a severe Typhoon. The "Juno" was an ex Australian vessel originally named "Cardross" built in 1927, and sold to Madrigal Shipping Company of the Philippines in 1955. She wasn't a very large ship, only about 1385 gross tons with a length of about 70 meters. I guess she would have been classified as a low powered steamship, even in those days, and at best I suspect producing a speed of only about 9 or 10 knots in favorable conditions. Obviously, for a small ship of those characteristics it was fraught with danger to be caught in open Ocean amid raging Typhoon conditions with little prospect of taking remedial action or outrunning the storm, the situation could quickly become catastrophic.

The ill-fated **"Juno"**, seen passing Kowloon Wharf at
Hong Kong, heading for Yau Ma Tei, around 1959.

Typical graffiti painted on the side of a ship by Red Guards in China during Mao's so called Cultural Revolution. It was politically unwise to try and remove the slogans whilst in China. Far better to wait until arrival at the next port of call then employ ship's crew or a side party to over paint it.

It did not take much provocation, especially by foreigners to trigger conflict with the groups of Red Guards. These groups varied in size from 10 or 20 agitators up to thousands. They were very intimidating and made one feel very unsafe since there was no Law and Order amongst their ranks, so it seemed anyway.

Mau's Little Red Book, this was a "gift" for all seafarers visiting the Peoples Republic of China during the years leading up to the Cultural Revolution. It was not unknown to have the entire ship's crew mustered during the night hours to have some shabby, official looking Chinese Commissar, rant and rave with quotes from the booklet. These sessions frequently lasted more than an hour and were designed to inconvenience and annoy foreigners rather than indoctrinate because no one really understood, or was remotely interested, in what was being said.

I became an expert on planes and ships, being able to quote yards of factual information right off the cuff, but when it came to the school books...well there was always tomorrow. Hence in later years, I had to spend many hours of hard study to catch up just to qualify for professional examinations. Nevertheless, this was a vital part of my worldly education and unlike many other teenagers of the era in Hong Kong, I knew very early exactly in which direction I was to go in terms of career path.

Up until the age of 14 or so I had always intended to be an airline pilot (I later did learn to fly and have gone on to log a noteworthy number of flying hours over the years) but a close friend had just been accepted into one of the principal nautical colleges in the UK. His stories, letters and photos of what it was like and the exciting career opportunities offered in the Merchant Navy stimulated a profound influence in my thinking at that point in my life and consequently it started to fire up and stoke my imagination. Hence in later life – flying became my passion but seafaring my bread and butter!

It is also true to say that whilst at grammar school a few pals had close family connections with the sea which also impacted hugely on my nautical aspirations. One close chum, his father was Master of the "Canada Fir", a tramp ship that was Hong Kong owned and based; another pal's father was Master of a ship belonging to one of the principal Hong Kong shipping conglomerates; whilst yet another was Danish whom I accompanied when visiting a very smart cargo ship, the "Michael Jebsen", engaged in Asian regional trades; his father was Captain. Finally, there was my closest friend whose old man was Engineer Superintendent for a large Dutch shipping company that had many vessels frequently calling Hong Kong – needless to say at weekends I was often found in mid harbor aboard one of their ships, by invitation of course. This was not to mention various other school friends whose parents had nautical connections, such as Shipyards or Liner Agencies

It was not unexpected therefore, that my career preference started to progressively deviate away from aviation and begin to focus more towards one in the Merchant Navy.

I approached my father about this change of heart; he hit the roof and did his best to talk me out of it. The more he tried, the more determined I became. Eventually after some 4 or 5 months he finally agreed to send me to the same nautical college as my pal in the UK (if I could pass the entrance examination that is…and was accepted). My course had now been set and from that juncture onwards I studied much more diligently and eventually passed the entrance examinations into the nautical establishment, although I still made time for my other social activities.

My father was happy because he had put pay to my notions to sign on some Panamanian Tramp Steamer as a Cadet, but rather, had reached a compromise, as he put it….sending me to sea well equipped and in the correct way. I respected my father for his change of heart and foresight. So without delay I went off to the Hong Kong Marine Department at Kennedy Town Praya for my mandatory Sight Test and Lantern Test (vision requirements needed to be verified as color blindness ruled out Merchant Navy entrants for Deck Officer Cadets). The accompanying Medical Examination was also very comprehensive.

Eventually that magical day came for me to depart Hong Kong and to fly to the UK to receive my nautical training. I boarded the shining BOAC Comet 4 airliner (yes progress had been made by this time from turboprop to pure jet). We took off on the newly constructed seaward protruding runway and I was in London only 24 hrs later. Little did I realize for the next few years it was the end of my comfortable and privileged lifestyle. Future life at nautical college became something of a shock to my system and sometimes difficult to endure.

For a period longer than I care to remember I was at pre-sea school, being taught and prepared for the role of a Deck Officer in the Merchant Navy. Suffice it to say I found the naval type discipline tough to accept after my colonial style upbringing in Hong Kong but managed to prevail, although it does not remain amongst my fonder memories, I have to admit.

In those days the selection criteria under which one entered into a sea going occupation was markedly different to that of today. More emphasis was placed on pre-sea training, leadership and compatibility to the profession and not purely based on academic achievement. One was required to have a solid and proven scholastic record with above average results all the same. GCE O and A levels in the sciences, being the bench mark. Upon reflection, I feel personally gratified and privileged to have seen the best of what the service had to offer over the ensuing years and most certainly I experienced the last of a maritime era.

Having completed pre-sea training all I now had to do was find a job with a shipping company that offered real prospects for a young enthusiast such as me! My preference and goal was on ships trading around the Far East.

My parents were home on leave at the time I left nautical college so I spent a short summer holiday with them at a wonderful country house in Steyning (West Sussex). During this period I had sent off many letters of application to various shipping companies. To my surprise it did not take long to start receiving the replies. I did attend a few interviews in London, underwent sight tests and medicals and after 2-3 weeks started to receive replies to my applications.

In fact I was very fortunate in having 3 firm offers as a cadet or indentured apprentice. One was a tanker company, this was trading worldwide but I did not really fancy tankers and had only applied as a last resort, in case nothing better came up, so that went to the bottom of my preferred list. Of the other two, one was from a highly regarded liner company, trading mainly from the UK to West Africa and Persian Gulf and the other from a well respected tramp company with a substantial fleet, of which a number of their ships I had seen during my days of playing truant in Hong Kong. I opted for the latter, hoping I would land a ship working in S. E Asia. It was a very exciting period for me

A week or so later, I received my Indentures thru the post, my father signed them as surety. Hence, I was suddenly an Indentured Deck Apprentice bonded for the next few years. My fate was cast. The articles of indenture were a masterpiece, being printed in old English script on parchment like paper. I still have those indentures till this day and frankly I treasure them. Upon reflection I find it hard to believe that my weekly salary was 3 Pounds and 10 Shillings. How things have changed since!

It was an anxious week or so for me before I was appointed to a vessel but the intervening time was well spent at naval outfitters getting kitted out with uniforms and working apparel and generally ready to embark on my chosen career. I finally received my joining instructions by telegram. I was directed to proceed to Immingham Docks to join one of the general cargo ships of 10,000 grt just completing a dry-docking. I was to board the vessel and report to the Master immediately upon arrival on 21st June 1961. My train ticket was prepaid and available for my collection from the ticketing office at Hayward's Heath railway station.

I said an emotional goodbye to my mother and brother and my father drove me to the station. I never forget his words as he shook me by the hand as the train pulled in – Take care son, look after yourself, write and don't come home with anything you didn't go away with!! He thrust an envelope that he had taken from his breast pocket into my hand. I jumped on board with my gear and waved as the train pulled out of the station. As the train moved away from the platform I sat wondering as to the significance of my old man's last remark, it was a little while before the penny dropped and I understood his inference.

I was my own man at last, more than anything else doing what I wanted most, even though somewhat apprehensive, inasmuch as I did not truly know what to expect. I have to admit that during the course of the train journey I did suffer the occasional moment or two of hesitation, when I asked myself if I was doing the right thing! I forced myself to overcome the fits of panic and sat glued to the carriage seat. Besides, I would not only lose face but also my father's respect if I defaulted. We had stopped at a few stations before I opened the envelope I had been given by my Dad. Inside was 200 Pounds (a considerable sum to me at that time) and a hand written note that simply said "To be used in case of emergency, God Bless and come home safely"; those few written words spoke volumes to me.

The remainder of the journey passed with me having flashback memories of my years growing up in Hong Kong and the factors that had influenced my wishes to embark upon a career at sea

It so happens that I did not see my parents for the next 16 months, when I signed off the vessel in Hong Kong and disembarked for my first home leave.

John Manners Group Hong Kong – Owners and Managers

A classic – Typical vintage Hong Kong tramp of the 1960s **"South Breeze",** light ship and in calm seas (perhaps the Malacca or Singapore Straits) I assume heading towards her designated loading port. I believe this vessel was a member of the well known John Manners fleet who were prolific ship managers throughout Asia during the 1960s and beyond, their operations being managed from their Head Office at Alexandra House in Hong Kong. They seemed to specialize in buying up older tonnage, overhauling and refurbishing to meet higher standards then running them for a few years before on selling for continued trading or demolition, usually on a buoyant market. John Manners' ships were always well maintained and nicely presented despite their vintage.

To be fair, not all of their tonnage was aged like that pictured. They had a good number of more modern vessels, including some new buildings. I also believe John Manners had significant real estate investments in Australia, shipping and ship broking being only one factor of their varied commercial interests. Manners was a renowned trading company in Hong Kong and had offices situated throughout the Far East and Australia. I later sailed with this company, finding them to be very decent employers. Hence, I retain good memories of the time I served with them, albeit not for very long.

John Manners Group Hong Kong – Owners and Managers

Above, a superb image of the **"Straits Breeze"** with a full cargo of dressed round logs, a common cargo in the 1960's for many a ship trading around the Far East. This was an ex Aussie ship, operated by John Manners – Hong Kong. Photograph was most likely taken at one of the upstream logging ports in Borneo, Papua New Guinea or Indonesia.

By the early 1970s purpose built log ships were conspicuous by their numbers. These ships could be seen at most ports, particularly in Asia with larger majority heading towards the Japanese logging Ports, such as Fushiki to discharge cargo. Although most logging was legal, reportedly there was a significant amount of illegal logging stemming from corruption at the highest level of government in some of the Asian exporting countries. Many of the corrupt officials cashing in with huge profits having no regard for the devastation of the forests they had caused and for which

53

they were responsible. Obviously this had a huge environmental impact and even today legal logging draws the closest scrutiny from environmentalists, worldwide.

I recall one occasion when in Papua New Guinea, being anchored off a river estuary waiting to load at one of the logging ports, seeing quite large log ships sailing from the roadstead unlit and under the cover of darkness. Only when outside territorial waters did they "switch on" their lights. Obviously this was illegal logging in the extreme. The illegal logging practice was widely known but so many were in the pay of the syndicates, nothing was seen to be done to eradicate the practice.

The carriage of logs on ships is considered to be precarious and much consideration must be given to loading, weight distribution and ship stability. Shifting of cargo is a real issue so a proper lashing plan is vital for safety. Therefore the carriage of logs and timber on deck is highly regulated.

John Manners Group Hong Kong – Owners and Managers

Above, an aged and well weathered old lady - **"San Miguel"**, also of the John Manners fleet navigating through Hong Kong harbor, somewhere around Yau Ma Tei. To me she gives the impression of being engaged in the "livestock" trade going by the structural additions and modifications about her upper decks. There was a thriving live Cattle, Buffalo and Sheep trade around the Far East during the 1960s. Date of image is unknown but going by the stage of development to the Kowloon skyline I suspect sometime around early 1960s.

Some of the major Asian ports engaged in the livestock trade during the 1960s were in Sarawak, Philippines, West Malaysia, Indonesia and occasionally Thailand and Hong Kong. In later years there was substantial change in regulations for the carrying of livestock by sea allowing for more humane handling of the animals during loading and transit. Large livestock carriers were built during 1980s, mainly for the thriving Middle East trade and the desire for live animals delivered "on the hoof" in large numbers. However, the livestock shipping sector has not been immune from criticism over the years and still remains a controversial topic to this day.

During the 1960s when live Buffaloes were carried on deck of a General Cargo Ship, typically from Thailand to Hong Kong, obviously all Buffaloes were tethered and whenever possible carried on the after deck in order to afford them better protection from elements of weather and hopefully to assist with the smell drifting away from main accommodation areas.

However, when live sheep were shipped, they were
carried fore and aft, due to the larger numbers. The
smell and noise was terrible and livestock ships could be
detected miles away by their smell. Therefore, whilst it
should be said that these were not frequent cargoes,
livestock was a trade to be avoided whenever possible.
Specialist handlers were carried to look after feeding
and husbandry of the animals whilst on board in transit.
From the late 1970s onwards much stricter regulations
were implemented that afforded more humane
conditions for the animals when in transit and being
loaded aboard.

Hong Kong's Victoria Harbor – A busy scene at Yau Ma Tei with Stone Cutters Island in the background. Shot early 1970s showing an assortment of craft, typical of any day in Hong Kong Harbor.

Above is a quintessential Hong Kong street scene. The popular Causeway Bay which is one of the main shopping precincts, going by the Tram seen lower left of the image, circa 1970s. Trams were only utilized as public transport on Hong Kong Island and proved to be a very cost effective and efficient mode of transport. Another action packed image by Karsten Petersen

Photo KP ©

Street vendor….Roast Pork or Peking Duck anyone? If bought freshly cooked this was top class tucker.

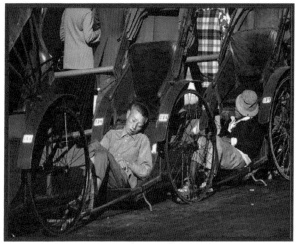

Photo KP ©

Waiting at the Rickshaws rank; it is obviously
exhausting work! This was still a common sight, during
1960-70s. Nowadays there are very few licensed
Rickshaws. They are used mainly as a tourist attraction
and as props for touristy photographs or the movie
picture industry.

Star Ferry – Highly colorful Star Ferry, not in traditional color scheme, a true Hong Kong icon and still going strong after 130 years of operation. The Star Ferry Company was Founded in 1888 by Dorabjee Naorojee Mithaiwala , an Indian businessman residing in Hong Kong at that time. Prior to the opening of the cross harbor tunnels it was the quickest and best way to transit the harbor.

3 Welcome Aboard

Upon my arrival at Hull station I was met by the company agent, a Mr. Cook, who advised me that I would not be joining the ship until the following day once she had been refloated from the dry dock. I was taken to a hotel for the night. I do remember being kept awake for some hours by whom I assumed were drunken Hull fishermen, all dressed in their distinctive and garish suits with bellbottom trousers. I watched their rowdy behavior and antics from the safety of my upper floor room, the window overlooked the court yard of the adjacent pub. There were more than a few scuffles I have to say. Anyway, it passed the time as I was otherwise unable to sleep due to nervous excitement.

I arose early the following morning, showered, downed a hurried but hearty breakfast and waited nervously to be collected by the shipping company's agent. Eventually he arrived and we bundled my entire luggage into his car. We drove towards Immingham Docks. The agent was a middle aged chap and very pleasant, but an incessant talker. He was somewhat inquisitive as to my background but kept assuring me that all would be fine and what a good company I had elected to join. The drive seemed longer than it really was but eventually we pulled up at the designated dock and there she was, freshly painted black hull with red boot topping, riding high, just out of dry dock. A few rust stains about the white upper works and buff masts and derricks but really quite smart in appearance. After all, she was a working vessel so this was to be expected. The ship was just as I had envisaged, I was thrilled to say the least. I had learned from the agent that the ship had arrived from Bunbury in Western Australia with a cargo of

Ilminite sand, prior to entering dry dock for hull maintenance and periodic surveys. It was planned that she work her way back towards the Far East by way of various ports and carrying different cargoes. To me this appeared the perfect scenario.

I thanked Mr. Cook and unloaded my gear from the car to quayside. No sooner had I done this when someone on board shouted down to me, "you must be the new apprentice – grab your bags and come on board". I followed as directed and staggered up the swaying accommodation ladder with my case and hold all.

I was met at the top of the gangway by a youngish fellow, perhaps a year or two older than I, dressed in overalls. "My name is John, I am the senior apprentice" he stated with a tone of authority, "welcome on board". He shook my hand, "please follow me". He took one of my bags. I was ushered to what was to become my communal cabin, where I placed my kit and was introduced to Michael, a fellow apprentice. There were three of us in the cabin. The cabin was situated on the officer's deck, starboard side, with two portholes, quite large, three bunks, one stand alone and a two tier arrangement. The showers and toilets were adjacent to the cabin. The accommodation was sparse but clean and livable." You are the junior so the top bunk is yours and so is that locker" he said gesturing with his hand. "Gather your thoughts then I'll take you to meet the Old Man and Harry Tate (common nick name for Chief Officer) the Mate", said John with an air of authority in his voice. I followed without question and as directed.

A short time later I was taken up to the Captain's deck. John knocked on the door. There was a sharp "Yes", "I have the new deck apprentice Sir" uttered John. I was feeling somewhat nervous. A moment later the Captain appeared at the door."I am Captain Banner" he stated, offering his hand. "Welcome on board – do come in". John departed and left me alone in the Captain's presence.

My eyes wandered and I was impressed with the highly polished woodwork and brass fittings about his accommodations. The Old Man was in his mid forties, graying hair and wearing horn rimmed reading specs parked at the end of his nose, he was clean shaven and of slight to medium build and wore an unassuming checked shirt and grey slacks (I had expected uniform but later learned that this was only donned on special occasions – general rig of the day being khakis at all other times whilst at sea)." Well young man, what's your name and where are you from" (I thought I detected a faint Australian accent) he enquired. I obliged with the information. I signed various papers, passed over my passport, seaman's book and discharge book for safe keeping. My Indentures had already been forwarded to him by the company in London. Being an Indentured Apprentice I was not required to sign ship's articles. Sea time, total earnings and length of service all recorded on the back of my parchment testimonial.

This was followed by a quick beginners guide to the rules and regulations applying on board, what was expected of me and how I should conduct myself. I was warned off drinking. During this briefing there was a knock on the Master's office door, it was the Chief Engineer, come to report something or other and dressed in a spotless white boiler suite. I was briefly introduced. The Chief Engineer was obviously a Scot, I would say early 60's and bore the evidence of being a heavy drinker going by the conspicuous veins in his whiskey nose. He soon went on his way and I was told to go down and report to the Mate who would give me instructions and who was most likely to be found in his cabin.

Harry Tate, the Mate, was much younger than I had expected, perhaps 28-30 yrs of age. Tall and lean with a crooked smile and piercing blue eyes. He was a man of few words as I discovered. Obviously an Englishman I thought, in fact I later learned he was from the Isle of Man. I was informed to go to see the senior apprentice, to get into my working gear and John would take it from there. All this I did without hesitation….so far so good. By this time it was approaching lunch time so I changed back into presentable rig, washed and was taken into the Officer's Saloon where I was allocated the end seat at the Captains table by virtue of my being the most junior. Seating was strictly according to rank. The dining saloon was mostly all timber bulkheads, comfortable, if somewhat limited in size, but well presented and snug.

The Engineers table was at the other side of the room with Chief Engineer at its head. There was a general introduction before we set about our meal. The stewards were all in black trousers and white mess jackets, with company house flag embroidered on their left breast pocket, the table linen was crisp and clean and the cutlery was of reasonably good quality bearing company emblem. Plates, cups and saucers also had the company motif clearly displayed. The Chinese stewards offered the menu in sequence according to rank. That first meal was well served although somewhat plain, but nevertheless both wholesome and plentiful. At least I wouldn't starve I thought to myself.

Following lunch, it was back into working gear. I was allocated an emergency station and shown all the lifesaving and firefighting features on the vessel, their respective function and how they were operated, what my emergency duties were and to which life boat I was assigned. A general familiarization tour of the ship was then conducted, during which further key crew introductions were made.

Having completed the tour, work began. All three apprentices were sent to No 2 hold tween deck to sort and stack dunnage. To my amazement there were stacks of it strewn about. Our job was to sort the good from bad and make up large slings of the timber. The good being retained in neat stacks at the forward and after ends of the tweendeck, whilst the broken and splintered was pre slung pending removal to the main deck for subsequent disposal. I was made to understand that this was the first of 5 cargo holds to be cleared of dunnage; this was a lot of work and was my introduction to the apprentice's lot on board a tramp ship.

Over ensuing days, we three apprentices plugged away from 7am until 5pm sorting the dunnage and checking bilge limber boards. It took us all of 3 days continuous work to complete the job. We were then assigned with the Chinese crew to sweep out all the cargo holds, after which we hosed down the Deep Tanks. The deck and engine ratings were all Hong Kong Chinese and I soon gained a few bonus points when they discovered I was relatively fluent in Cantonese. This served me well over the years to come as most of our crews originated from Hong Kong.

Sailing day was approaching but I did manage to call home to let my parents know all was well, the intended long voyage and that I would be out of contact for some weeks, indeed... Our voyage was to take us from Immingham across the North Sea to Bremen, where we were to load a full cargo of steaming coal for Noumea in New Caledonia. The ocean passage from Bremen, transit through the Panama Canal and Pacific crossing was calculated to take some 56 days all going well, at an average sea speed of 10 knots. I was awe struck by this prospect and feared how I would cope with such a lengthy first voyage.

Departure time finally arrived and being the most junior of the apprentices, my sailing station was to be on the bridge to keep the "Bell and Movement Book". This was basically a record of all engine movements and events so that they could later be entered into the ship's deck log book by the 3rd Officer, (a chap from Essex who had just obtained his 2nd Mates Certificate). I met the Pilot at the gangway and escorted him to the bridge where he introduced himself to the Captain.

It was not long before we were casting off and with the assistance of two harbor tugs, slowly departed the port into more open waters. This was all very interesting for me and I started my learning immediately as I had been told that it was expected of me. I at once recognized the difference between port and starboard hand channel buoys, the different helm orders given by the Pilot and various other nautical terms being used, which, until this point in time had all originated from a text book or class room.

I began to feel the throb of the ships engines underfoot and the "thump" thump" sound made by the Doxford opposed piston diesel engine. It was all very assuring to me. This ship was an 18 year old lady and was equipped with diesel main engines and steam auxiliaries, i.e. pumps, steam winches etc. We gained headway until arriving at the Pilot Station whence the Pilot disembarked. We transited seaward down river towards the Humber light ship. I began to feel the gentle motion of the vessel which caused me to reflect on my days on the old "Canton" and the sea sickness - I dismissed the thought! Once past the Light Ship, the Master gave orders and we set course for the next leg of the North Sea crossing. I was told to go below, to start work!

The passage across the North Sea was mainly in darkness and I had little time to take too much notice of what was going on about me as I was kept very busy most of the night rigging temperature sounding pipes in the various cargo compartments, along with my fellow apprentices. Since we were loading coal and it was combustible it therefore required regular temperature readings to be taken at top, center and bottom, morning, noon and night. The thermometer readings were all recorded in a special log and passed to the officer of the watch for the reference of the Chief Officer.

Despite the long hours of work, I was by this time starting to settle in and become familiar with ship board routine. My first unsupervised task was to be assigned as the ship's "sani pani walla". This in effect meant that I was the person in charge of ensuring the ship's sanitary water was regularly replenished by pumping up the various header tanks morning and evening, or as required... I was shown the various valves, pipe lines and pumps in the engine room. Initially I was to ask the duty engineer for guidance in their operation. This I did, but soon became competent in operating the various pumps and valves myself. After all not much that can go wrong with a steam pump as long as one remembers to drain it first and open the exhaust valve. It may sound quaint but this set me on the path to gaining a comprehensive understanding as to the operation of various steam and later diesel machinery used aboard ship. It was an excellent environment in which to learn, although being allocated the "Sani-Pani" job underscored my position on board as a very junior deck apprentice.

Thinking back over the years spent as a deck apprentice, I often complained quietly to myself about the low level tasks sometimes allocated to we apprentices but in retrospect I can now understand how important it all was to gaining a comprehensive understanding the fundamentals of the working of a cargo ship. It was all part and parcel of the excellent training I received during my apprentice years. I often chuckled when, years later, as a Chief Mate I found myself allocating the same sort of work to the deck apprentices.

A nice study of the first ship I served on as a Deck Apprentice – **"Weybank"**. I believe arriving in Risdon (Tasmania) early 1962 to discharge the balance of a cargo of Bulk Phosphate loaded at Christmas, Nauru or Ocean Island. It was quite common to have a two Port discharge for this type of cargo. The hull below the deck scuppers stained with phosphate residues after numerous washing downs to rid the dust that accumulated everywhere about the decks.

Bank Line Ltd - London

4 Foreign Ports

We arrived off the Weser estuary the following evening and at once proceeded up stream towards Bremen Haven, under the guidance of a river Pilot. Most of the day our Chinese crew had been topping all the derricks, of which there were 14 units, excluding the heavy lift or "Jumbo" derrick which was not prepared as it was not required, as well as checking stays, preventers, cargo blocks in addition to testing the steam winches and all the other things requiring preparation. The crew had also removed the canvas tarpaulins and hatch board (of which there were many) from the hatches, and rolled back the "King" and "Queen" beams in hatchways and tweendecks, to make ready for loading.

I was on the bridge again at my usual station recording all the events and proceedings. We at last arrived at Bremen Haven and tied up to the dolphins in mid stream. It was only a very short period of time before the coal barges and lighters were alongside. The crew swung out and plumbed the derricks and secured the derrick preventers and guys in readiness for the stevedores and loading to begin. We apprentices rigged the cargo clusters (lights) outboard and inside the hatch coamings.

Soon 5 gangs of tough looking stevedores came on board and started connecting up the one ton clam grabs to the union purchase gear. In a flash grab after grab laden with coal was being transferred from the barges into the cargo holds. It was an education for me to watch how skillfully the stevedores jockeyed the winches and gear, tweaking the steam valve and riding the brake. Aided by the hissing and clanking steam winches the grabs went in and out like clockwork, and fast – very fast. Even after all my years spent at sea I still believe that steam winches with union purchase gear, in the hands of skilled operators, is perhaps the quickest and most efficient shipboard method of conducting cargo operations. This obviously precludes containers, unit loads and the like.

Once cargo was under way the 2nd and 3rd Mates were set on cargo watches, likewise the apprentices. I was designated to assist the 3rd Mate on 12-6 watch. The Chief Mate was basically on day work, whilst our 2nd Mate was 6-12. I started to learn quickly and reveled in the variety of tasks assigned to me by the 3rd Mate; even down to cooking bacon and eggs about 2am when we had been working a couple of hours (those were always the best fry ups).

It was on my second night of such duties that my real exposure to a sea going life came about.

It was about 1am and I was walking down the main deck proceeding aft. As I passed the hospital porthole I noticed the light was on, this struck me as being odd at that time of night. The deadlight was down but sitting on the porthole lugs rather than being in a fully secured position. This left a large gap, through which I could see clearly, right into the hospital. My curiosity got the better of me and I peered in. I had not bargained for what I saw…

We had a Chinese Pantry Boy who did minor food preparation, the cleaning and washing up of cooking utensils and crockery for the officer's saloon. He was about 20 years of age. There he was, heavily engaged in aggressive lovemaking with two of the ugliest German whores imaginable. He was totally oblivious to me eye balling him. I stood there spellbound for about 5 minutes taking all this in – I had a ringside seat after all and this was uncensored to say the least. Once I had seen enough I hurried back to tell the 3rd Mate. Needless to say it's obvious who stood the remainder of the cargo watch and who did the eyeing.

We did not mention this to anyone for fear that we may miss out on a second performance, however there was no second round but we were both very careful for the next few weeks and steered well clear of anything the Pantry Boy had to do in terms of food preparation or handling. Hunger finally got the better of us.

The most lasting memory of my visit to Bremen Haven was the two magnificent frankfurter hot dogs I bought from a boat vendor who went up and down the river selling his wares to the ships. He did a roaring trade. Since that time I have never tasted such delicious hot dogs and for that matter, never been back to Bremen Haven!

As we were on cargo watches it made it almost impossible to go ashore so I opted to remain on board throughout the days it took us to complete loading.

At last the cargo holds were full with our bulk cargo, right up into the hatch comings with minimal broken space due to good trimming in lower holds and tweendecks, insisted upon by our Chief Mate. There was about a one foot clearance between cargo and hatch beams. The vessel was also loaded more or less to her maximum according to her Plimsol marks and load line.

During our port stay we had also taken fuel oil bunkers and topped up the galley coal. Our fresh water tanks were pressed up and our dry and cold stores had been completely replenished. In addition we loaded a substantial amount of deck stores, paint, mooring ropes, and bolts of canvas to name but a few items. We were ready for the long voyage.

6am arrived on our designated departure day, the Pilot was on board and the port formalities had been completed. We slipped our moorings and once again with the aid of two harbor tugs we inched away from the dolphins into the mid channel slowly heading in the direction of the river estuary. Yours truly, doing his duty on the bridge, diligently recording engine movements and sequence of events as we pressed on seaward. I immediately sensed the difference in sensation and ship motion, behavior and response between laden and unladen condition. So far I was enjoying every minute of my new found vocation and had no regrets whatsoever.

Prior to departure we had changed the Chief Mate. Apparently the one on board when I joined was only temporary whilst the vessel was operating coastwise. The new joiner was a Scot from the Isle of Sky. Duncan, 28 years of age and a fiery little character, although what he didn't know about his job wasn't worth knowing I later discovered. He had held a Masters certificate for two years and had been with the company since first going to sea as an apprentice, it was only a matter of time before he was awarded command because at that time the company fleet consisted of more than 60 ships. He and I forged a respectful relationship and I owe a debt of gratitude to Duncan for all his patience in teaching me principles of navigation and ship stability.

Years later, when I was a Pilot myself in the Solomon Islands, I once again came across Duncan. Master of one of the vessels I was Piloting. He was still with the same company. We had a roaring time reminiscing. Unfortunately he was unlucky to run his ship aground in some far flung and remote Pacific Island coral reef. The vessel became a constructive total loss. I never did hear the full account of the incident and sadly know not what happened to Duncan.

River traffic on the Weser River was heavy and it took us some hours to reach the pilot ground, where we disembarked our German Pilot. It was about then that I was first permitted to look into the Radar Consol. I did not understand the workings very well but was taken aback by the vast number of echoes which I assumed could only be ships. The Master conned the vessel whilst the 2nd Mate undertook the target bearings, ranges and aspect, plotting and reporting target appraisals and nearest approach data, obtained from the Radar set. All information was passed to our Captain. The majority of ships were only fitted with single Radar sets in those days and they were still rather elementary. In fact some older ships did not carry Radar at all. Seldom if ever did the more modern cargo ship or freighter carry more than one set, not like the mandatory two or more of nowadays.

It was well and truly dark by the time we had cleared the major traffic congestion. The Master had been on the bridge many hours, having eaten his meals on the bridge, along with drinking endless cups of tea that I had provided during my spell in the wheel house. I had been stood down earlier to have my dinner but at 8 pm I was back on duty with the 3rd Mate, armed with a pair of powerful binoculars, posted on the starboard bridge wing as an additional look out due to the persistence of conflicting traffic. It was still the northern summer but cold at night and it became necessary to wear an oil skin and "Souwester" to keep warm. Our Captain however was never far away during this period. The 3rd Mate was kept busy taking visual and radar bearings as well as a "compass error". This vessel was not fitted with a gyro compass so it was necessary to check the vessel's deviation in order to make the necessary corrections for each course we were required to steer. There was a deviation card posted close to the binnacle, however, as the ships position and heading changed, so did the deviation. This had to be updated in order to maintain an accurate compass course. Information concerning Magnetic Variation could be lifted straight from the British Admiralty Chars being used at the time for navigation purposes.

Our watches were complimented by our Chinese seaman who acted as lookouts and were always posted on the forecastle head – 3 rings of the ships bell signified a light or object ahead, two for the port side and a single ring for starboard. This code did away with any conflicts of language as it was the same to every tongue. These watches by the Chinese crew were religiously maintained during the hours of darkness whenever the ship was underway. In addition there was an extra Chinese Quartermaster always on the bride during night watches. He acted as the runner for the duty officer in case of need or emergency. One long blast on the duty Mate's pocket pea whistle made him come running to the bridge if he was elsewhere at the time.

By this time our diesel engine had been worked up to full power and was "thumping" away pleasantly and emitting that not unpleasant smell associated with large diesel engines working under load. The ship was alive and stoked and making a good 10 or 11 knots, heading into a slight westerly swell causing the occasional light sea spray to come on board. Every ship being an individual has her own character and this vessel was no exception to the rule. By midnight we were well out into the shipping lanes making a West South Westerly course. The 3rd Mate handed over the watch to the 2nd Mate and we both went below to hit the showers and then bunks. For me it had been a wonderful experience, despite the long hours of duty. I doubted if I would ever wish to do anything else for a living!

Our next point of call was to be the Panama Canal, thru which we would pass into the wide expanses of the Pacific Ocean. It was however many days steaming ahead.

5 Boredom and Routine

Another day saw us well out into the western approaches and nosing our way to the south of Ireland and into the Atlantic Ocean on a more or less westerly course. The weather remained reasonable and I did not experience any kind of motion sickness. By this time a strict shipboard routine was in place covering watches, meals, work schedule and rest periods. In fact it controlled one's life entirely. This was the hardest thing for me to come to grips with, the monotony, as one day merged into the next. Saturday, Sunday, Tuesday or Thursday, these were just days without any difference or special significance. The only way I knew the day of the week was by the menu, beef or pork on Sunday, chicken on Thursday, fish on Friday, kedgeree and selection of eggs or egg and bacon every morning for breakfast and so on. This only added to the monotony but I guess the steward's department had its limitations. Thinking about it retrospectively we were well fed and were seldom hungry.

Theoretically we apprentices did get Saturday afternoon and Sunday off but the reality of the situation was that there was always something that needed to be done so it seldom if ever happened. We were worked at weekends rather than the crew who had to be paid overtime, our services cost nothing. The only way to overcome the boredom was to become completely engrossed in one's work, read or tune into the radio if you were lucky to have one with a good band width. Transistor radios were in their infancy and early stages of development at that time and to get a good one with wide enough band spread cost an arm and a leg, certainly more than I could afford on my meager wage.

An apprentice was expected to devote a good few hours every week in study. The company enrolled apprentices in a correspondence course under a government training scheme. A certain number of assignments had to be completed within a specified period and mailed back to the UK periodically for marking and progress assessment. There was an annual examination in which one had to participate. Naturally all study was in one's own time. However, most benefit was derived from private tuition and practical exercises during watches, under the guidance of the respective Mates. Some Mates couldn't be bothered but on the whole most were very willing to pass on their hard gained knowledge. In retrospect, the quality and depth of training received by apprentices and cadets during this era was far superior to that of today, in my opinion. It taught practical application of theory, logic and fundamental understanding of the various aspects of professional applications, but above all else, built self reliance and confidence.

Our crossing of the Atlantic was uneventful as we edged further and further to the south west. We apprentices, along with the crew were tasked with removing all the running gear and cargo gear for inspection and maintenance. This include all head and heel blocks, topping lifts and runners, guys and preventers, the Safe Working Load were repainted on the derricks. Each block, shackle and wire was inspected, greased and its identifying mark and location identified, recorded and entered into the ship's cargo gear register. This was a tedious job but an absolutely vital one, all the same. As we entered the Gulf of Mexico, all the equipment was reinstated to original position and in flawless condition.

Slowly but surely we began to see large clumps of floating sea weed, a sure indicator of where we were. My frequent observations of the navigation chart showed a creeping passage through the Caribbean and passing exotic places such as the Virgin Islands with its powerful radio station located at St.Croix which we picked up easily on our radio receivers. It was with a sigh of relief that we arrived at the port of Colon situated at the northern end of the Panama Canal. Here we bunkered, watered and replenished food stores once again before entering the Canal and crossing the Pacific Ocean. Mail was also received and letters eagerly read – our written letters were passed to the Chief Steward who handed them to the ship's agent for posting.

The Canal Pilot was American and his jargon amused me, "give her thirty turns", "hard left rudder", "aback half speed", to name but a few. He did however demonstrate exceptional ship handling skills. He told me later he was trained on a Mississippi river boat. It was a marvel passing through the canal, first Gatun Locks on the Atlantic side, then Pedro Miguel Locks and finally Miraflores Locks on the Pacific side of the waterway. Passing the Culebra Cut made one wonder what hardship the original construction crews must have endured to achieve this magnificent feat of engineering. Eventually we cleared the Canal and proceeded out into the Pacific Ocean. Once only a few miles offshore I at once noticed the change in the color of the sea, it was now truly blue.

By now it was also starting to get much warmer as we headed towards the equator. As the ship was not fitted with air conditioning I took to removing my bunk mattress to the boat deck and sleeping under the stars. Talking of which, the heavens were brilliant. I lay awake gazing at the wonders above, night after night, watching the stars dancing about, the constellations, and shooting stars which seem to be prevalent in the Pacific. I occasionally observed satellites as they passed overhead orbiting our planet. Astro navigation was possible almost entirely throughout the hours of darkness as the horizon was very sharp indeed. Lying out under the heavens, listening to the faint drifting music from some off duty crew member's radio situated in a cabin below decks only added to the serene and relaxing atmosphere. Some folks actually paid for this sort of experience I thought, quietly to myself.

Occasionally we were awakened by a sudden rain shower but that was a small price to pay for such pleasure. Showers were relatively infrequent. However, when it did rain none of the water was wasted; we had rigged short sections of canvas fire hose from scuppers on the boat deck into fresh water tank filling pipes on the main deck below. We collected a lot of good quality water this way and it helped considerably towards easing the water rationing which by this time had been imposed. This was a common practice in those days during long ocean passages. Being the junior apprentice, it was my task to issue daily washing water to the crew from the deck pump on the poop deck and to lock it again once all had received their quota.

It was a Saturday morning when we crossed the Equator. This I remember very vividly as it was time for me to be initiated by King Neptune. Being the only one on board not having crossed the line previously I was chased about the ship and was finally captured by the other two apprentices who were dressed up like sea demons (no resemblance to Neptune). I was stripped, bound and head shaven. I was then covered from head to toe with non toxic paint as well as being dressed up for the occasion. Once I had paid homage to King Neptune I was hosed off with the full force of a fire hose. It was all good natured and harmless as well as being a fun way to pass a Saturday afternoon. Having completed the initiation and been awarded the usual certificate, signed by the Captain, I really did feel a fully fledged member of the crew.

The good weather signaled the time for painting ship. The Mate had devised a plan of action and passed this to the Chinese Bosun to implement. Over the next two weeks or so the ship was abuzz with chipping, scraping, priming and top coating. We apprentices were allocated the electric chipping machines, a job that we all disliked because it was dirty, hot and noisy.

The Masts and derricks were painted as was the funnel. The stays were dressed with a mixture of white lead and tallow. The accommodation was painted white overall as were the lifeboats, davits and railings, woodwork was sanded back and re-varnished. Work continued scaling the decks, hatch coamings and gunwales, but this was an ongoing and never ending task. Steam winches were overhauled by our engineers and then repainted black. Soon the ship was looking an absolute picture. The fact that in those days our company ships of similar class and size carried some 30+ very industrious Chinese deck and engine crew which enabled a lot to be achieved in a relatively short period of time.

Since departing from Immingham I had been religiously pumping the "sani pani" morning and night, by this time I was absolutely proficient in my handling of steam pumps, various valves and other associated machinery in the engine room in order to achieve this task and went about matters in my own way, no longer needing the guidance of the duty engineer.

I had also been taking temperature readings of our cargo of coal, by this time the temperature log was growing. Once the good weather was assured, each hatch had a corner hatch board lifted to aid thru ventilation. The large cowl ventilators situated atop of the respective mast houses designed to ventilate the cargo compartments, were frequently trimmed, in order to maximize every possible breath of wind to aid with the air circulation, or indeed backed if we encountered any rain squalls.

We were in our third week at sea since passing through the Panama Canal when we sighted the French administered colony of New Caledonia. We were heading for Noumea, the principal Port. We encountered a tropical down pour as we approached our destination which turned to steam as soon as the rain droplets struck our deck plates.

New Caledonia was tropical paradise indeed. Coral reefs with crystal clear waters and complete with the odd shark's fins breaking the surface as they cruised seeking a meal, golden beaches and lazy coconut palms swaying in the gentle sea breeze, coupled with schools of colored fish swimming about in large shoals close to the water's surface. This was all absolutely pristine. Looking over the ship's side one could see well into the depths for many fathoms.

We crew were horrified when the port agent informed us that due to wharf congestion we could expect to remain another 3 weeks at the outer anchorage before we were expected to berth and discharge our cargo. We had all been anticipating a good run ashore more or less on arrival. The anchorage was relatively sheltered but about 3 miles distant from the jetty and civilization! I guess this delay did not bother the ship's owners, since our ship was considered "an arrived vessel" it is likely demurrage would start to accrue in any case.

There was a hurried conference between the Mates and Captain, it was decided that one of the motor lifeboats could be used to ferry crew to and from the shore morning and evening. The 2nd and 3rd Mates would take charge of this operation. Engineers immediately set about checking and testing the respective engines to ensure reliability, even though they had been regularly operated during our frequent boat drills. Additional life jackets were placed on board and the duty boat swung outboard and lowered to the water. A Boat Rope was rigged and the lifeboat was secured alongside close to the accommodation ladder, all ready to be used as our own independent ferry service.

6 A Run Ashore

There was not a great deal of activity in the Port of Noumea. One other tramp ship from another British company lay at anchor not far distant from us. She was owned by Trinder Anderson's, going by a conspicuous black Swan motif painted on the buff funnel. Obviously, they were suffering the same fate as we, awaiting a berth. There were two French frigates hipped up alongside each other at one of the jetties and several smaller French cargo vessels. These French cargo ships were used I believe to transport some kind of Nickel Ore, to the various Pacific Rim ports.

After two days at anchor I was called by the Mate, he informed me that as I was a first tripper I could go ashore but only if I joined someone else. This was obviously out of concern for my well being due to age and vulnerability. I gladly agreed and that evening got dressed ready for the occasion. I was going ashore with our Welsh 2nd Mate and flamboyant 3rd Engineer.

We clambered aboard the motor lifeboat about 6pm, after dinner. The run to the shore took about half an hour, the boat being nicely handled by our 3rd Mate. Arriving ashore, I was surprised to find that my balance was a bit off, due I guess to the time spent at sea. My land legs soon recovered however.

At that time Noumea was a sleepy French style township, really too small to be called a city. It consisted mainly dusty streets and cafes with the occasional office block in their midst. The cafes I later discovered were mainly bars and brothels. There was a good few French sailors about the town drinking and making merry generally. None of my group had been to Noumea previously so we set off to find our way about.

We did not have that much time available as our ferry back to the ship was at 11 pm.

I followed my shipmates but being sailors, we ended up in more or less the first pub outside the dock gate. Actually it was quite reasonable and seemed to have a French proprietor. The only place of significance I can recall this trip ashore was the floral covered roundabout at the main junction with a large statue in the center.

I had been warned off drinking and was reluctant to break with this directive, nevertheless my companions assured me it would be OK, no one would ever know and they were insistent that I have at least one beer. The inevitable happened, one drink leading to the next. Being a shy and very inexperienced young man, I avoided the ladies that approached our table, obviously seeking business. The 2nd Mate and 3rd Engineer went about their business whilst I remained alone at the table. Soon, an innocent young lady came to sit with me for a while during which time she persuaded me to have a glass of wine. This was disastrous.

I had no experience of drinking and the mixing of alcohol made its mark on me. My head started to spin and I felt as if I wanted to vomit, which I did, having successfully made it to the toilet. I cleaned myself up but still felt very dizzy and like death. I staggered back to my table.

Not long thereafter my pals returned from their exploits, with half empty wallets I suppose. They took one look at me and laughed. "Don't worry Yule" they claimed, we will look after you. Yule was my nick name since having crossed the Equator when my hair was shaven off – it was decided by the officers I resembled the famous bald headed actor of the same name.

They sat down and continued their drinking and whispering to each other about their recent exploits with the ladies. I avoided further drink but did have to visit the loo again several times during the remainder of the evening. I felt awful but my two compatriots kept insisting I have more to drink. Fortunately I had enough strength of mind to refuse and sat out the rest of our time in the bar drinking strong black coffee and attempting to sober up, feeling rather ashamed and sorry for myself. Meantime, the bar was filling with French sailors who were becoming more rowdy. Several scuffles broke out between the Frenchies.

We three remained in the same bar until it was time to return to our ferry. I was still almost legless and needed assistance from the other two. They obliged, and I must say, did not abandon me in my hour of need. I was dumped into the lifeboat for the trip back to our ship at the anchorage. Once alongside I needed help to negotiate the gangway and made my way immediately to my cabin where I flopped on my bunk fully clothed. Luckily for me no one saw me in that state, the Mate and other apprentices being well asleep at that time of night.

I remembered very little of anything until early the next morning, even after a shower my mind was still fuzzy and I was nursing my first ever hangover. I dared not show this and turned to on time at 7am. When I was making up my bunk I discovered a pair of ladies knickers hidden under the bed clothes. Strong hints were made by my other two drinking buddies that they were a souvenir of my previous night's actions. I refuted this as I was not that drunk I was unaware of my actions. Besides I knew myself that I was just too shy for that sort of enterprise. Even though they later admitted to having planted them in my bunk the rumor spread amongst the officers and I was teased for a good few days. I swore off drinking until after I had completed my apprenticeship; I tried to convince myself without success. Obviously the lingerie had been someone's idea of a prank.

Several days later I came down with a severe case of tonsillitis. I was bed bound for almost a week until the antibiotics administered by the 2nd Mate started to take effect. The Master was obviously concerned as I had a raging temperature and was delirious at times so I was moved to the ship's hospital. He came to visit me morning and afternoon. Some of my earlier teasing obviously got about and met his ears as one morning he asked me, with tongue in cheek, if I had been with any ladies of disrepute. I assured him to the contrary. He departed my cabin chuckling. Slowly I recovered but was somewhat weakened for a number of days thereafter.

To our wonderment we did not have to wait that long at anchor for the berth to be vacated. It was just a week when we received instructions to proceed alongside the coal jetty. Discharging commenced and was in fact quite rapid, using our steam winches and union purchase gear and small grabs. I avoided any further excursions ashore and volunteered to do extra duties so my fellow apprentices could take advantage of the night life. After about 10 days our cargo holds were empty. They were subsequently swept and hosed down. Naturally, we apprentices featured prominently in all these shipboard activities.

7 The Pacific Islands and Australia Bound

Our next destination was to be a trip to Nauru Island to load a full cargo of bulk phosphate for Australia. We did not know exactly where in Australia other than our destination would be on the east coast. During our passage to Nauru we were kept busy about the ship along with the crew preparing holds and "bilge diving", so called cleaning the bilges and strum boxes ready for the loading of the upcoming cargo. We renewed the Hessian we had previously cemented over the bilge well gratings and made certain that all the limber boards remained intact and were well fitting. This work continued right up until our arrival off Nauru Island.

Nauru is an exposed low lying barren rock consisting substantially of phosphate. At that time most of the phosphate operations were run by Australian expatriates. It is a small island with little to offer other than its remoteness and of course phosphate.

The method of loading in Nauru is for the vessel to tie up fore and aft, to several buoys (all moored in very deep water). Two large, slewing cantilevers protrude from the shore and is the method by which the cargo is conveyed and loaded directly into the ship's holds thru a telescopic chute to the end of which is attached a rotating trimming machine that can throw product well into the hold or tweendeck extremities. Loading cannot be conducted for obvious reasons if the prevailing swell is too high. This was the case when we arrived so we steamed some 10 miles offshore to drift in open Ocean until the swell subsided enough for us to return and load. This was considered a prudent distance as the water depth was far too deep to even contemplate attempting to anchor. During this period I was introduced to shark fishing.

By this time I had been at sea almost 4 months. I was fit and bronzed, had managed to keep myself out of any real bother with the top brass and was still enjoying life on board.

For reasons best known to them and based on my observations, the sharks always seemed to congregate around the stern of our ship. There were dozens of them milling around just below our gently heaving stern. Large and small alike but all looking extremely sleek, dangerous and evil as they slowly cruised in incessant circles.

After work we would get an old heaving line, make up a trace out of seizing wire and affix a butcher's hook, which we obtained from the stewards department (being Chinese they were keen to lay claim to the fins for sharks fin soup).

With the aid of junior engineers and their machine shop lathe we fashioned a barb in the tip of the hook and introduced a semi twist. All this was attached together to make a very effective fishing line. We did not use bait but rather tied on a number of colored rags just above the hook to act as a kind of lure. For the sake of good order we did however empty some galley food scraps over the stern as well as a little offal to act as a sort of "chum".

The sharks became frenzied and we tossed our fishing line over the side. Soon we had our first strike. A medium sized specimen and hauling him on to the deck was not a problem. What struck me was how little resistance the sharks put up when hooked. Once landed, we clubbed the shark to put it quickly out of its misery. When dead the crew saw to the fins. The remainder of the shark was used as bait. Some of its teeth were formidable.

Over the course of the next week we hooked some 25 sharks ranging in size from 6 to 9 feet in length. At that time sharks were not protected anywhere but we were humane in our handling of the fish. By the time we proceeded back towards Nauru to prepare for loading there was a string of shark's fins stretched out about the poop deck, drying in the sun.

If one had fallen over the side whilst were drifting I have no doubt as to the fate that would become the individual concerned.

Loading at Nauru was very rapid, in just over a day we had loaded about 10,000 tons. Battening down was done as quickly as possible so we could sail as other ships were waiting to load at the island's single facility. The fine dust like phosphate gets everywhere so the entire crew (us included) spent many hours hosing down to rid the vessel of the powder like cargo residues.

As we had been busy all day we did not learn until after we departed Nauru that we had a female passenger on board, accommodated in the Pilot's cabin up on the Captain's deck. She was a school teacher working in Nauru and was on her way back to Australia for vacation. I must say over the next 10 days she kept very much to herself, the only time we ever sighted her was at meal times or when she sun bathed on the monkey island. A day or so after sailing from Nauru we were advised that our first port of call in Australia would be Cairns, followed by Newcastle (New South Wales), a two port discharge. There was an air of excitement on board amongst the officers as most had visited Australia many times and it was of course a favorite destination. I did not realize it then but I was eventually to become a naturalized Australian myself.

About a week after leaving Nauru we arrived at Thursday Island. This is the northern most boarding point for the Great Barrier Reef Pilot Service for ships arriving from our geographical direction. At that time becoming a GBR Pilot was the "crème de la crème" of jobs, offering high pay and much prestige amongst the seafaring community, worldwide.

Our Pilot boarded without any fuss and we set off southwards dodging in and out of the various channels and islands. The pilotage took two days or so and there was only one Pilot, so he was spelled from time to time by our Captain. The Pilot was always about when nearing any difficult spots or shallow patches. Wonderful descriptive names such as; Jardine's Point (old coaling station at head of Cape York used in the days of the first steamers), Cape Tribulation, Lizard Island, Magnetic island, Endeavour Passage, etc., most dating back to the time of Captain Cooke. The Pilot navigated us the entire route right up until our arrival off Green Island where the Cairns Harbor Pilot came out by launch to board us and take us into the port.

We were lucky and tied up to a jetty quite close to the town area. It was early on a Saturday afternoon and the stevedores were not intending to commence work until Monday. Hence I had a wonderful chance to stroll ashore unaccompanied and to explore for myself. The town was quite large if not a bit dusty and lay back. The streets were wide. The shops were all set back under verandahs and the pubs were full. The local cinema was an open air affair, one sitting in a deck chair under the stars watching the big screen. I saw my first Aborigine, bought a Kangaroo skin, fish and chips for my tea to satisfy a sudden craving, and then posted a few letters to my parents from the Seaman's club. The locals were very friendly.

On the Sunday we went on an outing arranged by the "Missions to Seaman" and made our way up into the rain forest and then to the beach at Yorky's Knob for a barbeque, before being driven back to the ship late afternoon in time for dinner. What a wonderful day. Soccer matches were arranged for us later during the week after our days work had been completed. Our goalkeeper was none other than our trusty Captain.

Once started it did not take the wharfies long to discharge and trim the designated amount of cargo earmarked for discharging at Cairns and after only a few days we were once again underway making our voyage south along the coast towards Newcastle, located just to the north of Sydney. Newcastle at that time was a major coal exporting port. This time we did not have a Pilot for the coastal passage south.

Arrival at Newcastle was a non event and we glided into the port early one bright sunny morning, to tie up to a wharf not too far from Hunter Street, the main drag. This time however the stevedores were about their work promptly, discharging into bins and trucks for transport to a distribution point elsewhere.

A number of our officers had been the Newcastle previously and knew the ropes. I was designated the ship's "entertainment officer" and was tasked with inviting the nurses from the large local Hospital, to come on board for a party. I was reluctant but knew if I did not follow thru with it I would not be a very popular sole. I can still recall the old phone number, B 3324 and ask for nurse……. To my amazement it was as easy as falling off a log! That evening we had a raging party on board in the officer's smoke room with many nurses attending. Music and enough to eat and drink, smiles and happiness all round. I was very popular; little did everyone know how easy it had been to arrange. From this point forward it would be a piece of cake for me.

The party ran most of the night. I will leave it to your imagination to work out the rest.

We were advised by our local agent that as soon as we had discharged we were to clean cargo holds and shift across to the other side of the harbor to one of the coaling berths where we were to load a full cargo of coal for Nagoya in Japan. At last we were heading back towards Asia.

The holds had been cleaned and hosed down in record time after discharging the phosphate. We had obviously done a good job with our earlier "bilge diving" the bilges pumping and emptying easily, then we moved across to the northern side of the port where we were to load.

Our ship squeezed into a berth between the ships "Baron Minto" and "Ridley"; on the next berth was "Fresno City" of Readon Smith's loading grain at the silo jetty. There was another old Bristol registered tramp steamer that had definitely seen better days, complete with a counter stern but whose name escapes me waiting in line for coal. It seemed to be a popular place for British tramps ships at that time.

Newcastle was geared up for quick dispatch of ships loading bulk coal. Complete railway wagons were run up a ramp of sorts, lifted and contents of coal tipped into the vessel's hold by a specially designed lifting device and chute. It was all new to me but very impressive and efficient. Loading and trimming took us about 4 days, but we did manage a couple more parties before we had completed our loading. Relationships were starting to blossom between some of the nurses and officers.

We went thru the same routine of rigging temperature sounding pipes in all the cargo holds. I knew the drill well by this time so we just went ahead and prepared even though it was only about a two and half week voyage to Nagoya. I was very excited about going to Japan and returning to Asia.

8 Heavy Weather

We set sail, all looking forward to arriving in the land of the rising sun. It was now November as we headed towards the north east. For the first four days the weather was kind to us and the voyage uneventful. Then without much warning the weather started to turn for the worse. The Master and Mate had received adverse weather reports so had us rig life lines about the decks and knock in extra wooden wedges between cleats and secure in place hatch batten bars across hatches to ensure none of the tarpaulins would come adrift or the cargo holds get broached. Various inspections were conducted to ensure the vessel was properly secured for heavy weather. We must have been well to the north of Brisbane when the winds and seas started to increase dramatically.

Obviously we had encountered the peripheral effects of a cyclone. Seas rose sharply and the decks were continuously awash, waist deep in solid green sea water. The ship heaved and groaned, rolled and pitched. Sea spray was continuously about the vessel. The seas just kept rolling in and it was not uncommon when on the bridge to look upwards towards the next incoming roller. Seas must have been thirty feet or more.. The forecastle deck was completely awash and often submerged under solid green seas. Nevertheless, our old lady kept plugging away although at a vastly reduced speed but the engines never missed a beat. Oddly I was not seasick at all, more than can be said for the Chinese Pantry Boy of Bremen notoriety.

This weather lasted for the best of a day and a night when at its worst, during which time we lived on soup and knocked up meals as it had been too rough to cook in the galley. Sleep was also very hard to come by. Then it started to abate just as quickly as it had arisen a day or two earlier. There was an air of relief amongst the crew. Two days later we were back to calmer seas as we ploughed northward towards the Solomon Islands and North Pacific Ocean.

Gradually, our speed increased and we were making good progress towards our destination.

It was at about this time I observed my first pod of whales, not far off the vessel to starboard, blowing with tails and humps completely clear of the water, all heading south. We watched intently for a good half hour before they disappeared over the receding horizon.

As we approached the Northern Pacific Ocean we came across fleets of tiny white fishing boats, really quite small to be so far out to sea. I thought this a little dangerous. It was later explained to me by Duncan, our Chief Mate, that they were either Taiwanese or Japanese fishing boats and operated from mother ships. They seldom if ever ventured more than 100 miles from the factory ship. Once they had filled their fish holds with Tuna or the like they would return to the mother ship to transfer their catch, take on water, stores and fuel before heading off again. This went on for months at a time until the factory ship was fully laden when they would all sail in convoy back to wherever they originated from. How the fishermen endured that sort of existence on those tiny vessels is truly amazing. I had experienced what it was like being on a long voyage but at least we had good food, a stable ship, warm bunk and adequate amenities!

I was now starting to receive training and instruction in the science of Celestial Navigation; I was under the watchful eye of the Chief Mate. I had to attend the bridge for morning and noon sights. Occasionally I would spend an hour or two on the 4 to 8 watch with

Duncan shooting stars, taking azimuths or amplitudes, but I was mainly with our Welsh 2nd Mate for sights and chart work. I was very fortunate; my father had bought me a micrometer sextant just before I left home to join the ship at Immingham. It was a lightweight job made from alloy and kept in a custom made wooden box, complete with brass plate bearing my name. I used the same sextant for my entire seagoing career until the introduction of satellite navigators and later GPS, when we all put them to bed, only to occasionally removing them from their boxes to dust them off during periods of nostalgia.

Days dragged by but after almost 3 weeks at sea we approached the Japanese coast. We could smell the fragrance of the land well before we sighted it.

The Pilot came on board as usual and we headed inwards, to anchor in Nagoya Bay. This was a crowded anchorage with ships of all types and sizes, and ashore mainly coasters laying stern to the wharf in a Mediterranean style mooring with two spread anchors leading forward and a couple of ropes aft secured to shore bollards.

Once again we were to discharge the coal into lighters but still using ships union purchase gear, not grabs on this occasion. Instead, the Japanese placed a hoard of stevedores in each of the holds, each armed with long handled shovel. The coal was loaded into large nets lined with canvas. The slings were spread out in various spots around the hatch square and loaded by hand. They were each filled to capacity and when lifted, the sisal ropes stretched and moaned under the strain. Having been swung over the side rail, they were then lowered into the lighters and emptied out with a single lift and immediately back on board. About 4 nets were used in every hold each with their own team. Hence, discharge was both uninterrupted and rapid. Trimming gangs in the lighters and our tweendecks did the needful. It was a monotonous process but nevertheless quite effective. At a guess I would estimate each lighter had a carrying capacity of about 200 tons. Coal barges were in abundant supply. The following year we used the same method to discharge coal when at Singapore Eastern Working Anchorage. It seemed the favored way throughout Asia.

Nagoya at that time, although being a major Japanese city, still retained many wooden buildings, as did most Japanese cities of the era. It should be remembered at this time Japan was still recovering from WW 11 and nowhere as affluent as the Japan of today. Citizens wore mainly traditional dress. Kimono clad ladies could be seen busily shuffling along the narrow streets with short steps in their wooden clog like sandals and exquisite silks. At that time there was about a thousand Japanese Yen to the British Pound. Crew, officers and ratings alike, had drawn heavily in respect of cash advances in anticipation of the entertainment ashore and of course, no doubt attracting ladies of the night, in some cases.

This time we did not have to rely on our motor lifeboat for transport ashore. A launch service was provided on a round the clock basis. Once ashore at the ferry landing, and outside the dock gate, one was greeted with a long row of Japanese style bars with their swaying lanterns and curtain covered doorways, tea houses, discreet hotels and of course bagnios; the latter loosely disguised to appear as some other form of business enterprise. The western music, bright lights and loudly dressed pimps at their doorsteps trying by all means to coax you inside with their promises of bliss in exaggerated phony American accents, gave the game away.

Being late November it was cold indeed and the rugged up appearance of most on the streets, and the warm inviting ambience of the bars and tea houses only added to the quaint atmosphere and encouraged one to venture inside.

We worked cargo from early morning until 6pm so we were able to enjoy some quality time ashore which led to a moment of weakness on my part, being succumbed to the special attributes of Japanese feminine hospitality. It was my first experience of the delights of the Orient, and I have to admit, Miyoko changed my life forever.

Time in Nagoya was far too short, although 7 days in all. It remained bitterly cold so I was not disappointed when our holds were empty and it became the day for our departure. This time we were ordered to proceed to Calcutta in ballast, on the way calling briefly at Singapore to replenish bunkers and provisions. My ship was to load general cargo i.e. Gunnies, Jute and the like in Calcutta, after which we would be proceeding to Colombo and East Africa. I would sail right past my beloved Hong Kong, so near yet so far.

After that it was anyone's guess as to where we would end up. This really was turning out to be an experience of a lifetime, and I was still only 17 years of age. I think not really knowing where one was off to next, only added to my overall excitement. My only regret was we were heading in the wrong direction for Asia.

Our sailing from Nagoya was delayed a day due to some last minute technical hitch with the main engine, but our illustrious team of Engineers under the experienced guidance of the Chief Engineer, worked round the clock to rectify the defect. During one of my visits to the engine room at this time, to pump up the "sani pani", I stood on the plates mesmerized at the size of one of the pistons that had been drawn for routine maintenance and remember wondering rather naively to myself how they would get all the components back together in correct sequence. The engineers obviously knew what they were doing as it wasn't much longer before we were heading out of Nagoya Bay, amid snow flurries which later developed into driving sleet.

The Captain was on the bridge for extended hours, as the visibility was considerably reduced due to the prevailing blizzard conditions. Our steam whistle sounding with monotonous regularity, indicating our presence to others, as we headed slowly through the murk. It was all very haunting and eerie. Radar sets during that era were limited in their capabilities and were not up to today's high spec for operating in such weather conditions. At best they could be considered a limited "aid to navigation" and used purely as such. Our Captain relied on the proven practice of fog signals, good lookouts and slow speed until well clear of navigation hazards and the heavily congested traffic areas, when visibility improved once again.

Our transit thru the South China Sea was uneventful and the weather was fair throughout with following winds and sea due to the North East Monsoons. Sporadic rain squalls prevailing from time to time. At night, between watches, I spent many hours with my newly acquired Sony transistor radio, tuned into the music originating from Radio Hong Kong when it was not being deliberately drowned out by Radio Peking's propaganda, which transmitted on a very close frequency. I guess for political reasons. I remember Ted Thomas was the resident DJ or pop music presenter in Hong Kong around that time.

The sweet smell of the approaching land was very evident as we came up on the Horsburgh Light House, situated at the eastern end of the "Singapore Strait". I was called to the bridge to practice taking sextant angles to determine our distance off as the ship steamed past – this was a good exercise for me.

This shipping lane is one of the busiest and one needs one's wits about them. The Singapore Strait is about 60 nm long by 8.5nm at widest point. It is bounded in the East from the North East tip of Bintan Island on the Indonesian side right thru to the Brothers Islands in the West at the commencement of the Malacca Straits. To the North is Singapore and to the South numerous Indonesian outlying Islands.

Junks, Dhows, cargo ships, tankers, passenger ferries, ships of every description and size are all present in their abundance. On this particular transit a few Indonesian warships were conspicuous, no doubt due to the developing political tensions between those nations on either sides of the strait around that time.

Singapore's Eastern Anchorage was crowded with many other vessels when we arrived. A British pilot boarded us and expertly guided us between the clutters of ships to a spot that offered us enough room in which to anchor. It was not long before the Bum Boats were milling around us, complete with young girls who carried small baskets in which were contained a few bottles of soft drinks. This pretext, I later discovered, was a front for their other more lucrative enterprises. It was all very discreet but fooled no one.

The bunker barge came alongside as did the lighter carrying our stores and provisions. The agent paid us a visit and brought long awaited mails from home. We only remained some 12 hours before weighing anchor and proceeding westward along the Singapore Strait, passing Raffles Light House and the "Brothers" (prominent small Islands) before changing heading to transit the Malacca Strait. Shipping traffic remained dense and the duty Mates were kept very much on their toes, as were we apprentices who had been placed on watch along with them, to act as additional look outs and gain valuable experience.

By this point in time, our senior apprentice was nearing the completion of his apprenticeship and kept checking and rechecking his qualifying sea time. He was expecting to be relieved soon and go back to England to prepare for his 2nd Mate's examinations. Co-incidentally, just as we passed Pulau Weh (mountainous Island and landmark at the head of the Malacca Strait) our "Sparks", Irish Radio Officer, received a message from the owners advising that John was to transfer immediately upon our arrival in Calcutta to another company vessel which was proceeding from India directly back to the UK. The Master officially conveyed this message to John, but there was an added bonus for him as well. The other ship was short of a 3rd Mate, he having had to sign off due to illness; John was to be promoted and join as acting uncertified 3rd Mate for the ship's trip home. Everyone was very pleased for John and offered congratulations accordingly.

We pressed on northwards, leaving the tropical Andaman Islands to port and Burma to starboard in our quest towards the delta of the Hooghly River.

Working cargo at Calcutta using ship's Union Purchase gear, cargo work was always so slow despite a dozen people to do every job.

9 India and Beyond

Christmas 1961 was spent at anchor off Sand Heads, the holding anchorage at the river mouth for vessels awaiting passage up the River Hooghly to Calcutta. It was a desolate place, quite far offshore with dirty brown muddy water, which by the way was renowned for its large sharks. At night the ship was infested by jumbo sized flying beetles, attracted by the lights and which if they flew into you, scared the hell out of you. During the day there was the circling "Shiite Hawks" that would dive bomb anything that looked like a free meal. As I was blonde, several times I had those dreadful birds dive and grab at my hair. I took to wearing a cap from that point onwards. I still got dive bombed occasionally however.

We had a joyous Christmas, all officers and apprentices receiving an invitation to the Captain's cabin on Christmas morning for celebratory drinks and merriment. Officially I was still under age and was not formally asked if I would like alcohol but a blind eye was turned when I went into the Captain's pantry and lifted a few tins of beer which I later enjoyed in my cabin. The Chinese cooks excelled and laid down a superb Christmas lunch, complete with all the trimmings. I suddenly realized I had now been at sea six months; how quickly time had passed.

We remained at anchor a couple of days (working off our Christmas indulgences) before our Pilot arrived to take us upstream.

An ancient steam powered launch came alongside from which the River Pilot alighted. He had his own minder who struggled with all his luggage but what I remember most was the Pilot's immaculate white uniform and plumb accent, which was more British than British. He would give orders to his peon who jumped at his every command. He insisted on being referred to as "Captain" rather than Pilot and was obviously very egotistical.

Our passage upstream was very uninteresting, the river being quite muddy brown and smelly, wide in the outer reaches with low lying banks. Now and then we would pass a grossly over laden barge being towed by tugs that had definitely seem better years and were obviously steam driven going by the dense black smoke they belched out from their long cigar like funnels. We slowed as we passed for fear of our wash swamping them and causing them to capsize. The river was strewn with filth and flotsam of every variety including carcasses of dead animals, so the stench was overpowering at times.

After a number of hours we eventually arrived at Garden Reach from where we could see Queen Victoria's monument. There were mooring buoys in the Reach to which some vessels were secured fore and aft by heavy chains. This was to ensure they did not break adrift during bore tides, common in rivers like the Hooghly, with large fan deltas. As we slowly steamed towards Kidapoor Dock I noticed two of our company ships in the Port. One was the vessel to which John would transfer. Both were at the buoys and going by their respective drafts, nearing completion of loading.

We entered the dock amid the frantic and comedy of orders conveyed between Pilot and Dock Master, also dressed in sparkling whites with very wide shorts that were rigid due to over starching. These were commonly referred to as "Bombay Bloomers" and had originated at the time of the "Raj" when used by British troops. The wide legs on the shorts intended to aid ventilation. Soon we were moored alongside our designated wharf and the gangway rigged. Numerous cargo lighters tied up alongside sometimes 3 and 4 deep; the ship was then inundated by hundreds of dubious looking officials, stevedores, coolies, ship chandlers, tailors and hawkers of every persuasion, not to mention the odd medicine man.

I had a good laugh when a leaflet was received from the Port Authority for posting on our notice board – it basically discouraged crew from bathing in the cool waters of the River Hooghly as it was infested with numerous sharks and crocodiles…going by what I observed if one was stupid enough to swim in that river a stomach pump would be needed urgently…otherwise curtains, no need to worry about sharks and crocodiles!

I had, for some months, been suffering with a "Verruca" (Plantar Wart) in my right heel. I guess picked up by walking on wooden decks bare foot. I had visited the doctors a few times previously but the lotions and ointments they prescribed did little to improve my anguish. In desperation I immediately collard one of the Indian medicine men who ventured on board and asked if he could do anything, he shook his head from side to side in confirmation and acknowledgement. He sat me down and brought from his bag a small animal horn. He placed the wide end over the painful spot and began to suck. After a few minutes of pain, the Verruca was out, complete with its roots. I paid him off with thanks and an additional bonus, a pack of "Lucky Strike", and then rushed to the medical locker to clean and dowse the small wound in antiseptic and cover with a dressing. After all, the surgery had not been conducted under the most sanitary of circumstances or perhaps by a medically correct procedure, it nevertheless cured me, the condition never reoccurred.

Soon after we docked, John left us and transferred to the other company vessel for his trip back to the UK. There was no replacement for him so I shifted to the lower bunk in the cabin and Michael to the standalone unit, by virtue of the fact he had been elevated to senior apprentice. John and I maintained contact over the years and he aspired to command many ships before sadly prematurely retiring from the MN due to illness. He later became an accomplished cartoonist.

Loading of the Gunnies and Jute Bales was very labor intensive. Vast numbers of stevedore labor, (so called coolies at that time) milled about the vessel. They seemed never to stop and the trail of rubbish and refuse they left behind was incredible. The crew was more or less fully engaged in hosing down the decks and removing their cast off trash from the cargo holds on a daily basis. For security reasons the ship was like Fort Knox, all locked down to avoid infiltration of the multitude into the living accommodation. Still, one found them sleeping in the most unusual places, such as the galley coal bunker, inside mast houses, curled up behind the potato locker and such. They were very imaginative.

I avoided going ashore much in Calcutta; it was just too crowded, smelly and squalid, but on one of my few excursions I did however enjoy an excellent meal at Firpo's Restaurant, this was a classy restaurant opened by an Italian – Angelo Firpo. The restaurant was frequented by the upper echelons of Calcutta's society. My dinner was followed by a movie at the Light House cinema. Chowringhi seemed to be the main district. I avoided "Isiah's Bar" due to its sordid reputation and my being alone, besides which it was regularly raided by Calcutta Police rounding up the crooks and whores that frequented the joint. I poked my head into the Great

Eastern Hotel but thought better of it when I saw how run down and threadbare it appeared to be.

Our stay spanned some six weeks. During this time we had all become honoree members of the Calcutta Swimming Club (CSC) and enjoyed a weekend now and again, swimming and eating. Up until about 1964 the CSC did not permit Indians as members. Occasionally there was a young lass, but always escorted by a parent to ward off the likes of us amorous sailors but that didn't deter us from looking, and drooling in some cases. We spent a few good times there until all MN Officer Personnel were bared due to some unsavory incident by someone from another ship. It was sad. Anyway, on my next call to Calcutta the ban had been rescinded because I am sure temporary members like us made up much of their revenue.

At the end of six weeks we were all ready for a move. The ship was about two thirds full and we were to proceed to Madras and Vizagapatam then Colombo to top off with other general cargo. However, before our departure from India there remained one more important job to carry out, fumigation. Rats where everywhere about the wharf areas and cockroaches were very prevalent along with similar creepy crawlies. Despite all our precautions we needed to avoid any kind of infestation on board. All the crew was assigned to laying baits and rat traps as well as cockroach repellants throughout the entire ship. It was an effective but necessary exercise and to our surprise yielded the required result. In fact we caught so many vermin it became necessary to engage a local rat catcher to clear the baits and traps.

Despite the smell it was wonderful to feel the fresh breeze on ones face as the ship headed seaward, down the River Hooghly towards the open ocean, under the guidance of a Pilot. This Pilot was somewhat less arrogant than the previous, but still very "pukka" and dressed in immaculate white number tens with his customary peon in tow. Finally, the fresh sea breezes of the Bay of Bengal sweeping away the smells of Calcutta from ones nostrils as we passed Sand Heads anchorage. Madras and Vizagapatam were much of a muchness, not dissimilar to Calcutta, a little less smelly. Our stay was shorter at these ports and time passed quickly.

Calcutta Port Trust

Kidapoor Dock Calcutta, sometime during the late 1960s or early 1970s.

No improvement - still chaotic. The smell lingered and could not be escaped when in the docks areas. Being moored to the buoys in Garden Reach was a slight improvement and a better proposition. The only problem being, the disgusting assortment of flotsam that gathered around the stern post or anchor chain which needed regular clearing for health reasons. The stench from this putrefying rubbish was so strong it was necessary for the ship's agent to engage local water boats to clear the debris. The crew of these small boats seemed immune to the smell.

Colombo by way of contrast was a different matter all together. It appeared far more organized and considerably less squalid. The port paid regular host to numerous large passenger vessels, calling en route to the Far East or Europe, to bunker and resupply so the port was correspondingly better equipped and organized. Colombo also seemed to be a focal port for the German "Hansa Line" as there were several of their heavy lift ships visiting the port at this time. My previous visit to Colombo was on the Canton when in transit to Hong Kong, years before, and which I only vaguely remember.

Kandy was the famous mountain resort but we neither had the time or funds needed to visit. Instead we were satisfied with the Missions to Seaman, Flying Angel and the occasional drink at the then named Grand Oriental Hotel (GOH), in need of a face lift even at that time. It was conveniently located close to the docks so a very popular haunt with ship's crew. Our stay was only about a week and soon we were on our way to Mombasa, in East Africa after having top loaded mainly Gunnies and Jute.

Below, the inner harbor at Colombo circa 1965 - 66
with what looks like John Manners' **"Asia Breeze"** in
foreground. The rather run down Grand Oriental Hotel
(GOH) is one of the large buildings at the end of the
dock basin, adjacent to the red roof. GOH was located
on the corner of York and Church Streets, right outside
the dock gates, it boasting a panoramic view of
Colombo Harbor. I understand in later years the GOH
was substantially refurbished and changed its name and
ownership

Sri Lanka Ports Authority – Port of Colombo

Rain squall after rain squall rolled in as we made our
way westward across The Indian Ocean. It rained and
rained for most of the passage. It was heavily overcast
much of the time which made taking sights less frequent
than would have been wished. Nevertheless, the Mates
grabbed them at every opportunity and plotted their
calculated positions on the charts. The rain meant that
Michael and I, as well as the crew, were engaged
working under decks or inside the accommodation. For
the first 3 days we were assigned to our Chinese Bosun

who instructed us in splicing of hawsers, rope and wires. He, along with his crew, was engaged in making up new cargo runners, mooring ropes and preventers for the cargo derricks. We had done this work regularly with him but it served as a good refresher. Additionally, over the ensuing wet days, we painted out the bathrooms and some of the alleyways that were not veneered, deck heads, the pantry and engineers duty mess. By the time we arrived at Mombasa much of our living quarters had been completely repainted. Even the Mate commented that it was not a bad effort considering there was now only two of us apprentices. Even if saying so myself, we did a good job, in record time.

Mombasa is the only major seaport in Kenya and is located on what the Africans call the "Coral Coast". It is a city steeped in history and at that time was crowded with Arab Dhows and ashore the Arab and Moslem heritage was further supported by the number of Mosques and Middle Eastern style architecture, especially in the old City and Port area which is dominated by Fort Jesus, built in 1593, a legacy of the Portuguese. There was also a significant Indian population, mainly proprietors of the numerous emporiums or traders of varying persuasions.

The modern Port goes under the name of "Kilindini Harbor"; it has a very picturesque entrance with a large white Hotel, I think named Oceanic Hotel – although I never went there, perched on elevated ground on the starboard side as you enter the port from seaward. The Port of Mombasa is only a few miles from modern down town Mombasa, with its inverted elephant tusks that act as a canopy as one approaches the city along Kilindini Road. Dozens of vendors peddling their wooden carvings of Antelope, Giraffe and animal skins flank the streets. It is also well known for its good hotels and resorts, many originating from the City's colonial past.

When we arrived there was a large American Aircraft Carrier moored to the buoys in mid stream. We headed for one of the wharves in the main Port. At that time there was still quite a European influence in Mombasa shipping circles and once secured alongside, a European Stevedore Supervisor came on board and headed directly to see the Mate, one assumed to discuss discharge plans. He was followed up our gangway by troops of laborers ready to handle the cargo. This time we were not restricted to using ship's gear for cargo operations, but rather electric cranes located on the wharf apron. Cargo was discharged more or less directly into rail wagons, obviously it was destined for somewhere other than Mombasa. There resided quite a number of Europeans and white Africans in Mombasa many of whom worked in the port.

It was a far cry from India where we had observed the coolies being abused, harassed and generally mistreated by their Indian employers. The African labor engaged in discharging were well treated by their European bosses and responded accordingly in terms of effort, although there was occasionally the harsh word or two intended to jig them along.

Mombasa boasted a very good Flying Angel Club so that is where Michael and I spend most of our free time, even though separately, as it was not often possible to go together because of our various duties and watches on board. However, there always seemed a reasonable crowd there from our ship. I think the American sailors from the Aircraft Carrier and support vessels had other priorities ashore, perhaps preferring to frequent the Casablanca, Rainbow, Sunshine, or Bristol Bars that were well known at that time for their hot entertainment. This was their likely source of distraction which suited us well enough as we had the seaman's club to ourselves.

We met and mingled with our contemporaries from other companies and ships, particularly Clan Line, T. J. Harrisons, Ellerman Line, British India Company and last but not least Royal Fleet Auxiliary, who had several logistics ships in port. We arranged soccer matches, barbeques and outings as well as ship visits. In fact they were mostly organized by the Mission to Seaman. If we went to church on a Sunday, the padre took a few of us to his bungalow after the service for a slap up breakfast of bacon and eggs; needless to say it was his only way of ensuring a "full House" on Sundays

The famous Elephant Tusks that spanned Kilindini Road in Mombasa, as I recall them during the 1960s.

We all enjoyed our stay in Mombasa (it was to become a regular port of call for me later) and were genuinely sad when it came time to leave.

Once all discharged and holds cleaned out we headed south down the African coast, past the Islands of Pemba and Zanzibar, off the coast of Tanganyika, slowly progressing towards the Portuguese administered colony of Mozambique and the Port of Beira where the Portuguese colonial influence still remained very evident.

Having anchored off the port for several days awaiting a berth, we proceeded inwards and made fast to the main wharf complex that could accommodate a good number of ships. The Portuguese were harsh colonialists and drove their labor hard from our observations.

Many stevedore laborers turned up to work cargo with only a Hessian sack as clothing, and bare feet. It was here that a very young laborer fell down a ladder in one of the tweendecks and injured himself. Our crew administered first aid but the young laborer was really more shaken than injured, although he had a few nasty cuts and suffered a heavy blow to the head during the fall. No one from the port administration seemed to be perturbed by this incident and they were really quite taken aback when our Captain insisted that since the incident had occurred aboard our vessel, the injured party be taken to hospital for more comprehensive treatment. This was finally arranged through our company agent. If we had not taken the initiative I believe the poor chap would have remained untreated and left to fend for himself.

We back loaded an assortment of general cargo, amongst other things, pallets and bales of salted Cow Hides which stank and needed to be segregated for fear of tainting other cargo, pallets of Carbon Black, stowed mainly in lower holds, high grade Sawn Timber and cased generals as well as a limited amount of bagged Coffee and bagged Nuts in the tweendecks. All this was for, you guess right…Calcutta.

My off time during our Beira visit was spent wandering alone up and down the wharfs looking at and studying the various ships, of which there were many interesting types and I clearly recall one handsome classic Norwegian cargo vessel adorned with highly varnished timber wheelhouse and surrounds. I never ventured outside the dock gate. I left that for future visits. It was about this time I discovered I was most happy when alone, doing my own thing. Besides, it was amazing how much could learn from observing other ships.

We apprentices were tasked with laying dunnage, arranging cargo separations, ensuring adequate straw matting was used to keep cargo off the steel work where there was no spar ceiling (timbers running fore and aft along vertical hull frames the entire length of cargo holds and tweendecks, held in place by cleats; holding horizontal timbers acting as a barrier between cargo and steel hull, the idea to keep cargo off the steelwork, sweating and from falling down between frames etc.) Michael and I were kept so busy as the back loading was so rapid, we had no spare time to venture ashore, other than for my evening stroll down the wharf.

We were completely discharged and loaded in just over a week and under way heading towards India once again. We dreaded the prospect of another 6 weeks in Calcutta and prayed we would not have to experience another extended period amongst all the squalla and we go elsewhere as soon as discharged. Unfortunately for us, our prayers were not answered and we did one further round voyage between Calcutta, Madras and East Coast of Africa before ending up once again in India.

Finally, our prayers were answered at long last, for having arrived in Calcutta and as usual discharged at Kidapoor Dock, we were given orders to proceed in ballast (light ship) to Christmas Island (there are two Islands bearing the same name but our destination was the one located just to the south of Java in the Indian Ocean) where the ship had been fixed to load bulk cargo of phosphate for Newcastle (New South Wales), Australia. We were all delighted to be heading back towards Newcastle, the nurses, parties and….

10 Our Luck Changes

Just before departing from Calcutta a strange turn of events occurred. It would appear that one of our company ships had discovered a stowaway on board soon after having left Australia, on passage to Calcutta. The Indian government refused to allow him entry into India and insisted he be deported and placed aboard the next one of our ships heading back to Australia. In this case the task of transporting him fell upon us, being the next cab off the rank heading in that direction.

The stowaway arrived on board under escort and was locked inside the hospital until after we sailed and were clear of Indian territorial waters. He was of eastern European decent, from Hungary. Over ensuing weeks we slowly gleaned his background and circumstances. He told us his name was Dody and that he was 26 years old. He was tall, slim, and blonde and wore specs; he suffered a slight impediment in his speech, nonetheless he spoke English rather well.

We had all been well briefed by the Master as to how the situation was to be handled and what security measures were to be implemented. Being more or less self sustaining by way of toilet and shower facilities, Dody was to be accommodated in the ship's hospital for the duration of the voyage. At night the door was to be locked and the keys kept on the Bridge, care of the duty officer, in case needed in an emergency. There was to be no freedom for Dody to wander about the accommodation or the decks and entry into the navigating Bridge, Engine Room or machinery spaces was strictly forbidden at all times. He would collect his own meals from the galley pantry and he would eat the same as everyone else. Officers and crew were discouraged from becoming over familiar with him and he would present himself on deck every morning at 7am and work alongside we apprentices. His daily reports to the Bridge, work activities and confirmation of his personal well being, were to be recorded in the deck log. Generally he was well cared for in every way.

During the evening gathering of officers in the smoke room following dinner, Dody became the topic of much gossip and speculation as can be imagined, nevertheless, our stowaway turned out to be a willing and enthusiastic worker with a definite mechanical aptitude. We later learned he was some kind of metal worker by trade.

In fairness to Dody, he never once complained or indeed shirked from any of his duties. Whatever job was allocated, he would try to complete as best he could, and he slowly became quite an asset to Michael and I.

We steamed south down the Bay of Bengal, past the Andaman and Nicobar Islands and the northern most tip of the Indonesian archipelago before following the southern coast of Sumatra and Java into the Indian Ocean and our ultimate destination. All the time we never lost sight of the very mountainous terrain of Indonesia to port and occasionally passed active volcanoes with tell tale wisps of smoke and ash rising from their conical summits. These were highly visible on the horizon due to the clear atmosphere, although some considerable distance away.

Christmas Island situated further to the South in the Indian Ocean, has as its port "Flying Fish Cove". The island was under Australian administration, which became evident by the fact that almost everything was run by Aussies. It was very tropical, far more mountainous than Nauru. Small houses or beach shacks were situated right down to the beautiful golden beach which skirted the cove, each veiled by swaying palms with the back drop of the dense undergrowth and dominating mountains. Colorful canoes with outriggers were hauled up onto the beaches, which only added to its tropical charm. It was everyone's notion of paradise, and the fishing was superb. Christmas Island is also renowned for its masses of red land crabs. The onset of the wet season around October and November stimulates their mass migration towards the sea in order to lay eggs.

The method used for loading was somewhat similar as in Nauru. We entered the small bay, or cove, and moored to several buoys, once the vessel was secured to buoys it was then slowly warped alongside the loading jetty. With our ship firmly secured in place the cantilevers were plumbed and the powdery phosphate began pouring in, amid clouds of dust. All doors, portholes, vents and other openings had been well sealed beforehand, in order to prevent penetration of the cargo. As usual it did not take more than a day to load to capacity and our seasonal load line. We sailed amidst a lingering sunset with avid red sky's, with a flat calm sea. By the time the sun had dipped below the western horizon we were well on our way. That night, as our hull glided through the water, the phosphorescence caused by plankton in the water, shimmered in our wash and wake.

Christmas Island Ports

Seen above, the remote and panoramic Flying Fish Cove at Christmas Island (Indian Ocean), courtesy of Christmas Island Ports.

The Phosphate Loading Cantilever is just out of picture to the right. A Beautiful landscape and easy for one to imagine the tranquil balmy evenings, with the drifting tropical scents off the land enhanced by the intense heavens dancing above as if alive. It had to be experienced to be appreciated, if you could dodge the phosphate dust that accumulated everywhere.

Being well laden, our freeboard was low. Early next morning our Chinese crew was on deck collecting the flying fish that during the night had been lifted by the sea breezes when they broke surface and had inadvertently become stranded on our deck. According to the Bosun they made excellent eating and were highly prized. At his invitation I sampled them later in the day, he was absolutely correct.

Four days out of Christmas Island, I was strolling along the fore deck early in the morning about 7am, ready to start deck work. Suddenly there was a horrific explosion behind me which came from the direction of the engine room and shook the entire ship, smoke belched from a few vents and the engine room skylight on the boat deck. I was shaken and somewhat frightened at this occurrence as I rushed aft towards my emergency station. The ships alarm bells were ringing and there was a hive of activity as the fire parties rushed down into the engine room. My emergency station was on the bridge, recording events, so that is where I proceeded. News soon came to the bridge from the Chief Engineer. There had been a crank case explosion, the main engines were naturally stopped, there were no injuries and the small fires in the engine room had been extinguished. He was assessing the damage and would revert shortly. We continued to drift for about an hour before the Chief came to the bridge, his overalls covered in oil and grime and he was sweating profusely. He went into the chart room with the Master to explain the situation.

We heard later that one of the thrust pads had melted and caused a crank case explosion, it was a major job to effect repairs. The entire engineering staff was grouped into two watches, one under the Chief and one under the 2nd Engineer. They worked around the clock. Our deck crew was assigned to clean up the mess in the engine room and assist with whatever other tasks that were necessary. I got the occasional first hand glimpse of the action as I attended the engine room to pump up the "sani pani".

Fortunately the weather was good and we drifted comfortably for the next 4 days. Late on the fourth day the Chief Engineer advised our Captain he was ready to start the main engines again but for the first few hours we would have to proceed slowly until he was satisfied all was well. The bridge telegraphs rang and the engines responded allowing us to gain headway and set course. Once again we felt the trembling underfoot, and the "thump" "thump" of the engines, it was very reassuring. Around midnight the engine speed was increased progressively until we reached our usual 10 knots.

During this crisis our Captain had been in contact with the Owners and it had been decided that the vessel would divert to Albany (West Australia), where we could get some engineering support and take bunkers and fresh water before continuing on our voyage to Newcastle, New South Wales.

When our stowaway heard the news that we were going to Albany, he at once became very quiet and subdued. We wondered why! It was not until the next day, when sitting on the boat deck drinking our tea at morning smoko that we learned the reasons. Albany was the port from which he had stowed away on the other ship, mistakenly believing she was heading for Europe. He had landed in Australia illegally a couple of years earlier and had an assortment of odd jobs during that time. He had got the daughter of one of the town officials into trouble and decided to fly the coop. Apparently he had deserted from the Hungarian Army a year or two after the Russian invasion in 1956. He had been 20 years of age at that time. Going back to Albany meant he would have to face the music, every which way.

About a week later, one chilly Sunday morning, we entered Ataturk Entrance and King George Sound in which the Port of Albany is situated. This is a natural harbor. Conditions were pristine. We anchored for a short while before proceeding into the port and berthing at one of the main jetties. Soon after we arrived two local police officers came on board and took Dody into custody. He was marched down the gangway under escort. We wished him well but we never saw or heard of Dody again. I often wonder as to his fate. Was he allowed to remain in Australia under political asylum and given a second chance in life or deported back to Hungary? I suspect the latter.

After only a couple of days we were underway once again. The trip across the Great Australian Bight was a bit choppy and decidedly rough passing through the Bass Strait, north of Tasmania. Conditions improved a little as we passed Eden and edged towards the north leaving Port Kembla and Sydney to port as we transited the coast, eventually arriving at Newcastle. By this time I had been on our trusty vessel for one year. The passage of time was moving quickly.

In my capacity as "entertainments officer" I did my duty in arranging all the parties and gathering of the friendly nurses from the hospital. In fact about a week before arrival the "Sparks" had sent off a telegram to his nurse girl friend advising of our imminent arrival. My phone call on behalf of the officers inviting them to join our partying was therefore not entirely unexpected on their part and we all enjoyed several memorable parties during our visit.

My girl friend was about my age and was a trainee nurse, one Saturday I called her and arranged for us to meet outside one of the cinemas in the town later that afternoon. After meeting and greeting each other, I suggested we go to see a movie! This did not go down too well; the young lady in question dropping numerous hints that she preferred me to take her back to my ship!! I was still very innocent, despite my independence and globetrotting experiences. I was too slow on the uptake as to the possible motives behind her suggestions, it only dawning on me sometime later. We did not go back to the ship but to the cinema instead….

We were destined to remain on the phosphate trade for one more voyage but this time we were to go to Ocean Island in the Pacific Ocean. Our port of discharge being Bluff, New Zealand, and then a short trip across the Tasman Sea to complete the balance of our discharge in Hobart,Tasmania.

I should explain, during this era it was not uncommon for officers and crew serving on British flag ships, to sign two year articles of agreement when joining a ship. In effect this meant that the shipping company could expect one to remain in sea going service up to a maximum of that period, before taking leave. This seldom applied as most shipping companies recognized the need for their crews to have more regular leave and generally rotated them as soon as practical after the completion of one year on board. There were however, some exceptions to the case, depending on ship's geographic location and circumstances.

If memory serves, there were basically only two main categories of ship's articles used regularly about that period, either six months or two years. It was just not practical in those days, to change crew any earlier, before the introduction of frequent worldwide air services that could be used to transport ship's crews about the world. This did not become the norm until after the mid 60's and even then the scope of air services was nothing like what we enjoy today. For ships frequently returning to the UK, plying the shorter Liner trades, then the lesser of the two agreements was used, the crew articles being closed and reopened before the Shipping Master at every ship visit to the UK, which gave the opportunity for those serving on board to sign off or remain as they so desired.

It was therefore not unreasonable that our officers were looking forward to being relieved in the not too distant future, but not this trip.

Ocean Island is a relatively low laying kidney shaped Island, only about two miles long and a small dot in the Pacific, situated almost on the equator. Its only export is Phosphate - "Guano" droppings deposited by birds over the centuries.

A large section of rusting wreck of an old freighter the "Kelvinbank" lies high and dry on the outer reef at Sydney Point, the shipwreck had long since broken in half. As one approached the loading facility the wreck's conspicuous prominence made an excellent Radar reflector and beacon, acting as a warning to other mariners to exercise caution for fear of succumbing to the same fate. The Island was administered by the UK, Australia and New Zealand. It forms part of what nowadays is known as "The Republic of Kiribati" and Ocean Island has since been renamed Banaba Island.

Due to its exposed location and after drifting well out to sea for more than 10 days, whilst awaiting the long ocean swell to moderate, loading at Ocean Island was monotonous and nothing at all special once commenced. The cantilever lived up to expectations. Perhaps the grade of Phosphate was different? The cargo had a slightly more grayish color with a few more lumps but remained equally as dusty. How anyone could live in this desolate place for any extended period of time is beyond my comprehension. We loaded quickly, in the small cove known as Home Bay, in the same old way, and were more than happy to depart and head for our destination of Bluff, New Zealand, followed by Tasmania.

Credit: John Beale

Seen above, a well photographed caption of the crippled **"Kelvinbank"** marooned on Sydney Point, Ocean Island. I believe this picture depicts the shipwreck not too long after stranding but in more recent times the wreck has disintegrated leaving only a single hull section as a visible reminder of the perils.

Our heading was predominately southerly and with every day that passed, the temperature dropped. By the time we were close to New Zealand, it was starting to get downright cold. Bluff is located at the extreme south of the "South Island" and can be considered somewhat remote, even by New Zealand standards. The nearest large town is Invercargill, but one must not neglect Stewart Island that lays not too distant offshore and is important in many ways to the local community.

Upon our arrival at Bluff, Michael and I were advised by the Mate that we apprentices, along with the rest of the deck crew, would have to assist the stevedores in sweeping out the tweendecks after being discharged. There was a severe shortage of labor to make up full strength trimming and cleaning gangs. Most of the lower holds were being left untouched for our next Port. It was dirty work and not one of the better jobs in keeping with our training. However, it did have its rewards. About two days after we started the task, we were very surprised to receive the princely sum of 40 pounds each for our efforts. This was huge money to us apprentices at that time. The crew was also compensated by the stevedores but exactly how much I am not sure – anyway we were more than satisfied with our lot.

The stevedores did not work night shift so I was able to run ashore occasionally. By now I was just legally entitled to enter a Pub in my own right. At that point in time pubs operated under very limited trading hours. I do recall them being open between, I think it was, 6pm to 8pm. Obviously they were crowded during this restricted period, so much so it was difficult to get to the Bar to recharge one's glass as there was some serious drinking taking place. This was overcome by the barman wandering amongst the crowd with a canister like contraption strapped to his back, to which was connected a short rubber hose. He mingled with the customers replenishing beer glasses and collecting coin as he went about it. It was a very effective way of overcoming the crowds and of maximizing trade. I never saw this method anywhere else during my travels. Take away Beer was sold in returnable glass flagons. It was amusing to watch the more ardent drinkers wandering off home with sacks over their backs filled with containers of the liquid amber.

The New Zealanders are very social and friendly types. We frequently experienced groups just wandering up the gangway to say hello and pay us a visit. Many Officer crew were invited to visit their homes for a BBQ or the like. They were extremely hospitable. It was not uncommon to see groups of young ladies standing on the jetty as the vessel secured alongside. Hence there was much partying. Some say the girls were primarily looking for the fathers of their abandoned children but that is not my personal opinion.

Thursday nights were worst in the New Zealand Pubs as that was pay day. At that time women were not permitted into the main Saloon Bars, so many wives waited patiently outside to get there weekly housekeeping before it was squandered on alcohol by some husbands. Later, bars were introduced for Ladies and of course nowadays the segregation no longer applies, quite rightly.

So this ended my first visit to New Zealand. We had discharged the amount designated for Bluff and now headed across the Tasman Sea towards Risdon (an area of Hobart) in Tasmania to offload the balance.

Later visits to NZ enabled me to see more of that wonderful country, other than from the inside of a pub. Years later I spent a wonderful 3 months residing in New Plymouth, whilst on assignment – a charming town with very hospitable people. The only down side was that my stay was during winter and as my residence was located on the coast facing the open ocean it blew a constant gale, rained, hailed, and snowed for the entire 3 months. However, the extremities of the weather were easily overcome due to the warmth and friendliness of the locals, not to mention the fine wines and beers.

A quintessential "six o'clock swill" in a typical New Zealand Pub during the 1960s. The restricted opening hours were finally rescinded about 1967 to the applause of so many avid drinkers.

11 Down Under Again

We were to complete one more phosphate run. Once the last grab full of Phosphate was ashore we wasted no time in battening down and securing for sea and Nauru. Having completed loading at Nauru we soon learned our allocated the discharge Port was to be Melbourne. Seas were quite choppy throughout the voyage, especially when passing through the Bass Strait in keeping with reputation. It remained miserable, overcast and rainy for the entire journey. We were arriving off "Port Philip Heads" just after sunrise on a Saturday morning. The Pilot did not linger in getting on board. The tide rips and races being very dangerous in this vicinity.

We entered Port Philip Bay, leaving Queenscliff, Geelong to Port and Sorrento, Frankston and St. Kilda to starboard as we progressed inwards towards the Yarra River at the mouth of which the Port of Melbourne is situated. It was turning out to be a beautiful warm day and visibility was unlimited. However, the Pilot did warn us about the Melbourne weather and how all four season could come and go in a single day. He was not wrong as we later discovered. After a few hours we secured alongside at Holden Dock, quite close to Appleton Dock, only a stone's throw from the City of Melbourne.

By now, all on board had become well accustomed to the clanking and banging of the grabs used to discharge this type of cargo, together with the incessant rumble and hissing of our steam winches. It was good to get ashore for a few hours to escape the monotony of life on board as well as the noise.

Melbourne is a wonderful vibrant city. It boasts some of the finest restaurants in the world and is extremely multi cultural and exciting. In fact at one point Melbourne claimed to have more Greek residents than anywhere else in the world outside Athens. It also has a large Italian community. All this contributes to the delights of the city, its night life and very friendly atmosphere. It also boasts an array of wonderful parks and gardens. Its quaint electric tramways serving the city and inner suburbs are a fantastic way to get about. We spent several memorable occasions exploring and shopping, eating, going to the cinemas and of course visiting the pubs at random. We enjoyed ourselves because once discharged and washed down; the ship was shifted to No 1 Victoria Dock, even closer to the city. Later we again shifted to South Wharf to await orders for our next cargo fixture. A delay such as this was unusual but we made the most of the opportunity in Melbourne.

During our stay we did receive a visit from two mysterious Chinese business men whom I met at the gangway and escorted to the Master's cabin as they were expected. They were from Hong Kong and were impressed to learn of my fluency in Cantonese when I was delegated, along with the Chief Officer, to give them a tour of the vessel. Their visit was very discreet as no one on board was advised by the Master as to the nature of their business. This obviously fueled speculation amongst officers, during evenings gathered in the smoke room. The consensus was that we may next be bound for China. We were to be proven wrong however when, after some two wonderful and relaxing weeks in Melbourne, tied up at South Wharf doing nothing, we received orders to proceed to our old stomping ground of Newcastle, to load coal for Singapore. This disappointed some of the officers who had half heartedly expected they may get relieved for leave, before sailing from Melbourne. We all carried on regardless.

Those officers and crew were not to be disappointed however; because upon our arrival at Newcastle the Captain gathered us all together and informed everyone that the vessel had been sold to Hong Kong interests and after discharging coal at Singapore we would sail direct to Hong Kong timing our arrival for the delivery date of 30th October 1962. At this time all crew would sign off – this was to include me and I would be granted leave in Hong Kong, it being my home. Everyone was ecstatic, most of all me. Even though the end of October was still a while away I was nevertheless excited as were the others of course, at the imminent prospect of being reunited with families and loved ones. It gave us something to look forward to. By that time we would have all been away from home over 16-17 months.

Newcastle came and went; some of us enjoyed the companionship of our nurse friends. Others decided to give it a miss and save their money for a big shopping spree in Hong Kong before going home. I visited one or two ships, a Chapman tramp and Baron Boat, both loading coal at adjacent berths. There was also another Cardiff registered vessel, Llew…something or other but she was a bit far away so I gave visiting a miss. My visits were more or less out of curiosity than anything else to see if my apprenticeship followed a similar trend as others. It did. I was also very interested to learn about other ships, companies, cargoes and trades.

We were now all ready for our voyage to Singapore. We had bunkered and provisioned and taken on board quite a bit of paint as the Captain had stated the Owner's had instructed the vessel be well pained before arrival in Hong Kong and subsequent delivery to buyers.

We cleared Newcastle and turned towards the north, following the coast over ensuing days until we arrived off the Port of Cairns, where once again we embarked the Great Barrier Reef Pilot. The weather was kind to us and we made good speed as we headed ever more to the north, dodging in and out of the tropical islands, various channels and passages. After a couple of days we arrived of the northern tip of Cape York but this time turned more to the west to transit the Torres Strait. Now we began to see the odd pearling schooner, usually with a white man as skipper and Aborigines as crew or pearl divers. We received the full history of the pearling trade from our Pilot. Booby Island approached and he disembarked thereabouts, then making our way past the Carpentaria Light vessel, before heading across the top end of the Carpentaria Gulf into the Timor Sea.

We steamed on past the Northern Cape of Timor and into the Java Sea. This was a very interesting part of the voyage. The seas were absolutely flat and shimmered in the sun and moon light. It was a wonderful experience and made one feel at peace with the world. We saw various vessels on distant horizons, mainly detected due to their rising wisps of funnel smoke. The occasional wreck on a remote reef as we passed clear and of course the smoking volcanoes to the southward, mainly located on Java and some of the off lying islands, all the more spectacular when viewed through the bridge binoculars. Arab Dhows sailed through the Java Sea in convoys of up to a dozen, all bound for a far off destination. At night they were poorly illuminated so keeping a good lookout was vital. They did throw sea water over the sails when they sighted another ship at night, this acted as a sort of Radar reflector and made Radar contact easier.

Michael, by this time was nearing the end of his apprenticeship so was permanently placed on sea watches with the 3rd Mate in order to gain more experience of bridge work before going to college to prepare for his 2nd Mates examination. Meantime, I continued alone with deck duties, reporting to Duncan every morning at 7am to get the day's work schedule. By this time I was well acquainted with what was expected of an apprentice and had no difficulty accomplishing my various tasks. I learned something new every day but enjoyed most the regular sessions I spent with our Chinese Bosun, splicing and working with cordage and wire. I became quite a competent splicer as a result of our Bosun's patience and regular guidance, for which I am forever grateful. After dinner, I would generally go to the bridge to receive instruction from Duncan in the various elements of mathematics, navigation, ship stability and of course not forgetting the "Rules of the Road". Life was very organized, even if somewhat repetitive and by this stage of the voyage the daily routine could easily have drained ones enthusiasm.

Eventually we nosed up through the Karimata Strait that separates Indonesia from the Island of Borneo (now called Kalimantan). The traffic was beginning to become much busier so I was placed on the 12-4 watch with our 2nd Mate to act as his second fiddle and additional look out. Finally a day later we came upon the Horsburgh Light House perched aloft of the rocky little islet called Pedra Branca (it was still there just as it was last time we passed it…) and entered the Singapore Strait. Ships were everywhere coming from all directions but somehow easily slotting into line astern to navigate the famous narrows. There was no compulsory traffic separation scheme (VTS) active in the Singapore Straits at that time, just the observance of good seamanship and obeying the anti collision regulations.

We arrived at the Eastern Boarding Ground and our Pilot embarked. He found us a suitable spot at Eastern Working Anchorage where we anchored, not far off the breakwater that bounded the small ship's anchorage, quite close inshore and in the vicinity of Amber Light which made for a good bearing point. This was close to where we had been anchored some months earlier.

Following completion of port formalities and being granted "Pratique" the lighters started to arrive alongside, together with hoards of stevedores and the odd bum boat with the usual milk girls peddling their wares. Someone must have given the local tailors a wink as we had several visit, all offering cheap suits stitched in 24 hours. This appealed mainly to the junior engineers in particular who ordered readily. The finished product looked quite good but with what I assumed to be single stitching due to the fast tailoring, durability had to be questioned. The Sew-Sew ladies also arrived, generally more elderly women who came on board to offer sewing, laundry and repair services. They were very useful indeed but they seldom spoke any English. However, they knew what was needed of them when it came to sewing and were all affectionately called "Mary" or "Aunty Mary" if language or name problems became an issue.

Our derricks had all been topped well before arrival so the multitude of stevedore labor had only to plumb them and start shoveling the coal into the large canvas covered nets, and load the lighters, exactly as we had done in Nagoya many months earlier. Each hatch had 4 gangs allocated. This went on from 6am to 6pm daylight hours, amid the rattling of winches, coal dust and chattering of the stevedores.

The Mates looked after day work watches, as did the Chief Mate. At night when there was no cargo work in progress I was given my first real task of responsibility. I was placed on the 8-8 watch unsupervised. I had become proficient at basic chart work and was therefore well capable of regularly taking bearings and charting the position lines to confirm the vessel was not dragging at the anchorage. I had a long list of instructions all written up in the Mate's Night Order Book and was under direction as to what I was to do, without hesitation, if a situation arose that caused me any uncertainty or doubt. It did wonders to boost my confidence. Looking back, years later, it was really no big deal but it was the turning point in me progressing from nothing into something! I could be trusted at last – not only restricted to pumping the sani-pani! I remember well watching the neon lights of the two "Worlds", in the wee hours of the morning watches. These were affordable amusement and entertainment centers for the mainly Chinese population. Both were clearly visible from our anchorage, as there were fewer high rise buildings in those days to obscure the view.

Meantime, there was a growing air of excitement on board, amongst officers and crew alike. Pay off time was now approaching fast and only a matter of weeks away. The Engineers in particular were busy trying to improve their "bronzy" in off duty hours; to us deck types it did not matter as we were already as brown as berries! This was always the envy of the engineers!

Over the ensuing days empty holds were progressively lime washed by the crew in readiness for the new owners. Our industrious Chinese crew had also painted the ship's topsides all around, cut in the boot topping very neatly and painted names fore and aft, as well as load lines and draft marks that were well above water. We were looking very smart indeed as they had also been kept busy with the paintbrush during our passage from Newcastle. The inventory lists and handover notes were also nearing completion in preparation for the imminent transfer of ownership.

One morning, after my watch I had the opportunity to go ashore for a few hours. I hitched a ride in the agent's

9am launch as far as Clifford's Pier and it was arranged I return in the next scheduled boat at 1800 Hrs; that would place me back on board in good time for my evening watch.

I meandered around the spots that were favorites amongst seamen at that time; Change Alley and the Straits Settlement Cabaret in Anson Road but being relatively early in the day it was closed so I wandered further down the street to Toby's Paradise Bar which opened early most days. A couple of Tigers later followed a quick visit to look at the notice board in the Cellar Bar, just across the road from Clifford's Pier. Whilst the Cellar Bar had an unobtrusive entrance once having descended down the front steps it was quite large inside and was famous amongst seafarers at that time for its notice board advertising jobs. If anyone needed a job in Singapore it was unnecessary to write letters of application, all that was required was a phone call to the various numbers that corresponded to the advertised vacancies on offer. It covered all ranks, from 3rd Mates to Masters, from Junior Engineers through to Chief Engineers, Electricians and Radio Officers.

After posting a few letters to friends from the GPO (now Fullerton Hotel) I then proceeded to enjoy a delightful lunch of my favorite local dish - mixed Satays on wooden skewers with Banana Leaf fish head curry – back at the popular Connell House restaurant. Whilst waiting for my lunch, beer in hand and with the bar virtually empty at the time, I had a great chance to study all the ship's crests, badges and flags that decorated the walls, as well as playing the Juke Box. I bought the latest "Sandoz" slim line, Swiss wrist watch, from my money earned in New Zealand but since time was now marching on I did not have the chance to visit the "Worlds" as was my original plan. I quickly returned to Clifford Pier just in nice time to board the prearranged launch back to the anchorage, very satisfied with myself and my outing.

I spent many memorable hours in solitude with my thoughts during those anchor watches, especially the morning watches. The lights of Singapore, quite close to hand, were always conspicuous and comforting, the coming and goings of all the small craft with the distant sound of their "put put" engines disturbing the stillness of the night and the wafts of smells and occasional noises drifting seaward from the shore. The host of vessels, both old and new, at anchor close by to us; ships owned by Blue Funnel Line with their names derived from Greek mythology, John Manners all named something "Breeze", Jardine Matherson - names prefixed by "Eastern", Williamsons, "Inch" something or other together with numerous ancient tramps sold off to the newly emerging collection of Far East operators. The list was endless. Amongst others the Straits Steamships' "Raja Brook" a small vessel that used to run a passenger cargo service exclusively between Borneo and Singapore, with her slightly larger sister "Kimanis" engaged on a similar trade to Malaysia, Singapore and Borneo.

This, coupled with those rapid Oriental sunrises, awakening sounds and now too familiar fragrances that aired with the rising sun, all made for a very good start to every day and I was thankful that Asia was my home. I just could not imagine living anywhere else or indeed ever wishing for any other chosen career.

As our ship was a relatively large and powerful freighter by standards of the day, our Captain opted not to follow the traditional charted track recommended for low powered steamers in the North East Monsoon, which hugged the Borneo coast most of the way before making a short northerly passage across exposed waters towards

Hong Kong; instead he decided upon a rather more direct track. We weighed anchor late one afternoon after we had delivered all the cargo, we moved slowly to the eastward leaving Singapore to fade in our wake. Soon, we had dropped off our Pilot and were proceeding at full sea speed towards Horsburgh and the South China Sea. Hong Kong was only 4-5 days steaming away.

12 Goodbye Old Lady

By late afternoon the following day we could clearly see the mountainous terrain of the Anambas Islands, off our port beam. We headed northeasterly into the South China Sea enjoying moderate conditions. The ship was alive with activity, everyone doing last minute things, whether personal or job related, in preparation for our arrival in Hong Kong. Telegrams were being sent to various loved ones advising of imminent return, perhaps in some cases to give warning and time to get the lodger out! Sadly, during our lengthy voyage there had been the odd casualty when some had received "Dear John's" from girl friends or fiancés, or indeed letters from wives revealing stressed relationships due to their lengthy separation. This was only human nature at work; but at that moment I could say with confidence, most crew on board were very happy at the prospect of being home in a very short period of time, not least of all yours truly. Even our Chinese crew was joyful and chattering away with big grins on their oval faces. There are some who declare that the only time a Chinese will smile is when they are either eating or counting money, the situation that prevailed on board dispelled that theory.

We experienced a reasonable passage and on the fourth day disconnected one of our anchors from the chain. The anchor was hung off with stout wire strops and robust shackles and the bare end of the anchor chain passed thru a Panama Lead in readiness for the coming day and securing to the buoy. That night, just before midnight, we were about 60 miles to the south of Waglan Island. All day the sighting of sailing junks and fishing fleets signaled our closing approach to Hong Kong so we knew we were nearing the end of our last passage. The Master was on the bridge at midnight and ordered an adjustment in speed in order to arrive at the Pilot Station precisely at 0600 Hrs the following morning. There was a tone of happiness in every ones voice.

I could not sleep, I remember I stayed awake all night and kept company with the duty Mates on the bridge. I was not the only one! The sunrise was glorious and as the Sun gained amplitude above the eastern horizon I observed vague shadows of Hong Kong Island to Port, which rapidly developed into the Stanley peninsula and not far ahead, Lye Ye Mun, the narrow opening through which we would pass before entering the splendid Victoria harbor itself.

Our Chinese Pilot boarded us from his sampan like motorboat exactly on time and navigated us through the last of the eastern approaches, thru Lye Ye Mun to Hung Hom immigration anchorage that was located in Kowloon Bay close to the Kai Tak airport runway. We were surrounded by the breathtaking views of the moment. We had truly arrived. Many on board had not previously been to Hong Kong and were frankly awe struck by the panorama.

Within two hours Pratique had been granted and we were underway again heading for one of the Typhoon Buoys that had been allocated to us and to which we would make fast for the last time. Our anchor chain was lowered to the water and the boatmen that were in attendance did the needful for us. I was home at last, after 16 months and 10 days. It was 30th October 1962. I stood on the bridge wing motionless for what seemed like an eternity eyeing the scene that lay before me, the changes during my absence seemed endless and my excitement at being home started to boil over.

Soon after our arrival my folks and brother came out in a launch to greet me. They could not believe how much

I had grown, how mature I had become and how bronzed I was. After showering and changing I took my father to meet Captain Banner. My folks and brother went ashore an hour or so later. I was to follow during the afternoon, once all the hand over formalities had been concluded and I was officially released.

After we had been at the buoys about two hours a group of officials arrived on board, they represented the new owners. Along with them came their joining officers and crew. We spent a good few hours showing them around the ship and familiarizing them with the various aspects of the old lady, she was now almost 20 years old after all, but solid as a rock. There was a new European Captain and Chief Engineer. As the sun was dipping all officers and crew signed off ships articles and were ferried ashore. Officers sent to hotels and crew to their respective abodes. The ship had officially changed ownership. As I boarded the launch that would take me ashore, I looked over my shoulder to say a last farewell to my old friend; her funnel by this time had been painted all black, looking like an inverted dustbin and a new name painted on the stern "Silver Moon" – Hong Kong, which I could just make out in the fading daylight. A new house flag fluttered atop her signal mast.

The Bank Line Ltd - London

The end of the road – a tired looking **"Weybank"** sold 30th October 1962 to Hong Kong interests for continued trading. She was renamed **"Silver Moon"**. I never did see or hear of her again except when she was scrapped in 1968.

In retrospect, the time I spent on board was some of the happiest and most productive days of my life. I owe much to those who devoted time and effort in passing on their knowledge and helping mould and prepare me for future voyages. I was no longer a first tripper!

I arrived home and Ah Kwan and Ah Wong broke down in tears, I must say I was a little unsettled myself. It was absolutely wonderful to be back, to wander out on to the veranda and just soak up the wonderful scenery with Stanly peninsula in the far distance, and the sea beyond through which we had sailed only 12 or so hours earlier. I had received news that I would be granted two months leave before joining my next ship in Hong Kong. Life was good to me I felt. I awoke early the next morning, it took a moment to reflect my whereabouts and I felt as if something was missing….then I realized, I did not have to pump up the "sani pani".

The officers had to wait 48 hours for their flight back to England; hence we organized a party at my home for the following evening. This had all been prearranged by my father when he met with the Captain on board. All the officers were collected by cars and driven up the winding roads to Mount Kellet, where we lived. All turned up and were stunned at what had been arranged for them. Our two "A's" had excelled and provided the most wonderful buffet, just like the old days I thought. The officers tucked in and thoroughly enjoyed themselves. There was plenty to drink and they all behaved amicably. Some other friends had been invited so there was plenty of non ship related chat. About 10.30pm the cars turned up to ferry those all back to their hotels. There were sad farewells, and then suddenly they were gone! I missed my friends but paths were to cross again with some in later years.

Most of the early days of my leave were taken up with tracking down old school friends (not forgetting girl friends). After all, I was keen to relay my experiences. I had initially thought that having been away so long I would have been forgotten, that was not the case and I was pleasantly surprised. Most of my male pals were either overseas at University, working elsewhere or uncontactable. It was mostly the females that were still about, some prettier than ever. I arranged to meet many of them at the "LRC" (Ladies Recreation Club). I spent many days with them, playing tennis, swimming and of course going on dates. I had no competition it seemed. My home phone was running hot and I was making the most of it. Privately, I think my parents scorned a little at my being constantly in the company of so many delectable young females, but if they did they did not say so openly.

November quickly passed as I was having such an enjoyable time. As Christmas approached I knew I must prepare mentally for my next trip to sea. By this time I had been fully informed as to my next ship. In contrast to the old lady I had joined in Immingham, this one was a brand spanking new motor ship only a few months out from the builders. She had sailed directly to the Far East from the builder's yard in Belfast. I had seen a portrait of her and her lines were very elegant and streamlined but in keeping with company traditional design which featured five holds and 4 deep tanks. She had a service speed of 16 knots, was powered by an 8 cylinder B&W main engine, and was to enter the regular Orient Africa Liner service between the Far East and South Africa. This would mean Hong Kong featured prominently in her list of scheduled ports, I would be home reasonable frequently. I started to look forward to my joining, in anticipation. Joining date was set for 1st January 1963, the date of her arrival in Hong Kong.

Christmas at home was a close family affair, although we did however attend a Christmas Eve party at my father's club and Boxing Day lunch was with friends at their home in Repulse Bay. I received several invitations from my regular female companions during this time but felt that I owed it to my folks to be at home, after all I still had almost a week remaining before I was off to sea again during which I could meet with the ladies. Carol, my favorite and who was to become a finalist in a well established beauty contest held in Asia, became very quiet and subdued as my departure date approached. Anyway, I made it clear that I would be home regularly and I would write every week (I kept this promise and we corresponded frequently). However, before my next return to Hong Kong she had been whisked off to the UK with her family where she had plans to attend University to read medicine, in fact several years after her graduation I received an invitation to her wedding in Scotland.

145

1st January arrived; I quietly packed my bags and departed to Blake's Pier, where I would catch a "walla walla" out to my ship which was now lying at one of the typhoon buoys, already working cargo. I was not to be disappointed.

The Bank Line Ltd - London

"Levernbank" – She was my new ocean greyhound. At Durban whilst engaged on the Orient Africa Liner Service captured circa 1963 or 1964. Unfortunately she was lost in 1973 at Matarani in Peru due to grounding whilst navigating in fog, where she later sank. What an ending for such a handsome and good working vessel.

13 New Horizons

My launch pulled alongside the accommodation ladder and I briskly hopped off taking with me my bags. I was very taken with the ship's sleek lines. I left the bags with the gangway quarter master and proceeded to the Captain's deck and respectfully knocked on his office door. Captain Stanton greeted me, sat me down and asked me a few questions about my previous experience. I passed my Passport, Seaman's and Discharge Book over to him as usual. As I was about to leave he mentioned that I would be the senior apprentice, the other two having only joined at Belfast and been at sea a couple of months. They needed a leader. I had not expected this but was not disappointed. This meant, being a new ship, as senior apprentice I would have my own cabin. Things were looking up.

The Chief Mate was next on my list; he was on deck when I caught up with him. Ivor Thistlewait was, a newcomer to our company and an ex liner Chief Mate. He seemed pleased to have me on board (maybe a bit relieved...) and as we walked aft towards the accommodation he told me that the following morning more or less the same Chinese crew with whom I had recently sailed would be joining. I collected my bags from the gangway where I had left them and followed the Mate to my cabin. The accommodation was very smart and well appointed. He gave me the key to my cabin and said I was to see him later once I had settled in.

My cabin was very comfortable and reasonably large. The bulkheads were veneered in light Teak; there was a single bunk with drawers below, settee, coffee table, large double locker, writing desk with chair and wash basin. The cabin was also carpeted. A large window opened out and overlooked the port side of the boat deck through which I had an unimpaired view of the sea. The ship was not air-conditioned but was instead fitted with a louvered cooling and ventilation system which was almost as good. I was the first occupant so everything had that new feel and smell about it. I particularly liked the matching timber work as well as the tasteful curtains and contrasting settee covers all carefully color coordinated. I was very impressed. Next to my cabin was the apprentices study and adjacent to that a double berth cabin where the other apprentices were bunked. The apprentice's toilets, showers and laundry were across the passage way. In effect we occupied the entire Port side of the officer's deck. Forward on the Port side was the Chief Engineer's suite and office, the Chief Officer enjoyed similar facilities on the Starboard side, also with forward looking windows. Between Chief Engineer and Chief Mate was sandwiched the Radio Officer. The 2nd and 3rd Mates were located on the starboard side. The Master occupied the entire deck above and the engineers the deck below.

I met up with the other two apprentices, "Ginger" naturally so named because of his flaming red hair and Max. Both were from the UK, Ginger from Yorkshire and Max from London. We hit it off immediately and for the next two hours Max showed me around the ship. I noted she was fitted with the latest electric winches; she did not have hatch boards but instead large sections of hatch slabs that were lifted and placed by derricks. This at least prevented the backbreaking work of opening and closing of hatches. Her decks were much wider and she had some 16 derricks. Looking fore and aft from the bridge her streamlined hull form became more evident. She was a beauty…through and through.

I was allocated my emergency stations and then was called to the Mates cabin to receive the usual "Pep

Talk". The Mate seemed an easy enough type to get along with. His concern was that the two junior apprentices were still "green" and often wandered about aimlessly. Being a general cargo ship on a Liner Service the Mates were very preoccupied with cargo work on her shake down voyage and the Chief Mate had not had as much time as he would have liked to devote to the trainees. That is where I came in. I gave the Mate assurances of my best efforts and went about my business. During the rest of the morning I introduced myself to the officers as our various paths crossed.

I had learned from the Chief Mate more about our scheduled run, it was to be from Hong Kong to Keelung in Taiwan, which would be followed by four ports around the Japanese coast. After Japan the ship would then proceed southbound towards South Africa, with occasional calls to Philippine ports but our regular loading ports being Hong Kong, Bangkok, Singapore, Port Swettenham (modern day Port Klang), Mauritius, Dar es Salaam, Beira, Lorenzo Marques, Durban, East London and Cape Town. We would then turn about, loading at all the same African ports on the way north, with the additions of Mtwara, Tanga, Zanzibar (occasionally - upon cargo inducement) before topping off at Mombasa and hence towards the Far East, until finishing off back around the Japanese coast, when the entire sequence would be repeated. This sounded great to me. A round trip was a tad over 3 months depending on precise port calls and rotation.

The following morning my old Chinese crew arrived on board, replacing the Indians that had brought the ship from the builder's yard. They were all surprised to see me at the head of the gangway as they alighted from the launch, I was greeted with " Nai Hau - Jo San Ho Pang

Yau" their eyes darting about surveying their new home as they clambered aboard under the weight of their kit. We briefly chatted amongst each other in Cantonese like long lost friends then I took the Bosun to introduce him to the Chief Mate.

That evening we sailed from Hong Kong, departing via the west, through the Lama Channel and as we did so I could clearly see my apartment block, conspicuous atop Mount Kellet silhouetted against a darkening sky line. As the ship built up to her 16 knots sea speed, it dawned on me how much of a greyhound and thoroughbred she really was; one could feel the reassuring throb of the engines underfoot and the continuous whine of the turbochargers. She lived up to my expectations in every respect.

We slowly altered course to the north east to bring us towards the Straits of Formosa, as it was then called. The straits were choppy and dotted with the odd man of war, originating from which side of the straits I do not know. It was not uncommon for merchantmen to be quizzed by the warships although it was slowly becoming less frequent by this time. That is why many merchantmen regularly plying the Formosa Strait and trading to North Vietnam and China had their national flag conspicuously painted on the ship's side and Monkey Island deck so it could be seen from the air.

At the height of the tension between mainland China and Formosa Island a few years earlier, north bound and south bound passages through the straits were restricted to certain days of the week, alternative days, for alternative directions. It was not uncommon for each side to shell each other across the channel on the days when there was no traffic. By the mid 60's tensions had eased somewhat but there still remained evidence of friction between Island and mainland. Formosa was more or less in a state of constant emergency as was to become apparent to us when we arrived in Keelung.

Taiwan at this time was under very heavy American influence, it had a strong US naval presence and amongst other things was reputed to be the center of operations for "Civil Air Transport", the Taiwan based airline which was later discovered to be the forerunner or connected with "Air America" which was operated by the CIA.

Upon entering the port it was alarming to see manned gun placements on top of buildings and there were frequent over flights of Taiwanese jets. Armed guards were placed at the foot of the gangway but other than that we were unhindered. One just had to be careful and not act rashly.

Being my first call I decided to go ashore with the 3rd Mate and one of the junior engineers. Had I have known their intentions I would not have accompanied them but nevertheless I did so. We ended up in a whore house, purpose built with perfume smelling cubicles, and complete with enterprising Mama-San (Boss lady) who lined up her girls from which to select. This was coupled by a summary of each advising history and specialty of the house. I was too embarrassed not to participate for fear of being ridiculed. I went along with the process and a young girl of about 20 years of age and I entered one of the cubicles. Despite the best efforts of the young lady to seduce me, I just sat there like a dummy until our time was up. I do not believe the girl ever said anything for fear that I would not pay her or she would receive a scolding from Mama-San. I escaped the ridicule of my pals but was out of pocket, which irked me somewhat.

We discharged a multitude of assorted general cargo over the ensuing two days, Coffee, Tea, Rice, Cased

Goods, Machinery and bulk Maize from the two deep tanks. The speed at which the stevedore labor toiled was phenomenal by comparison to others, with perhaps Hong Kong being the sole exception. The cargo was also carefully handled. We did not backload as the vessel was still cubically full. Loading southbound in Taiwan was subject to inducement and therefore not every trip.

We headed north towards Moji at the entrance to the Inland Sea. We loaded steel coils in the only vacant lower hold space we had. Highly planned and executed loading by very skilled stevedores, who handled little other than steel products. We only stayed at Moji one working day and departed the same night for the Port of Kobe. We passed Hiroshima and Kure leaving them to the north as we sailed eastward through the Inland Sea.

A considerable portion of the cargo was destined for Kobe. Here we discharged and back loaded as soon as suitable space was available. Several tweendecks were loaded with Japanese manufactured tractors for East Africa, more steel but this time Rebar and "H" beams, most of this being bottom stow. In all we spent 7 days in Kobe handling a multitude of various cargo types and parcels. During this time our 2nd Mate was kept busy every moment drawing up a very detailed cargo plan. It was about the size of an Admiralty Chart, was all color coded to depict commodity and port of discharge together with number of lifts, items or tonnage, being so recorded for ease of reference. It was a work of art for sure. This was virtually a full time and ongoing job because no sooner had he completed the southbound cargo plan, then he started the northbound, furthermore they were in triplicate; one for the ship, one for the Chief Mate and one sent to the company. It is claimed that the quality of a 2nd Mates Cargo Plan was a measure of his ability and on which future promotion prospects hinged to some degree. I am not sure as to the validity of this assumption but one thing is certain, there was a lot of competition between various 2nd mates on the liner trades and their cargo plans were absolute masterpieces. Without doubt 2nd Mates engaged on this class of vessel were the hardest working of all the Mates; not only did they have to keep watches but also were the designated navigating officer who was also responsible for regularly updating Chart Corrections from Admiralty Notices to Mariners as well as acting as the ship's medical officer.

At Kobe I was fortunate enough to be taken ashore by the Chief Mate; it was his birthday so he treated the apprentices who were not on duty, to a Kobe steak. This has to be eaten to be believed.

Soon after sailing from Kobe we arrived at Osaka, only a short distance along the coast separated the two ports. This was another major discharge and loading port. We stayed another 5 days, working around the clock. Here, the Mates and apprentices were kept very busy but the engineers enjoyed more time ashore. For those seeking the ladies, the usual arrangement was to strike a deal with the damsel of one's choice at first Japanese port of call, usually Moji, Hiroshima or Kobe. Having done so, the lady would follow the ship as it visited the various other ports around the Japanese coast. In all Japanese ports there was an abundance of drinking establishments and tea houses so selecting the right beauty was relatively easy. Some crew had permanent friends with whom they pre-arranged meetings, the vessel being on a regular run and operating to a reasonably accurate schedule, it was not difficult to coordinate social calendars.

Osaka was hard work. We back loaded various small parcels of generals, all of which needed to be separated by coconut matting, nets or dunnage and carefully recorded for inclusion in the cargo plan. This job fell to the apprentices.

Eventually, we departed and proceed south past Wakayama following the coast line until arriving at Yokohama at the foot of Tokyo Bay. On one of the infrequent clear days, from seaward one could see Mount Fuji with its snow capped peak. Yokohama was a good spot to go ashore, offering a vast selection of night life. Once was enough for me, in any event we apprentices were not flush with money and couldn't afford much, certainly not the ladies.

By the time we had been in Yokohama 5 or 6 days our cargo work was just about completed. We had discharged all the cargo destined for Japan and back loaded in place many different varieties for all points south, commencing with Hong Kong. By the time we sailed we had been on the Japanese coast a month, time was flying again and I was leaning my profession fast.

14 Heading South

We cleared Tokyo Bay bound for Hong Kong (we did not call Keelung sailing southward this trip). We had many tons of electrical and white goods for Hong Kong. This was high revenue general cargo. The ship was literally a floating warehouse by this time, one needed an inventory list which was the purpose of the cargo plan and manifests, after all said and done.

We sped through the Straits of Formosa again, engines never missing a beat, always with that gentle "whine" of the engine's turbochargers in the background. We arrived in Hong Kong in accordance with our advertised schedule in the shipping section of the "South China Morning Post". The anchor chain was parted as usual and one anchor hung off in readiness for securing to the harbor buoy. We wasted no time and soon port formalities were completed and we were all secured. The barges were alongside instantly, ready and eager to accept our valuable cargo. We discharged and back loaded simultaneously, back load consisting mainly manufactured goods and pallets of cotton items for east African ports.

In Hong Kong, many of the barges are privately owned and subcontracted to stevedoring concerns, in such cases the cargo barge is a family home having quite substantial living accommodation. Most are fitted with single slewing derricks and other than not being self propelled are otherwise generally self-sustaining. The family members act as stevedore, derrick operator, crew and so forth. Families take great pride in their barges and they are maintained in tip top condition.

I managed that evening at home for dinner but returned to the ship by 11pm as I had an early start the following morning and "walla wallas" didn't operate all night. My mother loading me down with goodies tins of biscuits, chocolates, etc. I took all this with me as I did not wish to offend but as I do not have a sweet tooth, offloaded most of it to the other two apprentices the next morning, who accepted willingly.

By now I was becoming acquainted with the duties of senior apprentice and reveled in that little extra responsibility. I believed I was doing a satisfactory job. I had received no complaints so assumed the best. Very conceited of me I felt. Our Bosun was always at my back in case I needed to know anything and I was not afraid to ask for his advice if I was uncertain.

Prior to sailing from Hong Kong there arrived on board an additional electrician, he was South African. He was a big talker and claimed to be of French decent and the Marquis de….or something or other. It may have been true but none the less no one believed him. If he was a Marquis, what was he doing in the MN as a junior officer we all pondered? After getting fed up with his romancing, one day a junior engineer procured a large piece of blue cheese from the Chief Steward. Whilst the electrician was on duty the engineer placed the cheese inside a small inspection panel below his cabin port hole and screwed it all up again. One could not even notice that it had been tampered with. Sunday was Captain's inspection and every week upon entering the electrician's cabin the Captain complained profusely at the smell and instructed the cabin be properly cleaned and the electrician do his laundry more frequently, this went on for a good few weeks until everyone started to feel sorry for the electrician and the cheese was removed just as discreetly as it had been placed. I think the electrician suspected something but it had the desired effect as his tall stories ceased, in fact after a couple of months he became a very likable and popular shipmate.

There was a raging electrical storm and heavy rain as we departed Hong Kong. I got soaked as my station was no longer on the bridge but rather on the forecastle with the Chief Mate. Once we passed Green Island heading for Lama and reconnected our anchor which had been disconnected for mooring purposes, we were stood down. We were bound for Bangkok, the capital city of Thailand. I had heard many stories but waited in anticipation of what to expect. My previous call at Bangkok had been for a couple of hours at Don Muang Airport during transit. Passage to Bangkok from Hong Kong is about 4-5 days and it is always rough when passing the southernmost tip of Vietnam. Once into the Gulf of Thailand it eases up a little except during certain monsoonal months.

Arriving at the Bangkok Bar at the mouth of the Chao Phraya River, ships usually have to anchor and await a rising tide or indeed high water to cross the river bar, depending on the ship's draft. This we had to do. Some ships which are very deeply laden are required to lighten into barges at Koh Si Chang Island anchorage in order to reduce sufficient draft to navigate up the river.

Two hours before high water the Thai Pilot came on board and we weighed anchor and started to move upstream. The river is very fast flowing and ships pass each other at what appears great speed. The delta is wide but the river quickly narrows and winds towards the upper reaches. We proceeded up stream to Pak Nam Immigration Anchorage where we underwent port formalities. I was amused by the long tail motor boats (so named because of the design of outboard motor and long propeller shaft) that darted all over the river carrying passengers, day and night. The method of propulsion is required in very shallow "Klongs" (canals) up which many of these craft navigate. Once clear of Pak Nam, we proceeded further up stream to our designated berth at Klong Toei, the main port area. The vessel was swung in the river, using our anchor, to face downstream, and then we berthed port side alongside at a wharf with many other ships ahead and astern of us. No sooner had we berthed and hatches been opened than we were inundated by boat loads of girls. Boats just kept coming alongside. The females climbed up any rope or ladder on to the main deck and then heading towards the crews accommodation area where they quickly disappeared. Try as we may (some didn't try that hard) we didn't win the battle, they soon infiltrated to the Officers accommodation deck.

Unknown to me it was usual custom for each to hire his own girl, she would clean the cabin, do the washing, sewing and ironing plus any other service requested. They slept in your cabin and ate whatever you gave them or you bought for them. They did not generally seek money but goods instead, mostly Lux or Palmolive toilet soap, one cake was the going rate for a day as was one packet of Lucky Strike cigarettes. For a carton they were yours for a week or as long as the ship remained, the same for six cakes of perfumed toilet soap. These items were more valuable to them than coin as they could be sold or exchanged for high returns on the black market.

In some ways it was pitiful. I was no different to anyone else; I followed the tradition and joined the others. It was the beginning of my discovering what a highly cultured race the Thais are, also the incredibly beauty and charm of their women. Having been raised within the Asian region I had hitherto ignored Asian women, but as I grew older I began to realize their delicate beauty, caring nature, high moral standards and femininity; not surprisingly therefore, my wife so happens to be of Asian origin.

I grew to respect these girls, they were not doing this because they wanted to, it was a simple case of "no money no honey"; if they made no money they didn't eat and in most cases that translated into their families and children going hungry as well. On this occasion we remained in Bangkok 5 days loading bagged rice and some veneers and packs of high grade sandalwood and teak. The method used at that time to load rice was very labor intensive. Coolies carried bags of rice on their heads in a never ending stream from warehouse to ships side; it was then lifted aboard in rope slings. In the cargo holds it was customary to lay wooden ducts fore and aft as well as athwart ships every few tiers of bags, to aid the through ventilation and stop the rice sweating and spoiling. Rush matting was used to keep the bags clear of ship's steel work. Consequently loading was somewhat slow. Nevertheless, the manner in which the rice was stowed was a work of art, every bag perfectly positioned to result in a tight stow. Over the years I can never recall discharging rice that had spoiled, when it had been loaded in this fashion.

Outside the dock gate at Klong Toei was the infamous "Mosquito Bar" and "Venus Room", both shabby dives that were basically a meat market but a firm favorite for visiting sailors. The girls seemed to have a pact between them, those from the bars did not board the ships and those on the ships did not encroach on bar territory. Business for the bar girls was brisk and transacted in dingy short time hotels close by somewhere further up town. I visited the Mosquito Bar and Venus Room a couple of times over ensuing trips, more out of curiosity rather than for any other reason. They both attracted too many hard drinkers and troublesome "Falangs" (at that time mostly down at heel Expats gone native) for my liking, there were frequent scuffles, in fact almost nightly, mostly women related. One of our engineers suffered the consequences of having allegedly started a brawl and ended up having stitches above his left eye and side of the head where he had been hit with a Baseball Bat being wielded by the Barman. It was a good place to steer clear of. I preferred the boat girls on the ship. Some years later the Mosquito Bar was demolished. I am uncertain as to its final fate but it was never rebuilt because the last time I visited the area there was just vacant land.

Close to these two establishments was the Mission to Seamen with a very different atmosphere but very welcoming to all.

After 5 days, we had to say goodbye to our lady friends. They would be waiting for us upon our return northbound. We raced down the Chao Phraya River towards the open sea, brushing aside large rafts of floating lotus reeds, lilies and various other vegetation that accumulated, as we approached the river delta and on towards Singapore.

Ports of Thailand - Bangkok

The Thai Logger cum General Cargo ship "Intan", captured whilst anchored at Bangkok Reach in the Chao Phraya River. The annoying rafts of Lotus Weed can be seen floating downstream. These floating rafts had root systems that protruded well below the surface and could be a nuisance at times choking ship's cooling water intakes.

Bangkok to Singapore was only a little over 2 days at our service speed. Being on a liner service we berthed upon arrival at Keppel Harbor. The wharfs and their adjoining warehouses lay along the Island side of the narrow channel that separated Singapore from Sentosa Island and was the demarcation and conduit between the East and West Port anchorages. There was a relatively large Dry-Dock and numerous general cargo wharves and warehouses. To the west of the channel Western Anchorage, Pulau Bukam (the large Shell oil terminal) and Sultan Shoal, to the east lay Eastern Small Ship Anchorage with its breakwater and the deeper water Eastern Working Anchorage.

As I had visited Singapore previously, I kept the nights on board and suggested where the other two apprentices may choose to visit. Singapore was a safe place in which to go ashore. Off they went all dressed to kill. They returned unscathed before midnight. They sat in my cabin and gave me a run down on their exploits which included visiting various bars in Orchid Road, Connell House and Change Alley, the "World" entertainment centers. Much as I had done on my first visit. The other highlights they would take in northbound. Singapore at that stage had still a sizable British garrison and therefore Orchard Road boasted numerous bars and girly dives. They enjoyed themselves and the run ashore did them both good.

By this time I was forging a good working relationship with our 2nd Mate Dave, who was teaching me a lot about making cargo plans, stowage of general cargo and the like. I particularly enjoyed being on cargo watch with him because of this. Dave held a Mates Certificate and nearly had sufficient sea time to undergo examination for Masters, which he intended to do at the conclusion of the current trip. He was an excellent all round 2nd Mate, very quiet and reserved but with a keen sense of humor.

We loaded more manufactured goods and discharged about 500 tons of bagged rice, also, loading some heavy machinery and a few Trucks on deck. Our stay was relatively short and we were underway by mid afternoon on the second day. Our next call being Port Swettenham up the Malacca Straits, located in Malaysia. Leaving Raffles light to starboard we skirted the Nipa Buoy and headed north, passing a few miles distant from Pisang Island (Banana Island) we continued on our way. The lights of Malacca City remained visible to the eye for some time as we passed then left them in our wake later that night. By first light we were approaching the Fairway Buoy marking the southern entrance to the long channel flanked by mangrove swamps which leads to Port Swettenham. This also being the point at which the Pilot boards.

At that time Port Swettenham only offered a few shallow water berths best suited to smaller ships and coastal traders, so we had to secure to mooring buoys mid stream, about a mile from the port itself. Port Swettenham was within the Malaysian state of Selangor and was the principal Port for western Malaysia, it being fairly close to the Capital, Kuala Lumpur. It boasted a very good rail terminus with services to many Malaysian cities and was the main arterial hub to and from Port Swettenham. It was strategically positioned mid-way up the Malaysian Peninsula on the Malacca Straits.

Here we loaded bundles of high grade treated sawn timber, veneers, and bales of latex rubber for South African ports. It amused me how the latex was just dumped into the holds by reeving out the cargo net causing the bales to bounce everywhere. These needed to be retrieved by the laborers then correctly and neatly stowed. Occasionally we would load parcels of loose timber planks which were very laborious. All was ferried out to us in lighters and loaded aboard using ships gear. One morning during smoko I stood on the boat deck in the shade of the awnings, sipping my tea and watching the cargo being loaded. There was no doubt in my mind, whilst the electric winches were quieter and cleaner in their operation; they were nowhere as fast as the old steam winches when in the hands of an expert winch man.

By this time Ginger and Max were settling down and becoming useful hands. Whenever possible I asked our friendly Bosun to take them for instruction in splicing and general seamanship, he was more than willing to oblige and being Chinese this gave him great face amongst his crew. Both these apprentices had joined direct from Grammar School without the advantage of any pre-sea training. Upon reflection, I realized the value of such training, particularly in mentally preparing one for a career at sea. My father had been right after all.

We spent a couple of days more loading at the buoys, not far from "Eagle Nest Point" flanked by the mangroves along the shoreline. By this time we were starting to fill the holds to capacity, cubically at least. When we sailed for Mauritius we were more or less full. Our departure was during daylight hours and we exited the Port via the southern channel which was used most of the time. There is a northern channel which, at that time was only used by small vessels. It was only a short time thereafter we navigated past the "One Fathom Bank", as the name inferred, a large shallow patch, that is very prominent in the Malacca Strait. As usual, we apprentices were placed on watch at night to act as additional lookouts as these waters were congested with ships, all heading towards or from the Singapore Strait and in particular heavily populated by small sampans and fishing boats, many unlit. The fishermen are most prolific during the squid season. Fishing nets where everywhere, which if wrapped around a propeller, given time, the fine nylon strands could work their way inside the hub, causing damage to the shaft seals. These fishermen, mostly from Indonesia, had no sense of danger and were very unpredictable in their actions, the rule of the road meant nothing to them and they did not seem to comprehend the dangers to themselves and their small craft if unfortunate enough to be swamped by the wake of a large, fast moving freighter, such as us. They could easily capsize. We remained on night watches until past Pulau Weh (approximately 5 50.2N 95 17.7E), having entered the Bay of Bengal

15 The African Coast

Our passage was across the Bay of Bengal, to transit
south of Dondra Head (Ceylon) and on across the Indian
Ocean to the small island of Mauritius, past quickly.
The ship was being painted and the new paint work
shone in the bright sun as we entered Port Louis, the
main sea port of Mauritius. Mauritius with its remnants
of British and French colonial rule is both serene and
beautiful. The harbor is very picturesque. The Island has
many resorts and magnificent beaches that attract the
tourists, not to mention the widest selection of French
style cafes and wine bars. Life is very laid back and
relaxing.

Like many other ports, one moored to buoys, fore and
aft. There was not an abundance of deep navigable
water in the harbor so ships were a little strung out more
or less in line in one area, but it was seldom that there
were more than four or five ocean going ships at any
given time. The main export of the Island is Molasses so
it was not unusual therefore that bagged sugar featured
prominently in its exports. We did not load this
commodity however, that came about when we were
northbound. Instead we discharged rice mainly, together
with assorted pallets and generals, mostly originating
from Hong Kong. No time for shore leave as our stay
was very limited. Then we proceeded across the Indian
Ocean towards Dar es Salaam on the East African coast.
We pushed westward into that long, low, lazy swell so
characteristic of the Indian Ocean at certain times of the
year. At 16 knots our sleek bow dipping and rising
gently to every trough and crest.

"Dar" as it was known, is one of my favorite East
African coastal ports. It has a quaint harbor which is
flanked on one side by a sort of sandy spit once inside

the lagoon like entrance. The town is close to the docks and set back a little, nestled behind a golden beach and the inevitable swaying coconut palms. The port has since grown and changed but at that time there were only a few cargo berths so one generally anchored in the harbor, only berthing alongside to load on the northbound sector of the round voyage. Being lowly paid apprentices we were not flush with funds so when ashore we tended to spend most of our time at the Seaman's Club, of which "Dar" could boast one of the best. It featured a bar, restaurant, wonderful swimming pool as well as many other amenities for the seafarer. Prices were very reasonable and the service and hospitality warm. Our other main entertainment was the Cinema. The "Young Ones" was released about the time of our call and was featuring at the local cinema. Ginger and Max took in the movie as I had volunteered for night duty during our stay.

The other favorite pass time was fishing, especially if at the inner anchorage. I have never seen so many Yellow Tails or Jacks in my life, all of decent size. Once the line was tossed over the side, the fish hooked themselves and surrendered. Our Chinese crew gutted and cleaned the fish before freezing for eating on a later day. This was regular evening entertainment in which most participated when not working or on duty.

Courtesy: Tourism Tanzania

Seen above, a ship entering the picturesque harbor of Dar es Salaam and the superbly sheltered inner anchorage as it was in early 1970s. "Dar" was founded as a fishing village in 1862 by the Sultan of Zanzibar.

From here on in, the voyage became intense, calling at a different port every few days during which cargo work became frantic, with agents and stevedores trying to meet with schedules. After Dar es Salaam, followed Beira and Lorenzo Marques in quick succession. Each of those ports having their own trait or particular characteristic. In both Beira and "LM" (as it was known), we spent only a day at each. The brown muddy waters at these ports were a contrast indeed to "Dar".

The Portuguese colonial masters again drove their workers hard. We discharged tractors from the tweendecks, part lot at each respective Port. Then we were off, no back loading until our return. We hugged the coast as we dashed ever more southerly. We were due to arrive at Durban at first light a day or so later but late on the night preceding our arrival we were drawn by the loom in the sky ahead of us caused by the lights of this large city, the glow on the horizon was very conspicuous at a very great distance.

Durban is a truly splendid place in all ways, great beaches (complete with anti-shark nets),good hotels, a modern city and a wide range of entertainment to suite every individual's whim. Approaching the harbor entrance which runs more or less East-West, we observed not one, but two of our company ships also in port. One was loading coal at The Bluff (port hand as one enters the Port) an area of jetties dedicated for the loading of coal over by the old disbanded whaling station and the other was also in the process of loading at one of the general cargo wharves. We tied up right astern of the one at the general cargo wharf. We expected at least 4 days in Durban as we had much cargo consigned to this Port. Hatches were quickly opened and as usual the stevedore labor all clambered aboard and were divided into gangs and allocated hatches in which to work, by their white deck foreman. Five hatches, plus deep tanks were to be worked around the clock.

Racial segregation known as Apartheid, with all its inhumane ramifications, was imposed by the governing regime at this point in South African history. Whilst none of us liked what we saw, we nevertheless had little choice but to comply with the regulations for fear of getting into serious trouble and retribution. Our South African electrician (the Marquis de…) was granted local leave and he was collected by his beautiful fiancé wharf side, arriving in a swanky late model sports car! Understanding a true South African or Afrikaner speaking English was not easy at first and it took me a little time to grasp. Their sing song tones and expressions are quite amusing to the unfamiliar ear. So when introduced to the electrician's lady, I did not understand a single word, but nevertheless smiled politely and shook her hand. She was stunning indeed.

We did not have the opportunity to visit our colleagues on either of the other company ships; the one ahead, sailed within a few hours of us arriving. We heard from the agent she was bound for Madras, India, (hearing this I had a considerable sense of empathy for all on board). She was a relatively modern vessel with pleasing lines and was a late addition to our fleet, (our company owned some 65 ships at this juncture) whilst the one loading coal at "The Bluff" was more aged and approaching the end of her no doubt productive service. She was also bound for India, Calcutta, heading seaward the following evening (my mental sympathies also being extended to her crew).

As customary, apprentices were assigned to watches with the Mates, me to the Chief Mate. He was very busy in the ship's office planning the upcoming back loading and feverishly going through cargo booking lists and specifications, calculating available space, etc. I acted as his runner and general factotum. I was up and down hatches, into tweendecks, measuring and calculating stowage factors and cubics, checking dunnage, separation materials, Checking with the Bosun to ensure hatches were swept and cleaned as soon as emptied, checking bilges, making certain that the two freezer compartments had been properly cleaned and the pre-chilled satisfactorily (relatively small freezer compartments, one located each side, port and starboard, in hatch number 3 tweendeck), cargo cages used for valuable items and mails were ready for use if required, etc., etc. I was appreciative for the opportunity to assist in a constructive way, always learning. The Mate was very experienced and took the time and effort to explain the reasons why he was asking me to do these various tasks, always giving me pointers and sound advice.

One evening I decided on an excursion into Durban for a few hours, it was a quick step ashore and I went alone. I was realizing by then that as a consequence of life on board and the daily routine; I actually enjoyed my own company and moments of occasional solitude. I was not a loner but needed a bit of space and opportunity to do my own thing from time to time. My main reason for going was to post a few letters at the Flying Angel, which I did. I also acted as the postman for the others on board who were unable to get ashore. On the way back I stopped at Officers Club in Alliwall Street then the famous "Playhouse" for a solitary beer, all very innocent, and I bought a cloth doll heavily beaded in bright colors, to replicate Zulu dress. This was a birthday gift for our neighbor's daughter in Hong Kong. I returned to the ship and was delighted to find half a dozen cold tins of Castle Beer sitting in my wash basis, courtesy of the Chief Mate. I closed my door, slowly drank 2, and retained the others for a later occasion. I turned in after reading a few chapters of "Nichol's Concise Guide", which I forced myself to read most nights.

The company doctor was aboard next morning, right after breakfast. He was vaccinating crew who needed booster shots for Cholera and Yellow Fever. I had the Cholera needle. Inoculation records and certificates needed to be kept up to date and current at all times. We never really knew what part of the world we would go to next, although in our case it was more a matter of conforming to company policy as we anticipated our trade route would remain the same for the foreseeable future.

Several more days of hard work followed; me doing whatever being called upon to assist our Chief Mate. The other apprentices were also kept fully occupied during their watches with the respective deck officers; I was not alone in my work effort. Both Ginger and Max did however get their opportunity to visit the "smoke", before we departed from Durban. Over ensuing voyages we all became very familiar with Durban, it being a favorite and very popular destination with all officers (and Chinese crew).

The day came when it was time to continue our voyage to Port Elizabeth and subsequently on to Cape Town. We cast off, aided by the usual duo of harbor tugs (beautifully maintained steam jobs featuring tall robust funnels) and headed out through the harbor entrance. We would return a few weeks later.

Port Elizabeth was a smaller or secondary port but it still managed to generate a substantial amount of cargo for us, as usual the southbound sector was mainly focused on discharge, back loading being reserved for our northerly enterprise when more cargo space was available. We off loaded the trucks from our main deck together with pallets of manufactured goods and bales of latex, from various cargo compartments. The scheme of things in Port Elizabeth followed more or less that of Durban but on a lesser scale. "PE" seemed to be a hub for South Africa's "Unicorn" Line – a prominent coastal and short sea trader company that plied the African coast. There were numerous vessels in port belonging to them, Those small ships were a delight to the eye, beautifully proportioned and nicely maintained.

By this time our Chief Mate had perfected his loading plans, they were very detailed and comprehensive. He explained his requirements in minute detail to the 2nd and 3rd Mates. A large cargo plan was posted on the bulkhead in the ships office. The intention was that as each consignment or parcel was loaded in its designated point of stowage, it was crossed off the plan. The mates were expected to maintain cargo logs that covered their individual watches. These tended to be very comprehensive indeed, more so when loading, and were reviewed morning and evening by our Chief Mate. Included were details of the cargo and stowage, any observed damage, working hours and numbers of stevedore labor engaged, any down time (i.e. waiting on cargo, trucks or rail wagons, rain periods, opening and closing of hatches), cargo pilferage and so forth. All intended for later inclusion in the Deck Log Book.

After 3 days, our cargo operations were done and we sailed off into the sunset, destination Cape Town.

Cape Town was the focal point for our South Africa to Asia service; this is where all the excitement started again with a return voyage to Asia becoming our next objective. Yokohama acted in the same way being our northernmost terminal. In Cape Town our company maintained a regional office, so it was not unexpected when we received a visit from one of our resident Superintendents, Captain Hargreaves; a man of high reputation and respect within company circles. He spent most of his time on board in the presence of the Master, Chief Engineer and Chief Officer. He did however find time to say hello to us apprentices, eager to hear how we were getting along and if we had any worries or needs. He urged us to devote time to our studies and assured us of a bright future with the company provided we obtained our certificates and demonstrated responsibility. This was encouragement indeed.

Cape Town with its prominent "Table Mountain" backdrop is surely one of the World's icons. It is a very vibrant city, windswept and prone to frequent climatic changes usually expected for a location in such an exposed position and southerly latitudes. Melbourne, Australia, was a comparable example with similar latitude (and changeable climate). Cape Town was a regular call for many of the large passenger liners plying the oceans, in fact there were two Union Castle Line ships in port when we arrived.

Our arrival at Cape Town was on a Sunday morning which hosted absolutely crystal clear visibility and brilliant blue skies, against which Table Mountain featured conspicuously in the picture postcard scene. We were brought back to the realities of the situation however, for no sooner had we berthed than we were once again heads down in discharging the remaining balance of cargo from Asia, and, starting to backload, as by this time our ship was nearing empty. A large barge came alongside, from which the engineers connected hoses to replenish much needed fuel supplies. Taking fresh water was ongoing and loaded progressively through hoses linked to shore connections. Stores and provisions were loaded simultaneously.

Below a grand spectacle of Cape town City and Port from above clearly showing the magnificent Table Mountain and Lions Head looking somewhat like sentinels at their posts.

Transnet National Ports Authority

We filled our reefer lockers with cartons of frozen sea food for Japan. Great care was taken in this, not only did temperatures of the chamber and cartons that were being loaded require constant monitoring, but good stowage was also essential. There were numerous parcels for various consignees so these called for proper separation and marking off. This became my job to supervise. Finally, the lockers were full, closed and sealed. For the entire voyage north, right up until point of outturn, constant observation of the reefer machinery and temperature control was undertaken by our two electricians. We did not carry a Reefer Engineer, having only modest freezer capacity. Consignees in Japan expected to receive their product in pristine condition, this being our objective, naturally.

We commenced loading a wide variety of bagged and general cargo for various Asian ports. It came in all shapes and sizes, large drums of electric cable, machinery, cased goods, personal effects (usually earmarked for the security of our cargo cages located in two of our tweendecks – one forward and one aft), bulk maize in our deep tanks destined for Kobe, pallet upon pallet of canned goods – mainly fruit, some bags of mail for Singapore and Hong Kong locked in the large tally office which was seldom used, cases of wine, beer and spirits (cargo lockers again…), bagged milk powder for Bangkok, the list was endless in its scope.

All this time the Chief Mate was juggling his stowage plan as changes and amendments, additions and cancellations to his original cargo manifest occurred. He had more than a full time job and so did our 2nd Mate, keeping track and drawing up an accurate cargo plan that reflected all this cargo activity. We spent about 10 days in Cape Town, which included one weekend but we in the deck department were frankly kept too busy, leaving the sightseeing and drinking ashore to the engineers, most of who were engaged on day work, carrying out routine maintenance to main engine and auxiliary machinery, thus enjoying most evenings free, except for the duty engineer.

16 Return to Northern Latitudes

Passing Cape Aghullas was a little unsettled but as soon as we skirted the southernmost tip of the cape the weather dropped away and we hugged the coast northbound until once again arriving at Port Elizabeth. This was another hive of activity with a diverse range of cargoes loaded. Our stay was restricted to one full working day but we achieved a lot in that time. This included the delivery to our gangway of our Marquis electrician, by his girl in her sports car. They had driven the considerable distance from Durban to Port Elizabeth so as not to exceed his leave period, due to expire on our departure date He came up the gangway with a smile on his face, from ear to ear, and seemingly very smug! We could all imagine why and were somewhat envious of his good fortune. Late evening saw us departing for Durban.

The ensuing weeks were spent progressively working our way, port by port up the East African coast until we arrived at Mombasa. By this time our ship was well laden and not a great deal of cargo space remained, but space enough in one of the tweendecks that had been reserved to load more pallets of those smelly hides, far away from other cargo so as not to taint. Into our cargo cages we stowed wooden crates of Cloves, which had been transshipped from Zanzibar and were destined to Singapore. There were the usual bags of Kenyan Coffee and crates of Kenyan Tea, bound for Mauritius and Port Swettenham. All this was good for topping off and filling what broken space remained

Again, whilst in Mombasa the favorite haunt was the Flying Angel, mostly spent lounging about the pool during our free time as well as playing the odd game of soccer, and attending the occasional BBQ arranged by the Padre; it followed much the same pattern as on my previous visit. I personally, tried to avoid too many shore excursions whilst on the African coast, preferring to save my meager earnings to spend in Asia. My only exception to the case was Durban and Mombasa. However, this did not apply to other officers and crew, who seized upon every opportunity to take advantage of shore leave at each port. The Seaman's Club was a good spot to meet other seafarers, to catch up on all the latest gossip and information, as well as being an ideal way to arrange to swap our ship's library with other ships.

Leaving Africa once again signaled the time to strip down all the ship's cargo gear for overhaul and maintenance during the passage North this was to be no exception. We started with the hatches containing cargo for Mauritius then moved on to the others once these had been completed. There was a lot of work to do and all crew and apprentices were fully engaged 10-12 hours a day. This was an important and essential undertaking as the wear and tear on the gear whilst being used at almost every port on the African coast, had taken its toll. We found it necessary to completely replace several cargo runners, preventers, derrick guys (complete with blocks) and numerous shackles. As usual all replacements had to be recorded for entry into the "Cargo Gear Register".

Our two electricians worked with us checking all the electrical components and contacts of our electric winches. The decks were a hive of activity with gear spread everywhere during our maintenance program. The weather was very kind to us and we improved our "Bronzy" no end due to the long hours we spent on deck under the sun; and whilst preoccupied with our various tasks it was always reassuring to hear the incessant drumming of the ship's powerful engines in the background as we ploughed onwards towards our destination. It is amazing how quickly one's ear becomes attuned to the music of the engines on a ship. One off beat or change in tempo becomes immediately apparent. Even if asleep at night, one was often awakened because of the slowing, stopping or changes in the engine beat or tone.

We experienced yet another brilliant day for our arrival in Port Louis, Mauritius. No time was wasted and our union purchase gear was proving its worth once again. The cargo for Mauritius was off loaded into lighters as a matter of course and we started to back load in its place several parcels of bagged sugar. The sweet smell of this commodity has always been pleasant, for me anyway. No time for shore leave and it was the next evening when we again sailed out into the Indian Ocean. The long low swell remaining with us until just prior to our approach to the northern end of the Malacca Strait, just off PulauWeh, when it dispersed and the sea became flat calm, like a mirror, as we turned into the Malacca Strait heading more southerly.

My first trip to South Africa had been a great experience for me but it was so good to be back in my part of the world. Somehow I felt more at ease and during my off time of an evening took to sitting in solitude on the monkey island, just taking in the serenity of those warm balmy tropical evenings, as we transited the Malacca Strait. These were halcyon moments and time passed quickly whilst sitting, deep in thought and absorbing the surrounds, to me it seemed like a different world, a world in which I enjoyed a sense of belonging. South Africa had been an interesting experience, as were the other east African ports but somehow I felt an outsider and alien to the environment, a bit like a fish out of water, even when mixing with my own kind. I could never see myself wishing to live anywhere in the world other than Asia. A day later we passed the "One Fathom

Bank" and a little further to the south, approached the meandering channel that leads to Port Swettenham. Even our Chinese crew had about them an air of excitement, being back in their own place.

Currents flow very swiftly through the Malacca and Singapore Strait but nevertheless the passage from Port Swettenham to Singapore Roads is only about 15 hours at a good speed. Upon arrival we anchored in the Western Anchorage, not too distant from Pulau Bukam, whilst awaiting a berth at Keppel. It was interesting to observe that one of the RFA ships was in the Dry Dock, the very ship on which my friend from Hong Kong, the one who had influenced my sea-going ambitions so much, was serving, by now nearing the end of his apprenticeship (called Cadets or Midshipmen in the RFA). Over the ensuing couple of days we visited each other's vessels and generally talked about so many things. It was good to catch up and somewhat unexpected. Our stay wasn't long enough when we parted company, but we had a scheduled call planned for Bangkok. However, before our Bangkok call we had a short stop off en-route, having received instructions to proceed to an anchorage off the Thailand peninsular, known as Bandon. Here we were to load about 30 large logs of very high grade quality, destination Taiwan, which were to be stowed equally on port and starboard after decks. Due to the weight the Bosun was busy rigging the derricks with doubling gear and "steam guys"" so a single swinging derrick could be used to load from the lighters

We arrived off Bandon and dropped anchor in good water at the pre-arranged co-ordinates, about a mile off the coast and three quarters of a mile off a small island. Soon a small diesel tug towed two barges out to us with the large logs and the lifting of the lumber was commenced.

Our ship was equipped with a sailing skiff for the use of the apprentices, basically intended for teaching the art of sailing. The craft was seldom used which was a shame as it was a beautifully built clinker boat, however on this occasion our Chief Mate told me to launch the boat, and sail it along with one of the other apprentices to the nearby island. There we were to fill a few sacks with sand and return to the vessel. There wasn't much wind about so it took a while to arrive at our designated golden beach. We dutifully filled the bags and were just about to return when something caught my attention out of the corner of my eye! About 30 meters away was a large lizard, rather like a Goanna, slowly waddling towards us with tongue flicking in and out. It must have been all of two meters long. I yelled out a warning and we both grabbed the laden sacks and fled back to our boat (for us to arrive back on board without the sand would have been a huge loss of face!) and paddled furiously until in deep enough water to lower the keel and raise the sail. We broke all records in returning to the safety of our ship. By which time the loading of the logs had just about been completed.

Later, I did make some enquiries as to the "Reptile's" likely species but the best I could derive was some sort of peculiar oversized Iguana like lizard relatively common in some remote areas of Southern Thailand! From that point onwards I was always (and still am) very cautious when walking along deserted sections of any beach, anywhere in the world.

Since last in Bangkok we had all diligently collected our weekly issue of "Lux" and purchased "Luckies" from the ship's bond, to pay off our Sew Sew ladies. Upon our return, true to their word, they were all waiting and most of us settled back into s somewhat domesticated existence for the duration of our stay. My girl's name was "Tasanee"; it always struck me as being a wonderful name. Tasanee was a beautiful but shy young lady, devoting her time on board strictly to housekeeping, laundry and sewing. I found her to be a wonderful companion. We frequently spent nice times together when we went ashore.

Some of our officers still preferred the excitement of the "Venus Room" or "Mosquito" Bar but like on our previous visit we had our casualties. This time our senior electrician went missing for a couple of days and caused everyone on board concern, not least of all, our Captain. The electrician had been reported as last being seen drinking "Mekong Whisky" in one of the dockside low life bars. Whilst inexpensive, Mekong was a particularly dangerous kind of concoction to those uninitiated. It could lay you out very easily and was absolutely full of "boxing gloves". We sent a party to look for him but to no avail so he was reported as missing to the Police and British Embassy. It was only after a couple of days he was picked up by the Royal Thai Police who found him slumped across some disused railway tracks close to the dock gate, still 90% proof. They somehow had managed to return him to the right ship. He was uninjured but filthy and try as we may he remained heavily intoxicated showing no signs of sobering. The final outcome was he had to sign off and be admitted to a Bangkok hospital suffering from alcoholic poisoning. He was still hospitalized when we sailed and eventually was flown to rejoin us in Hong Kong. Needless to say, he was not the flavor of the month with our company, or indeed either our Captain or Chief Engineer and he kept a very low profile as well as swearing off cheap booze for the remainder of his time on board. I think that resolution lasted until Japan!

We all said our goodbyes to the ladies and sailed down the sandy colored waters of Chao Phraya River, crossed the shallow bar and down through the Gulf of Thailand.

As we turned the corner of the southern part of Vietnam, the weather was, as usual choppy, but once to the eastward of Hainan Island it dropped away to become very calm indeed. The fishing fleets were prominent as we edged towards Hong Kong, our next port of call. This time I would not be taking leave, this would occur at the completion of our next round voyage. Meantime, ever since my joining the ship in Hong Kong, I had been persistently requested by the other two apprentices to talk with the Mate to see if we could all have a day off and I conduct a sightseeing tour for the lads. I approached the Chief Officer and was surprised that he agreed so easily to my request, stating he thought it a good idea.

I had not planned to go home during this stay, instead leaving that for our southerly call. Nevertheless, my father, mother and brother all came out in a launch to greet me and spent a few hours on board. The sightseeing tour for my fellow apprentices had been arranged for the following day.

Early morning of the next day we all hopped into a launch and headed to Blake's Pier. I had arranged with my father to provide a car and driver so as to maximum the time spent sightseeing. My dad had obliged. We clambered in the car and headed for Stanley village, passing through the crowded streets of Wanchai, Taikoo and North Point on the way. The driver waited for a while at Stanley whilst my chums bargained with the hawkers and bought an assortment of memorabilia from the market.. Then it was on towards Aberdeen via Deepwater and Repulse Bays. Finally our driver took us up to the top of the peak where we had refreshments at the Peak Café prior to boarding the "Peak Tram" for the 15 minute ride down to Garden Road where we all alighted. The chaps were stunned with the experience, exquisite views and the overall excitement. We strolled through the Botanical Gardens to Ice House Street then through the Central District to the "Star Ferry (oldest ferry company in the world, allegedly). Momentarily stopping off to post letters at the General Post Office. We halted for a snack before boarding the Star Ferry for Tsim Tsa Tsui in Kowloon. The harbor trip was great and we could clearly see our ship at the buoy in mid harbor as we traveled across the one mile stretch of water on the "Meridian Star".

We hopped a bus that took us in the direction of Tsim Tsa Tsui, via Jordan and Mong Kok. We offloaded somewhere in Nathan Road and walked down its entire length. By this time it was late afternoon and we wandered through the old pub areas of Mody Road, Hart Avenue and Chatham Road before heading off in the direction of Hankow Road and the Red Lion Inn located in Ashley Road (behind the old YMCA building).

The Red Lion was an institution in Hong Kong even at that time. It was the favorite watering hole for most of Hong Kong's seagoing community, which also included Marine Police, Harbor Department and the odd Airline Pilot.

The "Leon Rouge" as it was affectionately known, was on the same par as the Hong Kong Bar in Chulia Street, Penang. It was a real sailor's haunt.

Many a job was sought and accepted in the discreet nooks of the Red Lion as was a contract for the night with a Chinese "hostess". It was a place where one could sit for hours just absorbing the yarns of old "China Hands", "Soldiers of Fortune" and even the less scrupulous seafarers. No one bothered you and it was a safe place with a friendly atmosphere. The Red Lion, with its nautical patronage was nevertheless typical of the bars in Kowloon and Hong Kong of that era and therefore featured in many of the movies that were being shot on location in Hong Kong around that time. It was a very popular haunt and remains so to this day as the watering hole and gathering place for sailors, although **a** lot of its old atmosphere and nostalgia has been lost since its relocation to Lock Road and it becoming known as the "New Red Lion".

After the Red Lion we headed to the "Waltzing Matilda" in Caernarvon Road and then across the street to the "Hasty Tasty" for an excellent supper of fish and chips. Fleeting visits were made to the "Blue Peter Bar" in Nathan Road and "Fairyland Bar" in Hanoi Street. We made our last call at "Jimmy's", before finally heading to Kowloon Pier and a "Walla Walla" back to the ship. It was very late when we arrived on board but I believe a good, if not exhausting day was had by all. My friends were very satisfied with the excursion even though on this occasion time did not permit rounding off our tour by visiting the hot spots in Jaffe, Luard or Lockhart Roads in the Wanchai area of Hong Kong Island. That we scheduled for another time.

Meanwhile, aboard ship, things had been progressing without interruption. By the time of our return the first two barges had been loaded and were long gone. Others had replaced them and were filling fast; the first of the cargo to be loaded had arrived and their respective barges double banked, port and starboard, waiting patiently. As usual the Mate was kept busy planning the stowage, the 2nd Mate with his cargo plan and the 3rd Mate standing customary cargo watches. Everyone was fully occupied.

I realized, since first joining this ship in Hong Kong on 1st January, almost 4 months had elapsed and my qualifying sea time was accumulating quite rapidly. The need for study periods increased accordingly. I found that I was being placed on sea watches more regularly with the Chief Mate, even though we were also expected to complete 8 hours deck work each day (except Sundays). Despite the long hours, this did not matter much to me; I was young, enthusiastic and found the additional experience of watch keeping very exhilarating.

There was an additional port call in Taiwan this trip, Kaohsiung. This Port was located more towards the southern part the island. It was up a river, rather like a wide twisting creek with various industrial sites on each bank. Shipyards, ship breakers, wharves and factories of all descriptions being littered everywhere. Obviously, river frontage was at a premium. The number of scrap yards, each with ships of all kinds at various stages of demolition or others tied up in rows awaiting their fate and going under the torch. Amongst other things we off loaded the logs from the afterdecks, this was good as we regained all our deck space and did not have to climb over them again. When wet the logs were very slippery and treacherous under foot.

After Kaohsiung, it was on to Keelung. This time I did not go ashore remembering the costly experiences of my previous visit. The gun emplacements on the factory and warehouse roofs were still there and a dominant military presence remained evident. We discharged and back loaded some manufactured goods for Yokohama, but other than that our stay was uneventful. I was not sorry to leave; the state of emergency and very strict security was everywhere and disturbed me somewhat. It was a drab and dismal place.

The following month was spent around the Japanese coast, again calling at Moji, Osaka, Kobe and Yokohama, before heading towards Sasebo, where we were to dry dock (builder's warranty). The ship was virtually empty save for minimal parcels of light generals. We had received advice that we could expect a particularly heavy loading in both Hong Kong and Bangkok. This was music to my ears.

Sasebo was a big US Navy base and we were surrounded by all their war ships. We entered dry-dock but only remained for some 36 hours, during which time the hull was inspected, a few of the underwater areas lightly scraped and the entire underwater hull washed with high pressure fresh water hoses. Several zinc anodes were replaced the anti-fouling and boot topping painted as well as draft marks and load lines. Our anchors were lowered to the bottom the dry dock, where the anchor chain was flaked and inspected. The various shackle lengths being marked by twists of seizing wire and painted white prior to being re-stowed in the chain lockers. Soon we were refloated then sped on our way towards Hong Kong. No time for going ashore.

17 Our Second Round

By this point I knew exactly what to expect on our southbound sector but I was surprised to learn that there would be a change of officers upon our return to Hong Kong. Although over three months away it gave the officers something to look forward to, by then they should have been on board approximately 10 months or so and was in keeping with the company's recently declared policy to relieve officers within 12 months, even though two year articles were still the norm. I suspected this was in an effort to aid officer retention on an increasingly competitive labor market. I also received some good news; I was to go on leave now for about 3 weeks after which the company would fly me to Bangkok to rejoin. Needless to say, this was most unexpected. The reason was that as there would be a complete officer change next time in Hong Kong the company wished to retain the senior apprentice on board to assist incoming officers with vessel familiarization. This I believe was upon the recommendation of our Captain. Hence the rationale for my early leave. It sounded like sensible thinking to me.

Obviously once I heard the news I did not waste any time in coming ashore, leaving most of my gear on board, my cabin key with the Chief Officer and placed my two cartons of Lucky Strike and 6 cakes of Lux with my fellow apprentices for safe keeping until my return in Bangkok.

At this point my parents and brother were about to fly to the UK for 4 months leave, so I could look forward to having our apartment to myself, except for the company of our two "Amahs". To me this was even a better bonus, although my folks were somewhat hesitant at first they eventually decided to go ahead with their leave as planned.

Being a young man about the town and classified in Hong Kong as a potential eligible bachelor, I did the usual, frequented the night clubs and dance joints. One must remember this was before the "Disco" era really became of age but the cabaret and night club scene was at its zenith during the early to mid 1960s in Hong Kong.

There was a host of good bands that were resident at the nightclubs; a few names that come to mind were the "Corsairs", "D'Topnotes", "Anders Nilsson and the Kontinentals" "Astro Notes" and "Fabulous Echoes". The latter being the most successful. Others that influenced the music scene about that time, whether on radio or live were Ray Cordeiro's "Lucky Dip" and Giancarlo's "Italian Combo"

My favorite hangout was the "Bayside"; it was located in Nathan Road in the basement of one of the hotels (it has long since disappeared). The resident bands were all top line local groups that played the latest pop hits of the day. One of these groups had a lead singer "John" who had a superb voice. John was a super guy, very popular with everyone (especially the ladies). One evening I sat talking with him, it seems he originated from Shanghai where his father had been a shipping magnate. Little did I know at that time our paths were to cross professionally in later years. He became a trusted friend, and although I have now not seen him for some years, he still remains so. He later took up a career at sea, eventually becoming Master on large Bulk Carriers plying the North Pacific mainly on the grain trade from Canada to China, Korea and Japan. His wonderfully powerful voice continues to resonate in my ears. I miss his charismatic charm and vibrant company.

I latched on to one particular girl, who like me had been brought up in Hong Kong and for a long time been my neighbor (initially from my younger Kowloon Tong days). We had been to school together but there was no attraction at that time. She was very pretty, dark haired, beautiful eyes, tallish and slim. We spent much time together over ensuing weeks, mostly at the "Bayside" or "Go Down" (in the basement of Sutherland House) twisting away the hours. One thing developed into another, inevitably. We remained very close for some considerable time but then whilst I was at sea, she went off and married. That's life I guess. In later years when I was occasionally invited to her home in Hong Kong for dinner or a party, our eyes occasionally met. If I am any judge of character, there was always a look of sadness in those eyes and I am convinced the feelings for each other still lingered, although by this time too late to do much about it.

Another of my favorite venues was the Metropole nightclub in the central district of Hong Kong, close to Telephone House, the building in which my father's offices were located. This was a bit up market and was mainly frequented by snooty expats and would-be if could-be types, but the music was good.

One afternoon after shopping for shirts and trousers I decided to pay a visit to the "China Fleet Club" for a quiet drink before going home. It was the first time I had visited, although it had been a familiar land mark to me for years. Upon entering I was drawn directly to the "Kelly Bar", which until then I did not know existed; this was named after one of the ships on which my father had served under Lord Mountbatten, during the war. I was amazed to see a picture of the entire ship's complement, amongst which I saw a very young image of my father. I was pleased to see this, although I knew of my father's wartime service, he seldom spoke much of it. In later years I was able to get a copy of the photograph as well as a beautiful print of "Kelly", duly signed by the remaining survivors. It hangs tastefully framed in a place of pride, on my study wall to this day.

I enjoyed a wonderful leave and my three weeks passed far too quickly. The day came when I had to go to Kai Tak to catch the flight to Bangkok. It was a DC6 operated by KLM on behalf of, or in partnership with, some other regional airline. The flight from Hong Kong to Bangkok's Don Muang Airport had a duration of about four hours. It was late afternoon when I arrived and after being met by the company agent, I was whisked through heavy traffic with all the mopeds, Tuk Tuks and cars. I ended up at the Eriwan Hotel where I was to spend the night because I was to attend the immigration office next morning before rejoining the ship.

The Eriwan Hotel was a Bangkok icon, beautifully appointed featuring rich Thai style timberwork, high ceilings with slowly rotating fans, wicker furniture and a host of immaculately dressed staff attending to one's every desire. It was rich in Thai culture and was superbly located in the city center. I seized this opportunity to venture out, never having made it to the city which was some distance from our usual berth at Klong Toei. On the adjacent junction was the "Four Faced Buddha", a famous spot for tourists and not too distant from Chit Lom. Nearby were various Thai temples and other interesting places of historic significance. Shops were abundant and sold everything imaginable at bargain prices.

Next morning, after visiting immigration to have my seaman's book and passport stamped and authenticated, I was taken to rejoin my beloved ship. "Tasanee" was there waiting, she found out from the company agent when I would return, we only had a few hours remaining before sailing so in order to maintain the exclusivity of our association I gave her one full carton of duty free "Luckies" and 6 bars of "Palmolive", which I had left with my fellow apprentices for safe keeping Hong Kong, she was wrapped but still insisted in cleaning up my cabin right up until the moment of our departure for Koh Si Chang where we finished loading our rice due to our deepening draft. My abode looked and smelled wonderful; Tasanee had done a magnificent job! We arranged so she could maintain contact with our shipping agent's office. That way she knew when my ship would arrive in order to meet as usual next call.

I had now become very familiar with most aspects of the ship and I was asked by the Chief Mate to start preparing notes of salient information so that he could include in his hand over briefing for the incoming Chief Officer, next call at Hong Kong. This was done progressively over the ensuing months and was, even if I say so, comprehensive in content once completed handed to him.

Looking at the ship's cargo plan I noted we would not be calling Mauritius southbound, but instead "Isle de la Reunion", a small French colonial island more or less in the same vicinity as Mauritius, I had observed this on the Admiralty chart over previous voyages. Whilst in Bangkok, we had loaded 500 tons of rice and 100 packs of sandal wood for "Reunion". I surmised the sandal wood would be for transshipment elsewhere as I could not fathom why such would otherwise be imported into this small island – this turned out to be correct. No one on board had been there previously so it was all open to speculation as to what to expect. We nosed our way southerly through the Gulf of Thailand and past Tiomen Island until we picked up Horsburgh Light house on our radar before lining up for our entry into the Singapore

Strait. Our trip from Bangkok had been marred by almost continuous rain squalls, with rain droplets so large and the down pours so intense, our decks quickly became flooded and water took some time to shed through scuppers and freeing ports once the deluge had past clear. The Monsoons were on the change. The ship had also been struck by lightning on the foremast truck, no damage and quite safe, but one huge loud "Bang". Over the next hours, our Radio Officer and electricians went about testing all our electrical gear and equipment for resulting damage but thankfully all was given a clean bill.

Singapore was heavily overcast with rain when we arrived off the Western Anchorage. It always seemed to rain at about lunch time in Singapore and this followed the pattern exactly. There were no berths for us at Keppel so we spent a couple of days discharging and back loading at anchor. We were on the alert for Indonesian aircraft overlying as this was during the period of confrontation between Singapore and Indonesia (circa early 1960's). Our stay turned out to be uneventful and time flew by quickly, no sooner having arrived than being off again to Port Swettenham. The rain squalls followed us throughout, right up the Malacca Strait and into the Bay of Bengal.

"Isle de la Reunion" was picturesque but somewhat more run down than Mauritius. It had that "afternoon Siesta" feel about it. We berthed at a wooden jetty that has seen better days. Opposite on the other side of the narrow dock were two very swish looking French Cargo Liners (now I figured where our Sandal Wood would be going). The French ships were immaculate in every way. I doubt if the island had an airport so perhaps this was the only means of transport in and out.

Without warning a sudden cyclone approached the Island, this was either slow in being reported or unpredicted. The French Liners managed to depart whilst conditions still permitted but we were unfortunately not so lucky. We were trapped inside the harbor alongside the flimsy wharf. We set about maximizing the number of moorings in preparation. For 24 hours we were all kept flat chat replacing broken moorings, splicing up new ones, etc as the storm passed through and the vessel surged up and down the wooden structure. It was a demonstration of experience and excellent seamanship by our Captain, with occasional use of main engines which avoided the possibility of catastrophic consequences and brought us through this unwelcome event unscathed. No damage to ship or wharf other than a little of the paintwork on our hull needed to be touched up caused by chaffing of our moorings lines and wire springs. We never did see the two Frenchmen again.

After discharging our rice and sandal wood we quickly sailed for East Africa and our usual designated Ports. It was uneventful and more or less an image of our previous voyage except that northbound we called at Zanzibar to load cases of cloves. We uplifted quite a substantial amount of this highly valuable commodity, most being stowed yet again, in our tweendeck cargo cages to prevent risk of pilferage. Whilst there was no opportunity to go ashore, even from our position at the open anchorage, through binoculars, the quaint old city, narrow streets and Arab like dwellings was clearly visible to the enquiring eye. The harbor area was small and crowded, certainly not designed for vessels of our size or draft. The port was mostly frequented by Arab Dhows, many of them of a reasonable size, which plied the sea routes into the Red Sea, Persian Gulf and beyond. Additionally there was the usual fleet of small coasters and short sea traders that frequented the entire length of the East and South African coast, carrying whatever cargoes they could secure. There was the pungent odor of cloves everywhere on board until our electrical and natural ventilation systems became effective and dispersed the smell considerably.

Our last port was Mombasa, only a few hours run to the north. I think we were all pleased to be back into this welcoming port, especially the officers as it was the last port call on the "coral coast" before heading back towards Asia and the prospect of their well earned leave. There seemed to be an air of excitement amongst them which was perhaps the onset of the "channels" or sometimes referred to as "channel fever", in layman's terms growing excitement at prospect of signing off or, imminently proceeding on home leave. The padre turned up on board just before we cast off with a new batch of books for our library and to wish all those signing off a pleasant vacation, still some 5 or 6 weeks ahead. What were a few weeks when these officers had been on board some considerable time? We steamed out late evening and watched as the coastline and lights disappeared over the horizon in the darkening sky. On our way to Mauritius some days distant even at a sea speed of 16 knots. Frequent rain squalls hindered painting and deck work on the passage but as usual they abated as we approached the tropical island.

Port Louis had its usual barges of bagged sugar waiting and as soon as we secured to the channel buoys no time was lost. Being the last call for many, some went ashore. Upon their return, they had consumed their fill of French wine; we were ear bashed with the usual stories of dens of iniquity, Creole style food, the beaches and café bars; all the things that attract many a seafarer. One day and one night of constant loading and we had lifted our lot, we were ready to get under way, and Asia bound

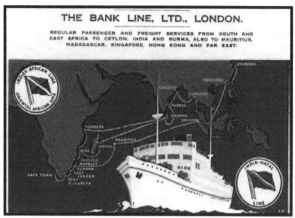

The Bank Line Ltd – London

A widely circulated Bank Line brochure advertising the Oriental Africa Line and India Africa Line services which the Company operated very successfully for many years. I was never on a Bank Line vessel specifically engaged in the India-Natal Liner Service although we frequently came across those that were, when we visited Durban or Mombasa, such as the "Isipingo" and sister ship "Inchanga" These ships were built specifically for the India-Natal passenger service. Both "Isipingo" and "Inchanga" featured many extra passenger facilities for the era such as En-suite Baths, Swimming Pool and Barber Shop, etc. They accommodated 50 First Class, 20 Second Class and up to 500 Deck or Steerage Passengers. Sadly they ended up carrying coal from Durban to India in their final years prior to demise.

The Bank Line Ltd - London

Bank Line's **"Inchanga"** pictured during her prime years

18 Malacca and the beckoning Orient

The usual sloppy Indian Ocean swell was again prominent for the entire passage until we made landfall at the northern most extremities of Indonesia and it's conspicuous and now familiar off lying island of Pulau Weh, at the southern end of the Nicobar Channel which separated Indonesia from the Nicobar Islands. The Nicobar Islands were for many years under Danish control which ended formally on 16 October 1868 when it sold the rights to the Nicobar Islands to Britain which in 1869 made them part of the then British India. The Nicobar Islands are thus Indian Territory nowadays.

Typically, once having passed Pulau Weh the swell suddenly disappeared and the sea became flat calm like shimmering metallic glass, with only light airs and lingering fingers of low lying heat haze which passed in an instant as we raced on our way.

Pulau Weh is situated about 9 nautical miles north of Sumatra and is separated by Sempitan Malaka or Malacca Passage. In about 1904 a Dutch trading company with a farseeing eye established a coal depot at the Port of Sabang, situated on the Island of Pulau Weh, at the extreme northeastern point of the Sumatra archipelago. A coaling station was established and controlled by the British enterprise of Hull, Blythe & Co.

Secluded and surrounded by tropical green mountains and headlands, the port is protected from every seasonal prevailing wind and is at best only two days transit from Singapore. Sabang is prominent in the track of every vessel trading between the Indian Ocean and Far East.

In itself a completely sheltered harbor with an entrance that calls only for the simplest of navigation, the Port of Sabang offers good depth and holding ground over a sizable anchorage with several relatively deep-water wharfs. During the days of "Steam" Sabang established itself as an important coaling port for ships plying the India-Asia route and rivaled Singapore in this regard. The prime geographical location of the original coaling depot at Sabang entrenched the Port's future expansion which eventually has been developed to become one of today's major regional transshipment hubs.

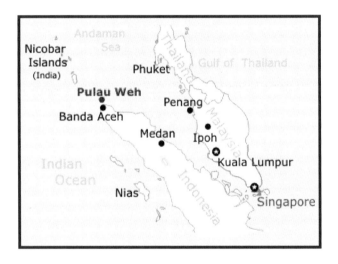

Map of Malacca Straits showing the strategic location of Pulau Weh at northernmost tip just off Sumatra

My evenings were spent doing what I enjoyed most in these waters, sitting alone on the monkey island soaking up the tropical environs, only disturbed by our thundering engines, whining turbochargers and fine lines of our bow piercing the shimmering sea ahead. Ships appeared on the approaching horizon and were soon lost out of sight astern, as I sat riveted, hour after hour. In bright moon light it was even more relaxing and balmy, the usual sweet tropical scent growing as we edged closer to land. The tranquility only disturbed by the occasional ringing of the ship's bell by the forecastle lookout, as he signaled the presence of lights ahead, to the bridge duty officer. I would generally turn in after midnight but even then I would lay awake in bed, cabin window wide open, just listening to the "swish" of the wake as it rushed by, before drifting into sleep.

I used these tranquil hours to reflect on my time spent at sea, it was by now well over two years. My apprenticeship was more than half completed already. I was now on the down side of the hill, not quite in the finishing strait but nevertheless well on the way towards the finishing line. I still enjoyed every minute of my chosen career and was thankful to be serving in a company which offered such solid training for its apprentices. I had learned much since joining my first ship at Immingham.

Our track again took us to a point some 2 miles distant off "One Fathom Bank" situated about 30km South West of the River Klang delta. The shoal was marked with a conspicuous black and white octagonal tower lighthouse. There followed a course adjustment that took us directly to the fairway buoy for marking the channel entrance for Port Swettenham

By this time the trade in which the ship was engaged was becoming second nature, we all knew what needed to be done, the quirks and peculiarities of each port of call, generally the types of cargo we would carry, the time spent in port and the navigation was now becoming somewhat repetitive. Chart courses and positions, fixes, and isolated dangers, almost indelibly imprinted on the various charts, despite frequent erasing. Passage plans were seldom changed except for logical amendments as there was no requirement; they were generally a carbon copy of those used previously, provided chart corrections were up to date. It was like running on tram tracks. For my part I looked forward to the officer crew change, not because of anything untoward but just to see some different faces, hear different voices, new topics of conversation, meet other people! I had another two round voyages, perhaps a tad more to endure, my objective being slightly more than 36 months total, before completing my sea time so a change was personally welcomed. I had taken to keeping a rough daily journal and I longed for new subject matter to record.

Port Swettenham, Singapore and Bangkok passed quickly, as the excitement continued to grow on board between the officers. Channel fever was rife by this stage. Bangkok to Hong Kong was usually only a 4 or 5 day trip and the day after we departed Bangkok the Master received telegram from the owners itemizing a list of incoming officers and apprentices as well as giving instructions in relation to those leaving. As pre-arranged I was the only one remaining behind, along with our Chinese crew. Much time was spent gossiping with those who knew some of the new joiners; my two apprentices were first trippers so I would have my hands full, certainly until they found their sea legs. The new Captain was a fellow called Fennimore, no one knew him. The Chief Mate was named Craven, also unknown to those on board. In fact with the exception of the Radio Officer and a couple of the engineers, it was basically a bag of unknowns. Not really unexpected in a company that owned and operated so many ocean going vessels.

The night before arrival in Hong Kong few of the outgoing crew slept. Except for those on watch most were gathered in the officer's smoke room, sharing their last few beers and chatting away like charged atoms. I slept peacefully as I knew what to expect over the next few of days.

The sun was rising as the Pilot boarded at Lai Yi Mun. As in all past visits we went directly to the immigration anchorage in Hung Hom Bay, adjacent to the airport runway. Once having gained Pratique we shifted to the designated harbor buoy, where the boatmen secured our barren anchor chain by means of a large shackle to the connecting point on the buoy. This was always accompanied by a slip wire. It could take a little time to complete the exercise but generally the boatmen were experts at doing the job so it was not laborious. The boat men used to curse and swear at those on the forecastle if precise instructions were not followed. Little did they know I understood every word and on this particular day I could not resist giving back some of their own, with a little additional dressing using such superlatives as "Diu Nei Loh Mo" and other expletives. They looked up at me with jaws agape, hearing this raw Cantonese from a Gweilo. This was much to the hilarity of our Bosun and Chinese crew who were on the forecastle at the time. The Mate was in stitches seeing their reaction, although not understanding a word I had said.

As 9am approached a large company launch arrived alongside the gangway bearing its precious cargo of new joiners. I greeted all at the head of the gangway, directing some crew to assist with luggage. All the officers trapped up the gangway. Having identified the Master I introduced myself and conducted him to the

Captain's deck. The two new apprentices were bewildered, I could see by their faces. I extracted names from these timid individuals first letting them know who I was, giving them assurances and confidence in the fact all would be fine and I would look after them. The taller of the two was Carl, from Berwick-upon-Tweed, whilst the shorter was Bernie, a well tanned individual who resided in the Wirral, just across the Mersey from Liverpool. Both were taken to their cabin to unpack and settle in, the outgoing opposite numbers being ready to ship out at a moment's notice, in fact they had been ready for the last couple of days. I left them to it, and then headed off to see the Mate.

Knocking on the Chief Officer's door I was asked to enter and sit down. I was introduced by the outgoing Mate to his relief. He was skinny as a rake and heralded from Leith in Scotland; it took me a moment or two to navigate my way through his broad Scottish brogue. Until the process of handover was completed I learned I would be the "officer" on cargo watch, as I had been well briefed by the outgoing Mate and knew more or less what was going on and what was expected. I went on my way. Meantime the two Mates were busy with handing over cargo matters, ship details and status, technical features of the ship, etc. Likewise with the 2nd and 3rd Mates were similarly occupied. I assumed the engineering staff was engaged likewise.

I kept bumping into new faces as they crawled all over the ship, introducing myself at every opportunity, (the ensuing days were to see me become the ship's centre of information for those needing to know the whereabouts, way things were usually done, what was going on, the ship's trade, what it was like, etc.). I was diligent in my duties about the deck. Near to 3pm that afternoon all the off signers had completed formalities and were ready to go. It was sad for me but that was a seaman's lot, goodbyes! I cheered them on their way and watched, waving discreetly, as their launch disappeared around our stern heading towards Kowloon Pier. I was overcome by a sudden sense of emptiness inside. At 6pm I was relieved by the new 3rd Mate and after explaining the situation I ventured to my cabin to wash up for dinner. The new Captain greeted me as I entered the dining saloon, generally introducing me to all and explaining if anyone needed any information about the ship then they should see me. Dinner dragged on a little that evening but after the coffee cups had been cleared the Mate asked me to visit his cabin as his "sounding board", he needed to go through a few matters with me.

The Mate I discovered was a very mild mannered chap indeed, a true gentleman. He claimed a background in "Banana Boats" He sounded me out then placed me on his evening watch. I also worked on deck during the day until lunch time with the two new apprentices. This was a good arrangement for me. My fellow apprentices needed to be led by the hand initially, this was only natural, and they followed me about the ship like a shadow. Slowly but surely they started to get a grasp of things. Sailing from Hong Kong the weather was kind to us but both were overcome with seasickness which I fear was more psychologically triggered rather than due to ship's motion. I remembered my days on the old "Canton" and could sympathize.

Our passage to Keelung and then Moji was placid and really uninspiring for me, although for the newcomers, many of whom who had not been to Asia previously it was an adventure in the making. Upon our arrival at Kobe, I once again became the local source of information for the "crowd", I persistently cautioned them against the abundance of rip off merchants, touts, pimps and other unsavory types that were still very prevalent throughout Asia at this time and who would seize every opportunity to con the unsuspecting foreigner. I also gave them the benefit of my experience when it came to the cost of "goods and services" and seriously warned my fellow young apprentices of what "Asia" could do to the inexperienced or unwary. First they needed a bit of controlled exposure before venturing out alone. Besides, unlike me, they had not enjoyed the benefit of growing up in Asia and were therefore totally naive in all matters pertaining thereto, especially differences in cultural and social values and behavior. I suggested the apprentices retain their unused cakes of toilet soap, although I did not venture the reason why! They would find out for themselves in due course.

It was about this time that I learned of a temporary change to our trading pattern. We were to load in Japan, Taiwan, Hong Kong and Bangkok with cargoes destined only as far south as Mauritius. We were to empty out at Mauritius and back load a full cargo of bagged sugar for a three port discharge; Bangkok, Saigon and Hong Kong. The plan was that we would then return to our regular route. This had apparently been brought about by less than attractive cargo bookings from the East African coastal ports. I thought this wonderful news, even though it meant about a two weeks stay in Mauritius whilst loading the bagged sugar. This was a reasonable prospect. As a consequence of this our time spent in Japanese ports was less than on previous voyages. Likewise our call at Keelung was short but in Hong Kong we spent 3 days during which time I managed a quick trip up the Peak to visit home, even though the folks as yet had not returned from their holidays in the UK. The two "A's" had baked the customary three large rich fruit cakes for me to take back, after so many years they knew my weaknesses very well. I couldn't eat all so gave one to Carl and

Bernie to share, put one in the officer's pantry and kept the third for myself. Mine alone kept me going for about two weeks!

Yokohama provided the ideal venue in which to introduce my fellow apprentices to the culture of Asia. It was a relatively safe haven providing one was sensible. Mr. Craven actually suggested I take the lads ashore for a spin but under strict guidelines; no drink (they were both under age), no women (naturally) and they were to be back on board by midnight. The Mate gave a pep talk the two uninitiated, and whilst none of this applied to me, I nevertheless felt obligated to take them under my wing and ensure their safe and timely return. At about 6.30pm, we stepped ashore and headed for the town, in fact I did not intend going into the city itself but one of the closer outlaying suburbs. This would offer just as much insight and action for my two charges on their first visitation.

We hailed a taxi outside the dock gate and after breaking the language barrier, off we set. First stop, a Japanese restaurant which I had visited before and which produced the most magnificent meals at an affordable price. After a lavish dinner (by shipboard standards) we browsed through various shopping areas, night markets and souvenir shops. Finally, before heading back, I introduced them to the joys of Japanese hospitality by way of a Japanese style "Geisha Bar" (so loosely named due to the Kimono clad hostesses that worked within) and the services such an establishment provided. I enjoyed several "Asahi" beers but the other two abstained and drank sodas.

The young lads, so white and pale – not yet having been tanned by the sun and by virtue of their apparent innocence, were an instant attraction to the various lady companions who by this time had managed to wriggle their way into our cubicle. In attempts to profit from their illicit trade they became very amorous towards my contemporaries in whom I could see that their eyes had been opened to the spoils of a life at sea, and some of the more shady attractions! Before matters got too advanced, I called a halt (much to their disappointment and indeed the Kimono clad girls and Momma-San), paid the bill, which was a bit heavy, and caught a cab back to the wharf with both my charges firmly in tow. I was thankful that we had not ventured too far from the docks and gone on to more well known bars such as the "Honey Bar", "Darling Bar" or "Blue Canary" otherwise getting my friends back may not have been so simple.

Once safely on board, we sat drinking cocoa for a spell and talking. From what I could gather they were both very taken by the ladies. Little did they know what to expect elsewhere. I kept that secret for another day and repeatedly reminded them to save their surplus issue of soap and smokes over the course of the next week or so.

Keelung came and went. The permanent military presence was always conspicuous. To me this created a feeling of oppression, gloom and spookiness to boot. We made a fast dash through the Formosa Strait, heading south towards Hong Kong. The only point of interest was the many heavy units of the US Fleet which we observed lurking within the straits. Several aircraft carriers and cruisers and no doubt many others just over the horizon, or below the surface, that we did not detect. I suppose a testimony to the confrontation that persisted between Taiwan and mainland China at that time and of course the onset of the Indo China conflicts that were to entangle the U.S. over ensuing years in Vietnam.

The weather remained choppy and overcast with a sort of restricted hazy visibility, for the entire trip; so we were pleased eventually to arrive in Hong Kong where things brightened up considerably. The weather was good and there was the usual dynamic and stimulating atmosphere about the place that enhanced an air of continuous excitement in everything one did, whether it is work or pleasure. Hong Kong was most definitely a unique location with an industrious population who gave the impression that they only existed to make money. The entire colony was "alive" from both commercial and social perspectives. Even though our calls were very frequent the changes that were observed never ceased to amaze, always something new and different to see upon each arrival. The skyline was changing with the rapid construction of numerous high rise buildings, continuously encroaching further up the mountainous terrain of Hong Kong Island. Mind you, Kowloon was not left out of the equation in that respect. The Tsim Tsa Tsui area of the Kowloon Peninsula was also under massive development. Large reclamation projects were commenced on both the Island and peninsula to satisfy the hunger for more land. The harbor became more crowded at each visit from which it was obvious shipping was booming and Hong Kong was developing into a major regional port and cargo transshipment hub. This was particularly so in respect of the China trade with Taiwan. For political reasons most of the good shipped to China from Taiwan were routed through Hong Kong.

Hong Kong was at that time the gateway for much of the Chinese exports and when it came to the mainland Chinese doing business with Taiwan, and vice versa, cargo was transshipped via Hong Kong in the interests of political correctness to maintain "Face" for both sides.. This went on for years and perhaps remains even to this day. The "Hongs" who established Hong Kong had incredible foresight as well as the British colonialists for their introduction of sound government and a good judicial system and civil service, which enabled the place to thrive and function effectively, providing international confidence, despite the occasional social unrest, mainly stoked by anarchists and professional agitators from across the border.

19 Changing Scenes

We spent almost three weeks loading our bagged sugar at Mauritius. It was unusual for this ship to carry such a homogenous cargo, mostly being engaged in a general cargo liner service. Nevertheless, I did not find the characteristically sweet smell of sugar unpleasant and the easy pace of cargo operations and break from the demanding general cargo trade allowed for considerable deck work to be completed. This included painting the ship's hull completely. We apprentices always got the job of painting the draft marks and names – hence we were always rigging Bosun's Chairs and Stages.

Over the course of our stay RnR had mainly consisted of a few runs to one of the many beautiful beaches that Mauritius had to offer, followed by the usual beers in one of the shanty bars, taverns or cafes, together with the odd sail in our skiff. The time was also well spent in lowering and testing our motor lifeboats and overhauling and painting the gravity davits, greasing the wire falls, renewing lifelines, and so on.

Our Chinese Crew seemed to like Mauritius because at the end of every working day there was always a steady stream heading ashore. Their attraction to Mauritius is a mystery so one can only assume there must have been a good China Town or abundance of Chinese women. Ahead of us there was moored a Hong Kong registered tramp ship, "World Pink", also loading bagged sugar, so perhaps some of our Chinese forged an alliance with their Hong Kong Chinese crew. In fact we had crossed paths previously when last in Cairns where she was also loading sugar. I recall one of our Chinese catering staff telling me she was loading for North Korea. We did come across one or two of her officers when on a sailing exercises, they were also testing motor lifeboats at the time and came alongside our skiff to have a sticky beak and brief chat. The Kampala (or one of that class of B&I passenger vessel) came and went during our stay. There was quite a large indigenous Indian population in Mauritius so no doubt there was quite a brisk passenger trade to India and East Africa, so I believe these ships were regular callers. The occasional Greek paid a visit to the port, most looking very down trodden and scruffy with their rust encrusted hulls. The only clean thing about them was the ensign, always brand spanking new and pristine, fluttering from the staff at their stern.

Cargo watches were rather boring, (after all there is a limit to how long one can watch slings of bags crossing the gunwale). Of an evening we engaged in our usual pass time of very good fishing. All we needed was a cargo cluster positioned over the side so the loom would attract our quarry. Good size fish were easy to catch and as usual our crew was always ready to claim whatever was landed on deck. One had to be a bit careful because the surrounding waters were overrun with large jelly fish and their tentacles became entangled with the fishing lines from time to time, so caution was needed to prevent getting stung. However, one of the crew was not so careful in his eagerness to claim a large Parrot Fish and ended up with painful red wheels on his arms as a consequence, which took over a week to disappear.

At last we were all done with our loading and made ready for sea and our passage back towards Asia. We were fully laden and therefore deep in the water, one could guarantee that the Chinese crew would be on dawn patrol around the deck collecting the "flying fish" that had become stranded overnight. It was not uncommon for the crew to collect a full bucket of these fish at the start of each day. These were often the subject of a BBQ and made excellent eating as I had earlier discovered.

Magnificent sunrises greeted us every morning as we progressively forged our way eastwards across the Indian Ocean and yet again that lazy, oily and confused kind of swell persisted; our sleek bow rising and dipping to each trough and crest in effortless fashion. This was the period of relative calm in these latitudes so conditions were therefore very placid. At night the heavens were aflame with dancing stars and planets all appearing so close one could almost reach out and touch them. As we transited the main shipping lanes smoke from the funnels of other ships far distant on the horizons could be seen rising vertically in the light airs. This is in far contrast to the strong Northeasterly Monsoons we would later encounter in the Gulf of Thailand and South China Sea.

As we nosed our way around Pulau Weh, with its amphitheatre of mountains encompassing the now familiar small port of Sabang, into the Malacca Straits, I again partook of my evening pleasure of sitting alone on the Monkey Island soaking up the tropical atmosphere and drifting sweet aromas of jungle foliage that swept seaward off the land. Upon reflection, these were my favorite moments, just sitting alone falling upon my thoughts in absolute solitude watching the world go by, without a care of any kind. Only the familiar shipboard sounds and occasional ringing of the forecastle look out's bell to keep me company. These halcyon times lasted until we passed through the Singapore Strait, at which time the effects of the building North East Monsoon started to become evident.

We had to lighten ship at Koh Sichang. As described earlier this is an anchorage off Siricha where ships that are deeply laden discharge partial cargo into lighters in order to reduce draft for crossing the Bangkok Bar. We only discharged about 1500 ton then proceeded up the twisting and muddy Chao Phraya River to Bangkok itself, where we discharged the balance of the sugar designated for that port. Of course Tasanee and all the others were there upon our arrival alongside and my two compatriots had by now discovered the reasons for saving their soap and smokes!

Our stay in Bangkok was to be short however, as the Thai stevedores worked endlessly to meet a daily quota set by their employers. After two days we had discharged two thousand tons from five hatches and again we departed this time heading down stream towards Saigon in Vietnam.

The entire Indo China region was embarking upon a politically confused state around about this time which would eventually escalate into the Vietnam War. The French had their day at Dien Bien Phu and it was now the turn of the Americans. American presence was building, in particular from a maritime perspective. It was not uncommon to see evidence of their growing fleet in the South China Sea, from Taiwan right down to the southern part of Vietnam and into the Gulf of Thailand.

We passed the southerly most point of Vietnam and started to head north towards the Mekong Delta and our upstream passage to Saigon. The Mekong is a massive river which generates very strong currents in the fan delta regions which extend many miles to seaward. The waters are muddy and relatively shallow so one must therefore be very cautious when approaching the Pilot Station due to shifting sand and mud banks. Channel buoys are either nonexistent or noticeably out of position in many cases. This is not to mention the fact that there are literally hundreds of small unlit sampans and fishing boats scooting every which way, each creating a mariner's nightmare.

The smell of putrefied vegetation increases as one closes the river estuary. This takes a while to overcome, but once in the river itself things sort themselves out somewhat. Other than Vietnamese, French is the preferred language which did not help with our communications with our Pilot as each spoken sentence consisted of a combination of Vietnamese, French and English. In more recent years there have been major improvements but at this time things were still a little primitive and unspoiled.

Eventually we arrived at the Saigon reach where we secured to mid-stream mooring buoys with the aid of a couple of line boats which struggled persistently with the swift flowing current. Pratique took several hours by which time the day was almost over so there was no work until the following day. The Mate initiated extra deck patrols and look outs during the hours of darkness as the river is infested with numerous pirates and vagabonds. Contrary to common belief, "Piracy" is a thriving business. Pirates are rampant in many parts of the world, especially throughout Asia and are the scourge of all seafarers. At this time ships were still ships and built with many brass fittings, portholes, valve Spindles and wheels, fire hose nozzles, ship's bells, fire hydrants, vent identification plates, to name but a few items. These were favorites targets for Pirates and the stealing thereof.

The story goes that one of our company ships, anchored off the port of Sandakan was stripped clean of all brass fittings about the decks, mooring ropes and paint, fire hoses and nozzles plus various other stores, in a single night. Not only are these pirates thieves but are generally very dangerous and aggressive if disturbed or challenged once on board and frequently they are heavily armed. Hence, the only solution to combating this is to have extra illumination about the decks (and over the ships side), all entrances secured with regular teams patrolling the decks and keeping a sharp look out. Piracy is rampant, particularly in such places as India, Indonesia, Singapore and Malacca Straits, South China Sea, Vietnam, Thailand, Philippines, etc., so it is very wide spread indeed. Now it is equally as bad in Sudan, Somalia and parts of the Red Sea, not to mention West Africa. The theft of ship's bunkers is also becoming a curse as well as kidnapping crews and high jacking of entire ships.

By most Asian standards Saigon was quite a clean city, unspoiled by the developing war, at that juncture. Living was cheap and there was a good variety of restaurants, bars and hotels as well as numerous sidewalk cafes from which to choose. There was never any problem getting a pedal taxi or transport to and from the city as most of the locals used pushbikes or mopeds (in their thousands) to get about. Saigon itself was a combination of Asia and France which created an "Oldie Worldly" atmosphere. Most of this stemmed from the French who had departed leaving their legacy very intact.

The females in their white or black native outfits and long smock like dresses with high splits in the side, pointed straw hats and deep rooted cultural traits only added to the mystery and charm of the place. I was fortunate to see Saigon in this unspoiled way because on later visits over subsequent voyages, prior to the takeover by the North Vietnamese; it only became a haven for many drunken, drugged and rowdy American servicemen on RnR from the War Zones who made themselves very conspicuous by virtue of their behavior, by which time Saigon had been spoiled forever. However this did not apply to all the American military, nevertheless to those whom it did made themselves very unwelcome.

Saigon Street Scene circa mid 1960s

Saigon Newport Authority (Port of Ho Chi Minh)

A typical Saigon River scene early during the Vietnam War years sometime around mid 1960s before hostilities became really bad prior to the departure of American Military in 1973 and reunification of North and South Vietnam in 1975. Most cargo work was conducted at buoys in mid stream, the limited amount of wharf space being prioritized for the US and Military vessels at that time.

My two apprentice colleagues had matured considerably since having joined in Hong Kong. They were fast learners, an asset about the ship and were now well used to going ashore themselves. However, the common practice amongst crew was to go in small groups which added a general safety net. There is much to be said for the buddy system. Both lads were becoming much better acquainted with Asian customs and culture as well as the manner in which things took place and were manifested in the Far East so were well capable of handling themselves

by this point in time. I believe they went ashore to sample the "delights" of Saigon having been introduced to the temptations of Japan, and of course Bangkok. They didn't say much upon their return but by this time I was becoming apt at reading them quite well in picking up their body language and glint in their eyes, which revealed the whole story.

All three modes of transport seen in this image - Bicycles, pedal Tuk Tuks and small Taxis in unspoiled Saigon during the early 1960s before the city lost much of its colonial charm due to the presence of foreign military.

Time flew by and after a week we were ready to depart for good old Hong Kong once again. As we transited down the Mekong towards the estuary the skies darkened, the wind increased and the heavens opened. We were delayed an hour in disembarking the Pilot and had to proceed further than usual offshore into deeper water where the sea was a little less steep and we could make a better lee, in order to disembark him safely. Our passage to Hong Kong was marred with this typical North East Monsoonal weather, windy and wet.

A Typhoon lingered off the coast of Luzon in the Philippines which did not help, conditions continued to deteriorate as we progressed to the North East due to the peripheral effects. Fortunately however, we missed the worst of it, as the Typhoon suddenly veered to the North and headed towards Taiwan and the Japanese archipelago. Nevertheless we encountered a rough passage until our arrival at Hong Kong. The adverse weather caused a conspicuous absence of the usual fishing fleets, most boats having taken refuge back in Hong Kong, safely hipped up in one of the several Typhoon Shelters the port provided, constructed precisely for the purpose.

The discharge of the remaining sugar took place at a wharf in the Taikoo area of Hong Kong Island. It was unusual to go alongside a jetty in Hong Kong as they were few in number, most cargo work being carried out by lighters in mid-stream, at the buoys.

The Taikoo Sugar berth at North Point was relatively close to the Shipyard and Dry-Dock. A couple of the smaller China coasters were high and dry on the slipways under maintenance but the Dry Dock itself was unoccupied at that time. It was a convenient location for me and made going home much easier. For the others, it was close to the red light district of Wanchai, which at that time was the red light district and home for most of the sex dives and bars on Hong Kong Island, such as the Top Bar, Ocean Bar and the Mermaid Bar, to name only a few. Luard Road, a highly frequented venue due to its inordinate number night clubs and bars. Wanchai and North Point's abundance of girly bars and dingy night clubs attracted our crew like Bees to a honey pot, which later provided the basis of many intriguing stories of lustful oriental seduction and pleasure being spun in the officers smoke room over ensuing weeks. More fiction than fact and grossly exaggerated in many cases I dare say. Nevertheless, there was no shortage of personal experiences portrayed.

The only down side to our visit was the heavy concentration of American Sailors and Marines from naval units that were visiting the port. They tended to concentrate on the areas of iniquity. Their loud, cavalier attitude, arrogance and boisterous behavior were in sharp contrast to the British and Australian servicemen whom we frequently encountered ashore. The need for the Americans to provide their own SP's (shore patrols – MP's) to oversee their personnel underpinned the situation. Frankly they were an absolute nuisance to all.

This port call was great for me as I was permitted to go home each evening after concluding the day's work. Friends visited me on board and I was delighted to see the return of our South African "Marquis" electrician who had been transferred back to us from one of the other company ships. He fitted in well, was good fun to be around and became a hit with all the officers who accepted him for what he was, a naïve romantic adventurer, with a heart of gold and not an evil streak in him.

Hong Kong was our Asian base where the company maintained a busy office, so we naturally stored heavily in preparation for our return to the Orient Africa liner service. Maximum quantities of Fuel Oil as well as fresh water were replenished. We were to sail empty (in ballast) from Hong Kong to Keelung initially, then to Japan, where loading would continue for our southbound voyage to Africa. All the cargo holds were cleaned and thoroughly hosed out before we set sail. Even though ballasted we were like a cork on the water as we sped up through the Formosa Strait towards Keelung. One night we were challenged on Aldis Lamp by a USN vessel patrolling the area but we satisfied their inquisitiveness and it became little more than nuisance value to us, so we continued on at full speed towards our destination.

That feeling of oppression was again very noticeable as we entered the port of Keelung. The local population were very friendly but treated everyone and everything with a distinct air of suspicion. The usual armed guards were placed at the foot of the gangway and painstakingly checked ID's of each person, in and out. Our Hong Kong Chinese crew in particular (many originating from the Chinese mainland) was all treated very suspect. Officially there still remained a curfew in place which appeared not to be too strictly enforced. However, we always complied as we never knew when it may suddenly become more rigidly applied. Everything was run by the military whose authority was obviously absolute, always hovering in the background continually overseeing all issues, consequently we never knew from one minute to the next if and when their attitudes may change for the worse or by whom we were being watched. This, together with constant over flights by Nationalist fighter aircraft, gun emplacements atop of many buildings and heavy navy presence offshore caused one feel uneasy at best. Hence, Taiwan was never to become a favored destination for us. This was in marked contrast to the Taiwan of later years.

However, during this period in the aftermath of President Kennedy's assassination in November 1963, the secret war in Laos, America's growing presence in Vietnam under LBJ coupled with the Indonesian and Singapore conflict, not to mention the tensions between Mainland China and Taiwan, the entire South East Asia region was aflame with political unrest and uncertainty. This made working in these locations a little hair raising at times so one always had to exercise caution in whatever one did when stepping ashore. Even the usually peaceful Hong Kong had been inflicted with riots during the early sixties, supposedly incited by those from across the border. Luckily they were quelled rather quickly and efficiently by the Royal HK Police and did not linger over too long a period, preventing detriment to the colony, as it then was.

Christmas and the Chinese New Year at sea were generally celebrated on board with much gusto. By nature of the circumstances these holiday celebrations aboard ship generally following the same trend; drinks with the "Old Man" followed by big eats, etc., as options are limited. For the Lunar New Year the Chinese Crew is usually left alone to celebrate and whenever possible given time off – their focus mainly being on feasting. Our Chinese crew considered me as a "Honkey", accordingly I was always invited to participate in their festivities and regularly accepted their invitation but having once eaten I left them to their own personal merriment and devices (usually Mah Jong Schools on the Poop Deck). For me to have refused their invitation, would have caused them "loss of face" and embarrassment. Besides which they were a good crowd.

Christmas 1963 was spent in Yokohama and the New Year at sea (complete with 16 bells being struck at midnight, 8 to say goodbye to the old year immediately followed by another 8 to herald in the new), whilst the Chinese New Year came about during our southbound call at Port Swettenham. However, for me this was all very significant since it well and truly marked the fact that I was entering the final strait towards the finishing line and completion of my apprenticeship – only one year or thereabouts, remaining to be completed. The end was in sight!

In Port Swettenham we had loaded significant quantities of palletized tin ingots and bales of rubber latex as well as veneers for several southern Ports. Upon departure the Master placed the vessel on high alert as he had received reports of recent and serious pirate attacks on several ships passing close to the Ache area off the Sumatran coast at the northern part of the Malacca Straits. Traditionally ships transiting the Malacca Strait closed the Indonesian coast in this area to minimize steaming distance. Reportedly one of the pirate attacks resulted in a fatality on board as a direct consequence. This was taken seriously so we rigged fire hoses about the decks and additional lighting was hung outboard as a precaution. Extra lookouts were posted during hours of darkness. This responsibility fell upon us apprentices, one of us being allocated to each sea watch whilst transiting the area. The Captain decided to give this region a wider berth airing on the side of safety. We passed without incident.

However, our vessel having a fast service speed we were a little less vulnerable to piracy than the slower steamers. During this era there were still many slower Empire, Victory, Liberties and numerous older type steamships frequenting and roaming the world's trade routes, particularly in Asia. Due to their slow speed of about 10 knots, these aging types became soft targets of choice for many pirates.

A high proportion of the world's older wartime and pre-war tonnage found its way to trade in S.E Asia which was becoming the grave yard for such vessels. Many were sold off to Far Eastern owners and reflagged under Panama, Hong Kong, Singapore, Indonesia, etc.; Greece also had a high number of elderly ladies within its national fleet, many of which tramped about Asia securing whatever cargoes that became available. That is not to say that the operation of such vessel types was restricted to these registries, Western European nations also had a fare share of oldies plying the Asian region but in most cases were better maintained.

Many pirate attacks were focused around the notorious Malacca and Singapore Strait, Philip Channel, Philippine and Indonesian Islands and the South China Sea, amongst other areas in the Orient. It was an absolute menace, as well as a real danger to all who tried to make an honest living from the sea. The various national authorities did what they could to prevent this criminality but poor resources and lack of political will (I suspect it often being regarded as someone else's problem), made their efforts impotent and hindered eradication in most cases.

Leaving our landmark of Pulau Weh in our wake we made our departure to the West to pass to the southward of Dondra Head (Sri Lanka) before setting a more south westerly course. The weather was up and down for most of the passage but it did not unduly hinder progress towards our destination the Mascarene Islands. This group encompasses the main Islands of Rodrigues, Mauritius and Isle de la Reunion; Reunion is the largest and still a French dependency whilst Mauritius was taken from the French by the British in the early 1800's but was to become an independent state in 1968. Rodrigues today is an autonomous region of Mauritius.

As we closed on the group we would occasionally get whiffs of the tropical fragrance in the air. It is amazing how far distant smell can travel across open Ocean if the prevailing winds are favorable. The mountainous terrain of the island of Mauritius was clearly visible to the naked eye as we passed some miles off to the north. This trip we were to miss calling at Mauritius and instead call at Isle de la Reunion which lies a further 120 miles or so to the south west of Mauritius and approximately 500 miles to the east of Madagascar.

Although having visited Reunion previously my stay had been short and marred by a cyclone, so I naturally hoped to have a better opportunity of sightseeing this time around.

The volcanic peaks of Reunion's interior, some still active, were obscured by mist as we approached the Port of St. Denis, at the northern tip of the island. What struck me immediately was how pristine the Island and its surrounding seas actually were. Peering over the ship's side one could see below the surface into the unknown abyss accommodating corals, fish and large dark eerie moving shapes, perhaps Manta ray or the like. We entered St. Denis Port and secured to the same jetty as on my previous visit. Coincidentally, the same two French Cargo Liners I had seen on the earlier trip were again tied up at the wharves opposite. Once all fast I remained on the bridge wing for a short while, eyeing the scenery through binoculars; scanning the colorful buildings, Creole architecture and numerous monuments and columns which made up the town, all were noticeably striking. I intended a trip ashore to see firsthand.

Lychees grow prolifically in Reunion and Mauritius and it was not long before the vendors were on board selling large bunches, very cheaply. Being brought up in Asia, over the years Lychees became one of my favorite fruits, so together with our Chinese crew we proceeded to make gluttons of ourselves.

We remained in Reunion for almost a week, during which we discharged most of the tin ingots and rubber bales. No doubt for transshipment, perhaps on our Frenchie cargo liner types, to France or other European destinations. Having completed our cargo operations we sailed for Dar es Salaam (then in Tanganyika, later to merge with Zanzibar and become known as Tanzania).

Dar es Salaam is a major port nestled in a natural harbor on the east African coast, to the south of Zanzibar. Its white sandy beaches, mostly isolated and deserted, flanked by swaying coconut palms and in some cases with a backdrop of mangroves and their thatch roof Cabanas, add to the tranquility of the place. It is a very picturesque harbor as I mentioned earlier and boasts wonderful fishing. Whilst in "Dar" there fell a public holiday on which there was no cargo worked. The local Seaman's Club arranged an outing for us apprentices, a BBQ at "Ras Kutani" which is a well known resort and retreat a relatively short distance away by car. I can honestly say that the BBQ'd fish, freshly caught, was the best I have ever tasted.

It was a wonderful outing but all three of us caught the sun badly and suffered from relatively severe sun burn for the ensuing few days. We were used to walking about the decks without shirts but in this case we underestimated the glare and sun's reflection from the white sands and sea. We learned our lesson for the future and for relief relied heavily on regular spraying with "Solarcaine", supplied from the ship's medical locker, to reduce the burning and discomfort. We soon recovered however and after a few days we all turned brown as berries, which once again made us the envy of the ship's engineers who were always trying to improve their bronzy but unfortunately for them, only tended to turn them pink!

We left behind the native poverty of the Ports of Beira and Lorenzo Marques (now renamed Maputo). Cargo had been minimal and thankfully so was our port stays. We had loaded cotton bales and bagged cashew nuts in the tweendecks. We were not calling at Beira northbound, but alternatively Mtwara, Zanzibar and Tanga before topping off at Mombasa The down trodden appearance of the Mozambique natives who came on board to handle the cargo, and the manner in which they were treated by their Portuguese masters always troubled me. I felt very sorry for them and passed to them the better galley left overs. They were always appreciative.

Then it was on to Durban, East London and finally Cape Town. It was time to start back loading and heading towards home waters once again.

Cape Town with its iconic Table Mountain was an interesting stay. We did the usual city roaming and pub crawling in our free time but this visit I was fortunate and managed a trip to the summit of Table Mountain. I can only say that it has to be seen to be believed. The unimpaired views east and west of the Cape are awesome. The Devils Peak and Lion's Head are very conspicuous and the entire city and harbor of Cape Town are laid out before you offering spectacular views. Looking towards the hinterland the height of eye made the visibility almost unlimited and it was difficult to differentiate between sky and horizon as they merged into an indigo blur some considerable distance away. One felt as if standing on top of the world but although the weather was fine the winds once at the top were quite fresh, mainly Anabatic and Katabatic in their nature. Katabatic being the down flowing winds from the mountain top as the surface cools and the Anabatic winds being the upslope alternative as the surface is heated by the sun. As they are caused by heating, cooling and vectoring of the surrounding surface areas, Katabatic tend to be night or early morning orientated whilst Anabatic are generally reserved for mid-to late afternoon. As my visit was late afternoon I was experiencing the Anabatic influence.

As usual our Chief Mate was heavily occupied with his loading plan and the same procedure followed as for the previous voyage. In South African Ports we back loaded pre fabricated steel work, steel coils and rebar as bottom stow. Our freezer chambers had been cleaned and tested before our arrival in Cape Town and were once again filled to capacity with cartons of frozen squid and shellfish for several different Japanese destinations. Each consignee being separated by fine colored nylon nets. Our tweendecks were partially filled with pallets of preserved canned fruit as were various parcels of assorted general cargo in crates. Additionally, we took on large coils of undersea telephone cable for both Singapore and Hong Kong the securing and shoring of which called for specialized squads of carpenters supplied by the stevedores. We said our farewells to South Africa and headed northward up the coast transiting the Mozambique Channel towards Mtwara.

Mtwara lies in the southern part of what is now known as Tanzania. It is a deepwater port offering a good sheltered inner anchorage and several deep water quays. Its "Spit" is a conspicuous feature. We remained a couple of days, long enough to top off several of our lower holds and tweendecks with bales of sisal, cotton, cashew and ground nuts. We were alongside the deep water jetty which assisted towards a rapid loading. Expert stevedores in handling the bales and bags made for perfect stows resulting in little, if any, broken space. We were told that there was quite a town at Mtwara but as we apprentices were kept very busy during cargo operations, alas we did not have the opportunity to do any sightseeing. So, amid one of those wonderful East African sunsets, we departed Mtwara and sailed northward towards the spice island of Zanzibar.

We approach the Island of Zanzibar from the South, transiting the Zanzibar Channel and passing numerous small off lying islands such as Chumbe, Nyange and Mutogo to name but a few. Proceeding towards the

227

anchorage off the Port we skirted the Prison Island of Changuu before dropping our anchor.

The Island of Zanzibar is as mystical as its name implies. There is a strong Swahili, Arab and Portuguese influence which adds to the Island's ancient mystique. First inhabited by settlers from modern day Tanzania, it then fell into the hands of the Portuguese and later the British before finally the Omani Arabs who ruled thru a Sultan well into the 19th century. It became a regional trading hub, especially with the Persian Gulf and Arab States. Consequently Zanzibar developed into a City State and was to become a major centre of the African slave trade, finally being abolished in 1873. In 1964 it united with Tanganyika to become part of today's independent Tanzania.

We spent well over a day loading quite a large parcel of cloves. Highly aromatic, even though all beautifully packed in superbly crafted plywood chests with consignee's details all beautifully stenciled on each. This was a high value cargo and accordingly was stowed in its usual secure location after being carefully tallied on board.

Tanga is the longest serving port on the East African coast. It is relatively shallow, hence most cargo is worked from lighters whilst anchored or secured to midstream buoys. Cow hides and carbon black were the main commodities loaded. This was all from lighters. We had to load small fork lift trucks (counter waits removed and lifted separately) in order to stow these palletized cargoes into the tweendeck wings. The holds nominated were numbers one and five so the tweendeck wings were not that deep, which made loading somewhat easier. It also meant that the stinking hides and dirty carbon black were well segregated from other cargo on board.

Like Dar es Salaam, the fishing in mid stream was excellent. I think all the crew participated and the overall catch was enormous, carefully gutted and filleted by the Chinese deck boys, the fish was frozen for future cating by all, as per the normal practice.

Arriving at the Kenyan Port of Mombasa we were almost cubically full although nowhere near our full deadweight cargo capacity. The intention was to fill last remaining space with bales of cotton, sisal and some additional nuts and coffee. Here we also learned we were to load a full deck cargo of pre-slung bundles of "pit props" up as high as the gunwales. The hatch tops were not to be over stowed.

Pit props are small timber stumps that have been partially dressed varying in size but on average about 2.5 meters long with a diameter of some 25 centimeters. I suppose their usage is as their name implies. Once loaded and stacked in parcels made up of about 20 bundles, each bundle consisting about 10 stumps, pit prop lumber being relatively light. Bundles were encased with a type of chicken mesh and well lashed with wires to prevent any movement. Hence each parcel was individually secured. On top was constructed a wooden walk way, from forecastle to poop, down both sides of the vessel. Care was needed to keep fire hydrants, filling and sounding pipes accessible.

Once our traditional general cargo had completed, the loading of the pit props commenced and took some 3 days or so to finally finish and lash. Their port of destination was Fushiki in Japan, a new port of call for us. Fushiki is located on the north Coast of Honshu Island on the Sea of Japan and is in close proximity to Toyama prefecture. It is a natural river port of small to medium size with a good anchorage for larger vessels. On clear days, which are few and far between in Japan, there are allegedly views of Mount Fuji even though somewhat distant. Personally I did not see the mountain from Fushiki.

Before sailing we visited the Missions to Seamen and paid respects to our friendly Padre, as usual we had our fill of his bacon and eggs after the Sunday service. We were now faced with a longer passage to Asia. Being absolutely filled to capacity with no vacant space remaining allowing for calls at the Port Louis or St. Denis; hence we sailed past heading for the One and Half degree Channel, south of the main archipelago of some 300 low laying coral Islets and atolls which make up the Maldive Islands located off the south west coast of India.. There are various channels thru the archipelago, many named after their corresponding parallels of latitude. From there we set course almost directly east to make our usual land fall at Pulau Weh. This again signposted my homecoming and signaled our entrance into the Malacca Strait.

As usual we three apprentices and the entire Chinese deck crew were kept busy on day work overhauling the ship's cargo gear after the serious utilization it had sustained on the East African coast. Of an evening, on the 4-8 watch, I was required to go to the bridge and practice, amplitudes, star sights and other navigation skills under the watchful eye of our Chief Officer. The Mate had now put in place regular classes of instruction for us learners. These were usually taken by our Chief Mate who drilled us in many things such as the Collision Regulations (Rules of the Road), math, chart work, ship stability, principles of navigation and seamanship. From time to time our 2nd Mate would stand in for the Chief Officer if he was busy. Far more emphasis was now being placed on the academic side of our training. For my part I was grateful as the time was soon approaching when I would be sitting for my 2nd

Mates Certificate of Competency and needed all the tuition I could get.

By this point in time both Max and Ginger were developing into good deck hands and we had all become firm friends.

21 Meeting Old Friends

Once in the Malacca and Singapore Strait there was never a moment without a small handsome "Straits Steamship" short sea trader far from the eye. We passed them frequently as they forged their way to and from the various ports on the East and West Coast of the Malayan peninsula. They ventured as far as Bangkok in the Gulf of Thailand, to Sarawak, Sabah (East Malaysia) and coastwise around the various ports of what is now known as Kalimantan (formerly Borneo Island). Their passenger ships and coasters were named after regional ports, provinces or places of prominence and were always immediately recognizable by their pale blue and white funnel capped with black. They were quaint little ships with a lot of character, numerous in number and iconic to the area. They did engage a reasonable number of senior British Officers and Engineers and a post with Straits Steamships was highly sought and considered to be one of the most prestigious sea going jobs available in Asia during this period, assuming one was fortunate enough to land one.

Straits Steamships had a Dutch counterpart, KPM, who tended to concentrate a little more on the Indonesian inter-Island trades, but nevertheless their ships were also regional icons. They were beautiful ships, impeccably maintained and presented. Included in their fleet were a number of smaller passenger vessels which had been the principal mode of transport for the Dutch colonials throughout the East Indies Islands and across the Singapore and Malacca straits, prior to Indonesia's declaration of independence. It is claimed, once a ship's crew joined a KPM vessel, they seldom if ever left. Like so many of the "Strait's" officers a number of expatriate Dutch in KPM made their permanent homes in

Indonesia, Singapore or Malaya. On our excursions ashore we often met up with these types, usually in a bar, they were never backward in coming forward with intriguing yarns of how wonderfully adventurous life was tramping around the various ports of S.E. Asia and the quality of the life style they enjoyed. I tended to agree with them wholeheartedly and was very envious indeed. Mostly, they personified "Soldiers of Fortune" in my personal view.

Our calls at both Port Swettenham and Singapore were generally uneventful. I did pay my usual visit to the Cellar Bar in Singapore, mainly for a cursory check on job vacancies posted on the famous notice board. I was not disappointed by the number of interesting vacancies. I wished to keep my finger on the pulse and abreast of opportunities. This was the bulletin board that one consulted if seeking a sea going situation in S.E. Asia. I have to admit, by this time, with only a relatively short period remaining to complete my Indentures, I was starting to get itchy feet; for once having obtained a 2nd Mates Certificate I was leaning very much towards joining one of the Hong Kong or Singapore based shipping companies in which to further my career. It was not that I was dissatisfied with my present lot, but simply a case of wishing to concentrate my sea going life more or less exclusively to the Asia region. This is where I felt most at ease. This notion of mine was even more stoked, when upon our arrival at our next port of call, Bangkok, I came across two old friends.

It is one of those co-incidences that seldom if ever happen, but upon our arrival at Bangkok I was astonished to find that two of my old friends "Michael Jebsen" and "Thames Breeze" were berthed fore and aft of us at Klong Toei wharves.

The "Michael Jebsen" I knew well from my earlier shipboard visits with the Captain's son, the first of several when she was in Cosmo Dry dock at Tai Kok Tsui in Kowloon.

Below is a nice shot of my fiend **"Michael Jebsen"** – Another good looking Danish Far East Trader. Captured in Chao Phraya River, near Pak Nam, loading Rice circa early 1960s. Note, although being tied up alongside the wharf she was also secured to a buoy with her anchor chain – this was because many of the private rice jetties at Bangkok, apart from being a bit rickety, were quite short which only allowed for working one or maximum two adjacent hatches at a time. Being moored to the buoy assisted in regular warping of the vessel up and down the jetty in the fast flowing downstream current, permitting alternate hatches to be worked as required.

Photo KP ©

The "Thames Breeze", Hong Kong registered and operated by Messrs. John Manners, I had come across in Yokohama and struck up a friendship with their 2nd Mate, an Anglo Indian chap named Ian.

As soon as I could wangle some free time I made my way over to the "Thames Breeze". It had been many months since my last visit so I was not surprised to learn that my pal Ian was no longer on board, he having signed off in Hong Kong earlier during the voyage, to undergo examination for his 1st Mate's Certificate.

This vessel was an ex British tramp, originally built for Newcastle owners. Her origins became immediately evident upon sighting her, the design being so characteristic of tramp vessels built in the UK in the post war years and throughout the 50's. The Master and most of the officers on board were old China Hands, either British or Australian. I made myself known and over lunch soon became engaged in a cacophony of table talk. I was particularly interested to hear of the company history, fleet and job opportunities and was given the address of the Chief Marine Superintendent at their Hong Kong office, mentioned as being the supremo who should be contacted by job seekers. The ship was a good feeder and lunch was extended that day as we were all so engrossed in interesting chat, so it was not surprising to learn of the number of mutual sea going acquaintances and friends we all knew from Hong Kong. It was good to keep track of various whereabouts and movements of my chums.

My visit on board had been timely for the vessel completed loading during the late afternoon and sailed for China with a full cargo of bagged rice the same night. I went down the gangway with the office address of a potential new Hong Kong employer in my pocket. It so happened that in later years I was to join this company as a junior deck officer being assigned initially to the "Asia Fir" (later renamed "Asia Breeze"). I was saddened to learn in later years that the "Thames Breeze" had run aground on Investigator Reef, in the South China Sea, sometime during 1969. The ship was abandoned by her crew and became a total loss. What a most unsavory ending for such a staunch vessel.

My next call was to the "Michael Jebsen" – a Danish China trader registered in Aabenraa with which I was well acquainted. I was disappointed that there was no one on board that I had known from my previous visits in Hong Kong. The regular Captain, whose son I knew so well, was on leave. Nevertheless, once I explained who I was and my past connection with the ship, the Danish crew was most hospitable and I soon gained an insight as to the whereabouts of many whom I had met previously. I was offered several strong Danish beers which went to my head immediately but fortunately they did not have a too devastating effect on me.

"Michael Jebsen" had been in Bangkok for over a week loading bagged rice for Hong Kong but still had a couple of days to go before her departure. At the conclusion of an entertaining evening on board I returned to my ship but before doing so took the time to study and survey the sleek lines of this fine ship. Her pleasing features, four cargo holds, bi-pod masts, streamlined silver grey hull and cream colored funnel sporting the company crest of three Mackerels, painted in blue encompassed within a circle of laurel leaves. From my point of view she was what a ship should look like from both a size and aesthetic perspective, this was further enhanced by her very comfortable interior accommodations. The Master and Officers invited me to visit again before they left Bangkok if time permitted, but sadly the opportunity did not arise.

My association with the ship brought back a flood of memories, reverting to my initial visit when she was in Cosmo dry dock at Tai Kok Tsui, Kowloon, so many moons ago. All this only served to enforce my determination to seek future employment on such a vessel operating within the Far East. It may not seem like much to readers but the length of time I was spending at sea was now starting to have its affects on me, so ship visits such as these were a breath of fresh air, they broke the monotony and spurred me on, encouraging me to see things through to the end with my apprenticeship, as well as affording an enlightening insight into future opportunities.

Bangkok seemed to be the hub for all these wonderful ships because just prior to my departure there arrived another Danish vessel, painted gleaming white overall, save for boasting 4 buff, and very prominent tall masts, with no visible funnel except for two exhausts mounting one of the masts. Her name was "Jutlandia". I understand she was a motor ship despite her vintage design and appearance. It looked as if she was a passenger cargo type and was reportedly owned and operated by the East Asiatic Company. I do believe it was the same vessel that had become famous when serving as a hospital ship during the Korean War and was later refurbished to once again become a freighter, which included superior passenger carrying capability, at the conclusion of the war. When I saw her she must have been nearing the end of her useful life because she allegedly went to Spanish breakers in 1964 or 65 for her inevitable demise.

Below: Chao Phraya River "A" showing River mouth and "B" Pak Nam Anchorage at Samut Prakan. The main Port at Klong Toei is further upstream towards Bangkok City.

So concluded a most enlightening visit to Bangkok and as we rushed down the now familiar Chao Phraya River as usual infested with long tail boats and large clumps of floating vegetation, towards the estuary, and ultimately on to Hong Kong, my thoughts started to focus on the future that awaited me in my chosen career.

The passage to Hong Kong was quite rough and we rolled and pitched most of the way. All the ship's upper works were encrusted in salt from the sea spray.

The weather was still miserable as we entered Victoria Harbor in Hong Kong. The passing aftermath of an unseasonable bad weather had caught many unaware and still lingered. The harbor was crowded, so much so we were required to remain at the western anchorage to await a vacant buoy to which we could secure in readiness for cargo operations. Our designated anchorage was distant and almost half way to Lantau Island, too far and expensive to go ashore in a walla walla or launch. We remained at the anchorage almost two days, as the recent inclement conditions had created havoc with the barges, most of which had taken refuge in the Typhoon Shelters. Besides, our ship was on standby in case a quick dash to the open sea was needed, should the Typhoon change direction. Finally the Typhoon dissipated over the land somewhere to the north of Hong Kong and life began to return to normal.

Gradually the port became better mobilized, and once again barging was underway. The passing adverse weather had caused a substantial number of barges to remain entrapped within the shelters until room was made for them to be towed out. To overcome the temporary shortage of barges these were supplemented by several large cargo motorized cargo Junks, expertly handled by their Chinese skippers as they were placed alongside. The fact that our decks remained loaded with "Pit Props" made operations a little slower than usual as our winch operators needed to be far more vigilant when operating the ship's cargo gear.

Two other familiar ships the "Clara Jebsen" and "Heinrich Jessen", both China traders belonging to the Danish Jebsen line, were at buoys over towards Stone Cutters Island. They were both masterpieces of design, being of about 6000 tons, perfectly proportioned in every way and very pleasing to the eye, even though the "Heinrich Jessen" was of an earlier vintage. I would have liked to visit them both but unfortunately there would be no opportunity due to our heavy work load on board.

It took us 3 days to discharge a variety of cargo at Hong Kong, namely, pre-formed steel, cashew nuts, sisal, cotton and pallets of preserved fruit. Thankfully we had discharged the stinking cow hides and part of the carbon black earlier at Singapore. We were very busy and I did not visit my home so had to make do with several hurried phone calls from Blake's Pier. Anyway, next visit would be different as I intended to talk with the Chief Mate and request a day off in order that I could visit my family. The expected duration of the round trip before calling Hong Kong again southbound, would be in the vicinity 7 weeks or so. After Taichung in Taiwan we were then scheduled to be on the Japanese coast a full month, calling first at Fushiki (Toyama) on the north coast of Honshu, to discharge our deck cargo of pit props. The rotation was then to back track into the Inland Sea, for Kobe and Osaka, before calling at Shimizu and finally Yokohama, to discharge and commence back loading for another round voyage to southern latitudes.

Taichung is the main port for Taipei, the capital city of Taiwan. It is located on the west coast of the island, about half way up. It was a port built around an industrial complex, grey and boring to say the least, the overkill security still in being throughout Formosa only increased the usual oppressive atmosphere of the place. We discharged the last of carbon black, ground nuts, various generals and some bagged coffee. It was a short visit so no time to go ashore, not that anyone was really planning on doing so anyway. We were a long way from any sort of civilized township and there was no value in visiting an industrial area. Besides which, the hassle of the Port security just to get off the ship for a few hours was not worth the effort.

The port was in its early days of establishment at this time but I do believe that in the years since this visit there has been huge development and Taichung has now become a major port, ranking amongst the busiest in Taiwan and possibly Asia as a whole. This was to be my one and only visit to Taichung (until many years later when serving as Master). Again, we were not disappointed to depart and head towards more interesting parts, namely exotic Japan.

Angry skies, choppy seas and moderate visibility accompanied us all the way to the Korea Strait. We passed the Korean Island of Cheju-Do with its volcanic peaks, leaving it to port as we pressed forth, northward, skirting the Japanese Island of Tsushima before entering the Sea of Japan and following the coastline of Honshu towards Fushiki. I was assigned to the Chief Mates watch as an extra pair of eyes due to the intensity of traffic and marginal visibility that prevailed. My fellow apprentices being similarly allocated to watches with 2nd and 3rd Mates.

Having rounded the headland we entered Toyama-Wan (Bay) and was guided to our designated anchorage by a Japanese Pilot. Fushiki is a small to medium size port at the foot of the Bay but is very prominent for logging, with its paper pulp mills and holding ponds for large quantities of floating logs. It is a principal Japanese importation point for logs and a significant timber handling facility. The general area around the township is heavily industrialized in respect of its sprawling iron and steel works. We were required to anchor off the port and discharge into lighters as the port of Fushiki itself is located a little way up stream and too shallow for a vessel of our size and draft to enter. It all forms part of the Toyama prefecture, with the actual city of Toyama being relatively close to hand.

We arrived early morning to find the entire coastal region heavily overcast with a pinkish colored smog, one had to assume due to pollution caused by the local industry and the associated factory chimneys each belching out pollutants of one kind or another. Needless to say everyone wore cotton face masks. No time was lost and as soon as port formalities had been concluded the stevedores and lighters arrived. Unlashing and discharge of the timber commenced, using ships gear to handle the bundled log stumps directly into the barges.

Doubling wires had been rigged before arrival so swinging derricks could be used port and starboard. A couple of small Japanese coasters arrived alongside and we discharged directly into their empty gaping cargo holds, their respective crews acting as stevedores for the purpose of stowing the bundles below decks.

Whilst discharge and dispatch of the coasters was quite rapid, the same could not be said for the barges. There appeared to be a chronic shortage of lighters. Once loaded they were towed to the shore where they waited their turn in a queue to be discharged before returning empty to our ship for the next load. The slow cycle of lighters tended to hamper the speed at which the cargo could be discharged from us. After the first day there had not been much progress made and it became clear it would be a slow process. Discharging was only between the hours of 6am and 6pm because of the poor infrastructure and limited number of lighters, so we had the opportunity for shore leave and our stay was likely to be about a week based on quantity discharged on the first day. I volunteered to remain on board the first night and keep the anchor watch. Whilst I kept the watch on the bridge between 6pm and 6am a duty officer was always available and on call. I had never been to Fushiki or Toyama before so there was method in my madness in staying on board; the others could check out the town, then I would decide whether or not to go ashore myself based on feedback received.

Curiosity got the better of me so the next evening I opted for a run ashore myself. Fushiki itself was a clean small affair, very quaint with a high number of timber buildings and was mostly undeveloped. Amongst the multitude of narrow streets, all the tea houses, bars and restaurants were decorated with their quintessential hanging advertisements painted on cloth curtains draped across their doorways. This, coupled with numerous swaying lanterns outside respective establishments all added to the magic of the place in the eye of a foreigner like me. After wandering about the township for a while, I decided to go to the larger city of Toyama to sample the action it supposedly offered. I jumped a cab and set off as it was not too distant. One town seemed to merge into the next, Toyama's only difference being more of everything and considerably more neon lighting. It was a vibrant city going by what I observed.

I meandered through the winding streets, window shopping and soaking up the surrounds. This town was very different to the large metropolises of Kobe, Osaka and Yokohama. It was very "Oldie Worldly" with many locals, both male and female, wearing traditional national dress. Eventually I entered a typical Geisha Bar (I refer to them as Geisha Bars – although the ladies were not true Geishas, they were all adorned in traditional Japanese kimono and extended the most wonderful company, entertainment and hospitality – hence my loose reference). To start language was a problem since no one could speak English; nevertheless the language barriers were easily overcome amidst much laughter and merriment. I shall not go into detail, sufficing to leave it to the imagination of the reader.

I had been so engrossed with the goings on in the Bar and extravagant attention imposed upon me by the hostesses, I clean forgot the time and when I eventually looked at my watch I had already missed the midnight launch back to the vessel, the next was 0600 hrs. The Bar Momma-san took pity on me so I ended up in a Japanese Hotel that night, absolutely typical Japanese in every way. Small as a postage stamp but immaculately clean, sparsely furnished, thick quilt on the floor as a bed, sliding wall panels made of flimsy materials instead of doors, etc., slippers and kimono's provided, not to mention the adjoining communal bath.

I arose early at 5 am, hailed a passing taxi and headed for the jetty to catch the ferry back to the ship. The launch departed exactly on schedule and I was sitting in my cabin aboard ship drinking a mug of tea by 6.30am, ready to turn too at 7am. I had not even been missed and no one knew I had stayed ashore that night (except for the Chinese quartermaster on duty at the gangway when I arrived back on board – a few cordial words in Cantonese made certain my secret remained safe). Apprentices staying ashore overnight was frowned upon by the Company and ship Masters alike. I got away with it completely.

Striding out on deck that morning I was taken aback by the unexpected progress made to the discharge of the pit props, most of the afterdeck had been cleared and they were starting with more gangs forward. It seems that the stevedores had extended their working hours the previous night to compensate for the slow progress. We apprentices, along with the crew spent most of the day cleaning up aft, unlashing the securing wires and stowing them away in the forecastle. We hosed down the decks and by lunch time the after decks were clear and one would never have known that the lumber had ever been stowed there. The forward deck cargo was to take another two days to discharge, for whilst additional barges were procured by the stevedores, which aided the speed of actual discharge, the turnaround of barges ashore still remained pitifully slow. Eventually the last props were offloaded. We secured for sea and departed Fushiki bound for Kobe and Osaka, followed by Shimizu and finally Yokohama.

The passage around the Japanese coast and thru the Inland Sea to Kobe was both slow and hazardous. We encountered dense fog over most of the route. It was as thick as an "Old Boot" and our speed was reduced accordingly. As usual, Radar plotting and extra lookouts posted on the Bridge wings, the monotony of fog signals sounding from our ship's siren, not to mention orders given to the Engine Room to remain alert and on standby for unexpected engine movements all added to the intense eeriness of the situation. Traffic density was very high, causing stress for all on board, in particular the Bridge team.

Our Captain spent many hours on the Bridge catching the odd catnap whenever possible in the Pilot's Cabin situated next to the chartroom. However, all our precautions and strict adherence to the rules did not prevent us from almost being run down by a rogue Panamanian Tanker that was steaming at full speed, not sounding fog signals and which cut across our port bow missing us by the narrowest of margins. Luckily our Captain had been monitoring and plotting all this on Radar and had stopped our engines in anticipation of a close quarter situation developing. It was a narrow escape but hammered home to me, especially being an apprentice, the importance and value of obeying the international regulations for vessels proceeding in restricted visibility. These rules being for the guidance of wise men and disregard of idiots, the tanker Master clearly falling into the latter category. We only caught the shortest glimpse of the tanker as it sped across our bow; it was visible only momentarily before disappearing again into the dense fog banks. This close encounter unnerved us a little but for me this incident remained clearly fixed in my mind for all my future seagoing years, serving as a stark reminder of the consequences if the regulations were flouted.

As we entered the Inland Sea the visibility improved to about 2 miles which was a relief. Shipping remained denser than ever and the prevailing conditions, still required extreme caution for the remainder of our passage. In this era there were fewer compulsory traffic or separation schemes (VTS) for high volume shipping lanes, as compared to today, so traffic tended to be going every which way. It came with a sigh of relief when we anchored off Kobe to await allocation of a berth, inside the port. It was several days before the fog lifted.

All the Japanese ports were very similar, Kobe, Osaka etc., I found the only one being somewhat different was Sasebo due to its large American Navy influence and presence.

Shimizu was also smoggy, like other Japanese ports it did not experience too many days without some kind of smog or air pollution impeding the atmosphere and limiting visibility. However it was not as bad as could be experienced in those cities located in the Inland Sea. The township of Shimizu itself was once again a smaller clone of many of the other places we had visited in Japan.

However, one interesting aspect of Shimizu was its historical connection with the Samurai beliefs and culture which was the ancient Japanese military nobility and officer class code of obedience, honor and service to their Lord. This elite class dated back to the 12th century in feudal Japan. Samurai was finally abolished in 1868 but from Samurai stemmed "Bushido", a discipline of moral principles, obedience, loyalty, self control and chivalry which became the traditional way of conduct and virtues of many modern Japanese people. Finally, we completed our business on the Japanese coast at Yokohama and headed off, southbound once again.

22 Passenger Medics

Our arrival in Hong Kong met with some interesting news. We would be embarking two passengers for the voyage to Durban. Mr. and Mrs.Van De Doel were medical practitioners and were returning to their native South Africa at the conclusion of their working contracts in the colony. Traveling on a cargo freighter was starting to become a novel idea amongst the professional set at that time and whilst we did not often carry passengers, our ship was nevertheless fitted with quite a luxurious "Owners Cabin" located adjacent to the Captain's accommodations. This cabin offered very comfortable facilities, including a large double bed, en suite, private pantry and attached dining area. It was relatively quiet and secluded being on the Captain's deck and was indeed ideally suited for the purpose of carrying fare paying passengers.

The Van De Doels (both being medics they were immediately nicknamed VD^2 by some cheeky junior engineer) came on board the day we arrived in Hong Kong with all their luggage but once having deposited it on board returned ashore until just prior to our departure. One of the Chinese stewards was assigned to look after their needs and cabin cleaning whilst all the catering staff turned out in extra special garb, crisp white mess jackets. The same applied to the table linen in the officer's dining room. Officer's smoke room and dining rooms were also spruced up, carpets shampooed and bulkheads which consisted of real wooden paneling were highly polished, as was the brass work. The Officers laundry was also given a special "once over".

I was able to spend a day and night at home whilst in Hong Kong. I had not seen my folks and brother for a while. My father took us all for dinner at Landaus restaurant; this was one of my favorite eating spots. Landaus had been around since the year dot and was a Hong Kong icon in terms of fine dining, being on a par with "Gaddis", another top restaurant, which was situated in the Peninsula Hotel in Kowloon. One of Landaus' signature dishes was an excellent Madras Curry – full of spice and body, it made you sweat. Following dinner we went to the other extreme and visited a night market in Kennedy Town for some late shopping, as I recall my mother wished to buy some kind of knick knack.

These night markets never ceased to fascinate me, you could buy virtually anything and everything and the sounds and smells were unique to Hong Kong. One could browse for hours without getting bored or spending a cent.

My favorite market was in Kowloon at Temple Street in Yau Ma Tei, located quite close to the Tin Hau Temple, hence the name.

A couple of hours before sailing our passengers arrived on board and settled into their suite. We were scheduled to depart late evening so during dinner our Captain seized the opportunity to introduce all the officers and apprentices to them. Our departure from Hong Kong was perfect for the Doels, Hong Kong's illuminations was at its best. As we glided through the busy port towards Green Island and the Llama Channel; the eye was feasted with a magnificent and spectacular panorama of all the harbor lights for which it is so renowned. Additionally, the harbor was a buzz of busy shipping, whether underway or working cargo at the typhoon buoys, their lights, sounds and smells all added to the hive of activity and excitement of the port.

I suspect the Doctors were in their early forties. They appeared a somewhat sophisticated duo, and initially I considered them as a little aloof and snobbish. Nevertheless, there was a long voyage ahead of them and perhaps they would mellow a little I thought to myself.

I soon revised my opinion of Mrs. Doel; she was exceedingly courteous and generous towards me from the outset. I think she took a bit of a shine to me. She regularly dropped off all sorts of things to my cabin; books, cans of cold beer, cakes she made herself whilst on board, toffees, etc., and she always remained for a chat. It was a little embarrassing for me at times but I have to admit I was a willing recipient. Her husband on the other hand was just the opposite, a studious and quiet type, reading books incessantly. Whenever he spoke he raised his eyebrows, lowered his head and peered over his gold rimmed spectacles. He had steel grey hair, penetrating green eyes and neat black moustache – looking and acting very much the part of a Doctor. His only other interest seemed to be his movie camera which was always close at hand. They were each so different in their personality but then I guess they were like a magnet to each other, different poles attracting. He kept very much to himself.

This voyage we did not go upstream to Bangkok as the port was congested. Instead we anchored off Koh Si Chang and our cargo was transported out to us in lighters. Loading was a slower process and further marred by heavy rain squalls. This was not a very good start for the Doels as it was just not practical for them to go ashore by boat to Siracha and then by road to Bangkok, the road trip alone being something of a hazard. The weather was so unpredictable and sea conditions at the anchorage so choppy at times we were required to cast off the barges for fear of sustaining hull damage to both ship and barge, this also made traveling in launches completely out of the question since it was too dangerous. In fact we did hear that one of the barges coming downstream capsized when crossing the Bangkok Bar. This really came as no surprise considering the weather and the fact that more often than not the lighters were frequently grossly overloaded. Still, Mr. Doel's movie camera was working overtime. Sadly, Tasanee was conspicuous by her absence because I had been collecting my washing and ironing for a week or so by this time, in anticipation.

The loading of rice and crates of veneers was eventually completed and we weighed anchor and headed off towards Singapore at our full sea speed of 16 knots. The weather was still inclement as we approached the Horsburgh Light House. Even though only a few miles off the coast Singapore remained out of view, it being engulfed in heavy rain. Rain drops the size of golf balls it seemed and many of the scuppers could not cope with the deluge of rain water causing temporary flooding on many of the upper decks. The ship was receiving a very good wash down indeed.

Conveniently for us the down pour eased as we approached the Pilot Boarding Ground and by the time we were secured alongside the wharf at Keppel things were starting to dry out somewhat. As usual the stevedores stampeded on board and started to open the hatches. The labor must have been placed on some kind of incentive as they made it obvious that time was of the essence and cargo soon started to turn up at ship's side ready for loading on board.

This was a memorable visit to Singapore because one evening whilst ashore, paying my usual call at the Cellar Bar (yes to check the notice board!), I ran into a very interesting character. He just so happened to be sitting next to me on a stool at the bar and introduced himself in a casual sort of way. He was a slightly rotund

American with drawling accent, thinning sandy colored hair, mild ruddy complexion and at a guess in his mid to late 40s. He went by the name of Sandy Stimson and was allegedly an old China hand having spent many years as a nomad wandering throughout the Far East, in particular Indo China and the Philippines. His home was wherever he was at any given time, being of no fixed abode, although he alleged to have originally heralded from Amarillo, Texas. He was conspicuous by the solid gold Rolex watch and heavy gold ID bracelet he wore.

He appeared a shady, complex cove and was definitely a man of many faces. Sandy claimed to be working as a flight Captain flying C-46s and C-47s for some nondescript airline operating out of Taiwan and was in Singapore on RnR. We sat drinking beer for a while during which time he drifted into a litany of stories and yarns of his past flying experiences. Initially I took this with a pinch of salt, considering it to be just bar talk; until he dropped a few names that were known to me from within Hong Kong's aviation circles, which made me take a little more notice. After about an hour he departed and went on his way.

I quizzed the barman as to who he really was because he most certainly came across as a truly colorful character. The bar tender informed me that Sandy regularly visited the bar when in Singapore, and he had overheard him being referred to as "China Sandy" by some of his closer acquaintances that had visited the pub with him on earlier occasions. He was supposedly based somewhere in Indo China at the time and was undoubtedly the aviator's equivalent to a sailor with a girl in every port; totally adventurous, a romantic with wonderful charisma and gift of the gab; one of those types that remained fixed in your memory.

The barman pointed me to a spot on the wall upon which was posted numerous photos. Sure enough there was a few of "China Sandy" with his C-46 together with several other dubious looking characters sporting shoulder holsters. I never did find out what actual airline he worked for but as the Indo-China conflict was rapidly developing in retrospect one could be excused for suspecting that somehow he was linked with clandestine activities in Vietnam or Laos. Our paths did not cross again but for some inexplicable reason the image of this guy remains with me. Perhaps this is because he was so deliberately evasive about most things when questioned. I often wonder what happened to him because although giving the impression of being a "China Bum" I believe he was well read and somewhat more intelligent than he cared to divulge. I am sure there was considerably more to this mysterious character than initially met the eye and his country bumpkin façade may have just been little more than a cover for other activities.

Soon after my return aboard I was sitting in the officers smoke room drinking a mug of cocoa when Mr. and Mrs.Van de Doel walked in. They seemed very satisfied with their days sightseeing in Singapore and eager to share their experiences. They had obviously been busy going by the number of venues they had visited – no doubt all chronicled on movie camera by Mr. Doel. I was given a private showing of many the handicrafts they had bought; this included some smaller items of rosewood furniture with inlaid mother of pearl fashioned in typical Chinese style and intricately carved rosewood chests with camphor wood lining, not to mention some fine ceramics, all exquisite and no doubt expensive. It was getting late so I excused myself and went to my cabin where I quietly studied the list of job vacancies I had lifted from the Cellar Bar's notice board. Thus ended, an interesting day for me in Singapore.

The next day we were due to sail but before hand we were visited by some people from the British military (there still being quite a garrison in Singapore at this time although progressively reducing in numbers). Apparently we were to carry deck cargo consisting of about 20 refurbished Army trucks. These were bound for East Africa and were similar to what we had carried on an earlier voyage. The army personnel were responsible for the logistics of getting them to ship's side and seeing them safely loaded on board. Needless to say, we apprentices were engaged in assisting the crew with the chain, wire and bottle screw lashings that were necessary. These were the last items of cargo to be loaded so it took a good few hours to finish the lashing which needed to be completed to our Chief Mate's entire satisfaction prior to departure. Mr. Doel was watching proceedings from the bridge wing, his movie camera operating in top gear.

By the time we sailed the weather had cleared and as we passed Raffle Light House on our starboard side and entered the Malacca Straits, I reflected on the tranquility of the moment. Everything was so placid, sea like glass with only light airs, good visibility and the that sweet smell of coconut and palm oil that lingered in the air about this section of the Malacca Straits. To top it all we were treated to another magnificent sunset which complimented the tropical ambience. How could I possibly wish to live and work anywhere other than in Asia I thought to myself yet again!

We spent the night forging up the Malayan coast towards Port Swettenham. The squid must have been still running because once again we spent most of the night dodging a vast number of small squid fishing boats. During the squid season these very small boats venture well offshore, they anchor or motor about in the calm and relatively shallow waters of the straits and usually display only a single bright light. They tend to be very erratic in their movement and intentions; the single bright light being their only illumination, serving both as a warning of their presence to approaching ships and to attract the squid to the surface. They generally carry no navigation lights since in the main they are little more than motorized canoes. On many occasions the fishing fleet spans from horizon to horizon and number in the hundreds. Whilst it is traditional fishing for the coastal population, this nevertheless poses a hazard to larger vessels navigating these restricted waters, which calls for extreme caution and I may add causes considerable stress at times on the part of Bridge watch keepers and Captains. Such is life at sea.

The Bank Line Ltd - London

My ship **"Levernbank"** pictured transiting the lengthy channel leading up to Port Swettenham. Taken about 1963 when she was still quite new and whilst I was serving on her as a Deck Apprentice.

There was a light morning sea mist as we transited the long channel leading to Port Swettenham. Once at the inner anchorage the lighters were soon alongside but we were delayed about an hour in opening the hatch covers due to a sudden tropical down pour. It was noon before we were able to commence our cargo operations but the wet weather did not prevent the Doels from hitching a ride ashore in the agent's launch and catching the train up to Kuala Lumpur for the day. As usual it was late evening before they returned, worse for wear and worn out, but once again loaded down to the gunwales with all kinds of expensive and quality native handicrafts and memorabilia.

Having finished loading our typical cargoes of Veneers, Sandalwood, Latex Bales as well as a varied assortment of generals, we sailed seaward and then set course northwards, passing the One Fathom Bank as usual and eventually Pulo Wei slowly falling from view as we progressed toward the Bay of Bengal. We experienced good weather most of the time, dawn till dusk, so our illustrious Chinese crew spent time painting ship; whilst we apprentices were engaged in numerous other tasks such as maintaining lifeboats, lifesaving appliances and firefighting apparatus. During my evenings and time off I was also starting to spend more and more time studying in preparation for my 2nd Mates examinations as time was approaching when I would appreciate these extra hours I devoted to learning.

The Chinese calendar is full of festivals and auspicious days. One such festival fell during our passage across the Bay of Bengal. It was the festival to commemorate the birthday of the Goddess – "Madam Tin Hau", which falls in April or May depending on the Chinese calendar. This called for colorful banners and the burning of Joss Sticks together with gifts of paper flowers and offerings of various foods and fruits to the

Goddess. "Tin Hau" the goddess and protector of the seas, was born to a fisherman from Fuzhou during the Song Dynasty. Her ability to predict weather soon brought her fame in the eyes of the fishermen and sailors in general and she has been highly revered by the Chinese sea going community ever since. There are a number of temples in Hong Kong and outlying islands dedicated to this Goddess in one way or the other. Perhaps the most visited are those situated at Causeway Bay on Hong Kong Island – this location once having been a fishing village, another is the one at Yau Ma Tei, close to today's Temple Street night Market. The Temple at Tai Mun Wan (Joss House Bay) remains the most sacred however.

The ritual continued most of the morning on the forecastle and it would have been unheard of to interrupt proceedings. Having been raised in China this sort of ceremony was common to me but was of particular interest to Mr. Doel for his movies .Once completed everything was cleared away and our crew immediately commenced working again. I was assured by our Bosun that our ship and all on board would be protected and blessed with very good fortune as a consequence of the ceremony and offerings. In hind sight, this good luck was only to be a temporary blessing because some years later long after I had departed, this ship was stranded and subsequently lost when she hit an uncharted underwater obstruction one mile North of Matarani in Peru, whilst navigating in dense fog, on a voyage from Chittagong to Buenaventura. It was a shocking loss of a fine ship.

By the time we passed to the south of Dondra Head the ship was looking grand. It was usual practice to paint ship southbound and devote the northbound passage to deck and cargo gear maintenance The Doels spent most of their days lounging about the Captain's deck; Mrs.

Doel enjoyed sunbathing and devoted a lot of her time clad in a bikini laying on a towel or sitting in a deck chair soaking up the UV. Her favorite spot was on the Monkey Island, I guess because it was out of the view of most prying eyes. During the evenings they would spend time in the officer's lounge, reviewing and editing their documentary movies, of which much footage consisted of our officer's and crew at work during the voyage and the odd interview with the "Chinese Bosses", namely; Bosun and No 1 Engine Room Fitter. This of course gave them "big face" in the eyes of their other Chinese subordinates.

We did not call Reunion this voyage but rather proceeded direct to Mauritius. Our ship sparkled under all her new paint as we entered the port, she was a picture, even if I say so myself. We were a sharp contrast to other down trodden old tramps, mostly Greeks and Panamanians that regularly frequented Mauritius to load bagged sugar for China or North Korea. This visit was no exception; at least 3 motley looking tramp steamers of various flags, all having seen better days, were loading at the time of our arrival.

Some religious holiday in recognition of one of the local Saints was celebrated by the inhabitants on one of the days during our port stay. Since there was no cargo work, Mrs. Doel (in cahoots with our chief steward) organized a BBQ on the boat deck that evening. BBQs were the favorite pastime and form of entertainment on board and did much to foster good relations between officers and crew alike. On this particular occasion it was quite an elaborate affair complete with colored fairy lights, music, and plenty of food and drink. Most of this was courtesy of Mrs. Doel, who had spent most of the day ashore shopping for the occasion. The Captain had invited the agent and several other port officials who all turned up in colorful party suits and shirts, together with their families, which by the way, happened to include a couple of very attractive daughters in their early 20s. Obviously these young ladies caught the eye of everyone and were the focal of the party which continued until well after midnight.

23 Mozambique and the Southern Cape of Africa

We left Mauritius in our wake as we plowed through the characteristic low swells, passing the southernmost point of Madagascar at Cap Sainte Marie, at which time we altered course more to the North West to transit the Mozambique Channel in order to close on our destination of Beira.

The Mozambique Channel is an important commercial seaway for vessels sailing the East and South African coastal trade routes. The channel itself is about 1000 miles long and varies in width between 300-600 miles and is considered to be the notorious breeding ground for some of the Southern Hemisphere's most devastating cyclones. It is also very deep and the origin of the strong ocean currents known as the "Agulhas" and "Mozambique". These currents, which mainly run parallel to the coast of Africa, are generally fast flowing and have a very significant influence over a large distance of the African coast, from the South African Cape northwards towards the Comoros Islands at the top end of the Mozambique Channel. Such currents and tidal flows can be treacherous unless understood by mariners and treated with the respect they deserve.

Our crossing of the Mozambique Channel turned out to be very fortuitous for Mr. Doel's cinematic documentary. We came very close to a large pod of Whales for which the area is renowned, likely Humpback or Right Whales. It was a great display which went on for what seemed like an eternity before we passed clear. During this time we came really quite close to the pod, one large specimen passing down our port side only about 30 meters away. We experienced a brilliant view of the Whales and their calves at play. Everything stopped on board, the crew being very excited at the spectacle. The whales were so close that when they surfaced and exhaled the smell of their breath was very pungent. We had previously sighted the occasional pod but this was by far the best seen to date. Mr. Doel was in his element with his movie camera

The red brown waters were a tell tale sign that we were approaching the African coast and in particular the estuary of the Pangoe and Buzi Rivers at the mouth of which Beira is situated. Having first anchored off the port for a day awaiting a berth, we transited the long buoyed channel and entered the bustling port where we berthed at one of the general cargo facilities The port was very congested and most of the wharfs for ocean going vessels were occupied. There were also several large Portuguese passenger ships present at the time.

Beira, being the 2nd largest port in Mozambique, had quite a significant passenger trade during this era, with many regular services to and from Mozambique, mainly to Europe. This was primarily because Beira was a transit center for two way passenger traffic between central African nations that bordered Mozambique and the rest of the world. The City port was well connected with its octopus like rail links to neighboring countries which acted as a conduit in support of its passenger ships. Additionally, Beira was a significant regional hub for transshipment of cargo to other African destinations and for coastal shipping, by virtue of its ideal geographical location and sprawling rail network system.

We spent two days offloading our cargo in Beira before we departed for Lorenzo Marques. Our stay was really routine and I spent my off duty hours doing what I enjoyed most, wandering the wharfs alone, looking at and studying other ships. By this time I was starting to become quite bored and frustrated with the repetition of life on board the ship. The only stimulus to keep going was the realization that I now had very few months to go before completing my indentures and the prospect of working out of Hong Kong or Singapore once becoming qualified. I have to admit I was also starting to ask myself if this was the sort of life style I truly wanted for myself and spent many private hours soul searching my thoughts over this issue, endeavoring to seek a meaningful answer.

However, living and working in Asia was my salvation, finally concluding that I would keep going; besides which, if I gave up now I would miss out on my future qualifications and the time I had so far spent at sea would have been to no avail. I consoled myself by starting to draft letters of application to various ship owners situated in Hong Kong and Singapore, seeking future employment. This uplifted my spirits considerably as I planned to post my letters from Durban.

We paralleled the Mozambique coast heading south down the Mozambique Channel towards LM.

At Lorenzo Marques, in contrast to Beira, the harbor was almost deserted with only very few ocean going freighters alongside. The limited shipping in the port meant that there was no shortage of stevedore labor so our cargo operations, which mainly consisted of discharging, were expedited as a consequence. This was the last port of call for the Doels before they disembarked in Durban so they made the most of their time sightseeing, visiting places of interest and no doubt adding to their considerable collection of artifacts and memorabilia; the rest of us crew only experiencing the monotonous repetition of the daily work schedule on a busy cargo ship in a port already visited many times. There was little to make the days memorable, the only saving grace was time passed quickly and it soon became time for us to move on towards our next destination. Unusually, we departed early morning, however, most of our sailing so far throughout this voyage having occurred at evening time or during the hours of darkness.

In any event I had used my off duty evenings in port to finalize my letters of application to selected Asian ship owners. The letters had been drafted and redrafted, edited, checked for spelling and grammar many times over and were already sealed in their envelopes. Apart from the postage stamps they were ready to dispatch – if I did this immediately upon our arrival in Durban, I pondered, perhaps I would be lucky enough to receive replies by the time of our next arrival in Singapore.

I had calculated and recalculated my sea time and estimated that I would have accrued sufficient to complete my apprenticeship and subsequently undergo examinations, by the time of our next call at Hong Kong, with the slimmest of margins, with about 10 days up my sleeve. This gave me a real boost and feeling of exuberance because it was not that far off, this prospect progressively dawning on me more as every day past, it was becoming a reality at last. The timing of my letters seeking new sea going job opportunities was therefore appropriate I thought.

In Durban we all said our goodbyes to the Van de Doels because soon after our arrival in port they left the vessel and went ashore with all their luggage and mass of collectables. Mr. Doel's movie camera was last seen swinging from his shoulder on its strap and brown leather case, as he went down the gangway. It was sad in some ways to see them go as they had been good company. Before leaving, I was given a totally unexpected gift of a gold fountain pen by Mrs. Doel, with my name engraved and a small notation – "Good luck - Now you have no excuse for not writing". I still have the pen to this day, but sadly have lost contact with the VDD's over the ensuing years.

As I could not get ashore the first evening in Durban I requested Mrs. Doel to post the letters I had so carefully written, seeking a new job. Mrs. Doel obviously kept her promise as was evidenced by the replies later forthcoming.

The realization that I would soon be "out of my time", for some reason caused me to lose interest in going ashore at Durban. I was very excited and volunteered to stand in and cover duties for the other two apprentices, who made the most of it. It just so happened that one evening I was late into the dining saloon for dinner, having been delayed on deck for something or other. The Captain was sitting alone at his table drinking coffee when I walked in.

I greeted him respectfully and settled down to eat. As I was half way through my soup he mentioned that he had been going through his crew files and had noted that I had very little time remaining to complete the qualifying sea time. We chatted on the subject for a while during which he encouraged me to remain with the company emphasizing solid job prospects and career path. I nodded and agreed, not daring to give any hint of my recent correspondence with other owners; but did take the opportunity to inform him of my intention to attend the Hong Kong Polytechnic and sit for my exams in Hong Kong. As he was leaving the saloon he mentioned that he would contact the head office in London to let them know and confirm if and when their plan was to relieve me in Hong Kong. This stoked me even more!

East London was our next port and my first call. This is a smaller city of the East Cape Province and is South

Africa's only river port being located at the mouth of the Buffalo River. The beaches to the north and south along the adjacent coast are open to all the elements of the southern Indian Ocean and are considered a surfers dream due to the frequent high rollers; consequently the outer anchorage is also very exposed. However, our Captain had timed our arrival for first light so we could enter the port immediately, thus avoiding the necessity to stand off awaiting entry. Once safely inside the port we tied up to one of the jetties which was designated for the handling of both grains and generals. Our stay was to be less than one working day but during this period we loaded bulk grains into our deep tanks and some high grade lumber, all nicely bundled, into several tweendecks. We apprentices had been engaged for over a week cleaning and preparing these cargo spaces for this purpose. Both the timber and bulk grains were destined for Taiwan (Keelung).

There was no time for anyone, except the Radio Officer, to go ashore but we had learned that East London was a place that could occasionally be subject to potential unrest as a result of racial and tribal differences, particularly during the apartheid period that prevailed at the time. Hence, there was no real urgency, or desire, on the part of anyone other than "Sparks" to venture into the town. As usual late afternoon saw us depart and head further down the coast towards Port Elizabeth.

Again our stay at Port Elizabeth was very short, just about one day and therefore just enough time for me to dash to the post office to mail a couple more letters of application that I had written to Far East ship owners. I was hoping for the replies upon our arrival at Singapore.

Arrival in Cape Town was mid afternoon on a very crisp and clear day. As we nosed our way into the port I could not avoid staring in awe at the majesty of Table

Mountain framed by surrounding mountains and brilliant clear blue skies. It was quite spectacular and never ceased to amaze me; second only to my beloved Hong Kong in my opinion. However, I was somewhat biased.

As we approached our allocated wharf, ably assisted by two harbor tugs, I recognized our resident Marine Superintendent standing on the wharf apron. He appeared in deep conversation with our port agent, and was flanked by immigration and various other Port officials, all awaiting our arrival. Once port formalities had been concluded we wasted no time in opening our hatches, rigging derricks and commencing cargo operations. I could see we had quite an amount of cargo this call as the wharf sheds were full and the surrounding lay down areas stacked with various parcels of cargo awaiting shipment. As usual our reefer spaces had been thoroughly prepared and pre-cooled ready for receiving freezer cargo, which usually arrived towards the end of our loading schedule. It was going to be a busy time for us, no doubt about it.

Within a short span of time after receiving "Pratique" our ship's cargo gear was in full swing, with fork lift trucks scurrying about the wharf feeding our hungry cargo hooks. At hatches one and five shore cranes were being used. The ship was a hive of activity; our Chief Officer was on deck with the duty officer, giving instructions to the Cargo Supervisors. As I walked down the fore deck towards the cargo office I was hailed by our Chief Mate who told me that I would again be acting as his general factotum during our port stay and once we had departed Cape Town I would be standing permanent cargo and sea watches with him until I completed the remainder of my sea time. This was encouraging news because it made me wonder if the Captain had already received a reply from head office confirming my anticipated signing off. If so, it was quite understandable he said nothing to me at this early stage. I would just have to wait and see what transpired but the reality was that this would be my last call at Cape Town as an "Apprentice".

24 My Farewells to East Africa

Our port calls at Cape Town, East London and Durban came and went with what seemed like the blink of an eye, progressively loading as we worked our way again up the African coast. In Dar-Es Salaam we loaded quite a quantity of cotton bales in four of our five hatches. As per normal number 5 Hatch was as usual reserved for the stinking cowhides and pallets of carbon black in the tweendeck. As on most occasions at this part of the northern voyage the ship was filling up cubically save for lower hold of number two hatch as this had been reserved for heavy lifts from Mombasa. Hence the short passage between Dar-Es-Salaam and Mombasa was spent rigging our "Jumbo" derrick.

Because generally a heavy lift derrick is not used that frequently it is usually left unrigged, save for the head and topping lift blocks, which are well greased and wrapped in canvas covers to prevent corrosion and deterioration due to weather. Rigging was a full time job as we had to break out all the heavy runners and wires for the steam guys, most of which were stored in the focs'le head. Much time was spent checking to ensure all were well greased and in tiptop working order before rigging.

The Bosun and I were the two who volunteered to work aloft on the cross trees during the rigging process, carefully observing the reeving and checking everything conformed with the rigging plan. It took the best part of two days for us to complete the job but the Chief Mate was happy with the end result.

The plan was that we would load 3 large steam boilers, very old and heavy, about 50 tons each, which were to be placed in number 2 lower hold on suitable spreaders to distribute their weight evenly over the wooden sheathed tank tops. They were destined for Taiwan where we understood they were to be scrapped.

As soon as we arrived in Mombasa our heavy lift gear was broken out in readiness for the three boilers. Underwriter's surveyors attended on board to check and inspect all our gear and observe the lifts and their stowage below deck. Everything went without a hitch, under the direction of our Chief Mate with us apprentices along with our own crew operating the winches and attending the gear throughout the course of the operation. It took only about two hours to get them safely on board. The stevedores then swarmed below into the holds to commence chocking and securing the three units. Due to the temporary listing caused by the heavy lifts, only once the 3 boilers were on board did the other cargo operations take place. This was good experience for me, coming just at the right time with the completion of my apprenticeship and pending examinations just around the corner

We spent the next few days greasing and checking all the runners, blocks and various tackle used on the Jumbo derrick – it was unrigged and all gear meticulously stowed away in the forecastle stores since the boilers were to be lifted off by a floating heavy lift crane once we arrived in Taiwan.

Before departing Mombasa I paid a visit to our friendly Padre at the seaman's club, to say my goodbyes as this would be my last visit for a while, He had been very good to us over the past 3 or so years during our frequent visits so it was a sobering goodbye, although he did mention to me that he had made a request for a similar appointment somewhere within Asia. Perhaps our paths would cross again.

As we were carrying quite a lot of baled cotton we apprentices spent a good amount of time engaged in frequent cargo inspections below decks to check for spontaneous combustion, as cotton is susceptible to such chemical reaction. Fortunately there was no problems and aided by good ventilation and careful monitoring we traversed the Indian Ocean to Mauritius without incident. There was a Molasses Tanker loading as we entered Port Louis and the stench of the loading product was quite strong as we glided by towards the buoys to which we would moor.

Soon after we had tied up the barges came alongside and we wasted no time commencing the loading into hatches 1 and 3 tweendecks. We were only expecting to lift about 500 tons of bagged sugar so our port stay was not expected to be protracted. The weather was fine and the port was unusually busy both in respect of general cargo and molasses vessels.

During our visit a second very smart Norwegian molasses tanker arrived to await her turn to load, mooring at buoys quite close to us, whilst waiting to berth. She was not overly large, perhaps 10,000 gross tons but of typical Scandinavian design, with smart lines, very well proportioned and of course meticulously maintained being Norwegian. Her bottle green hull and red boot topping shimmered in the sunlight and was complimented by her cream painted accommodations and masts. A red funnel sporting crossed multi colored flags made her picture perfect. I placed this vessel in my category of favorites along with the "Michael and Clara Jebsen", for pleasing lines. One of her officers came over in a launch to see if we had and books to exchange, he was grateful for our English language contribution but all he could offer us in return was in Norwegian text which we politely declined except for a parcel of glossy picture magazines. During his stay he mentioned that his ship was bound for Nagoya in Japan to discharge a full cargo of molasses, after calling at Singapore for bunkers. Perhaps we would meet again!

We sailed from Port Louis early on a windy morning, spray coming aboard due to our low freeboard, as we butted into the oncoming weather. The ship was well laden and very solid under foot. Our slender bow rising and dipping as we increased to full sea speed. The bluster only lasted a few hours then dropped away and by the time the sun was setting it was almost flat calm with the lowest of monotonous swells. We were making our usual 16 knots as we progressed towards Dondra Head and then on to Pulau Weh. I recall, as I stood my watch that evening, wondering if upon arrival in Singapore I would receive any response to the various letters Mrs. Van de Doel had posted for me in Durban. But first we were scheduled to call at Port Swettenham and Singapore was yet a couple of weeks away.

On our way to the Malacca Strait we had the 3rd Mate come down with Malaria. He was very sick for almost a week. He did recover in time for our arrival off Pulau Weh but was still very weakened and gaunt. I had been keeping the 8-12 watch and assuming his duties during his incapacitation and whilst I wished it had been under different circumstances this boosted my confidence no end. I began to realize the value of what I had learned over my past few years at sea. Putting much of it into practice was a very satisfying exercise for me.

Dawn broke and we could clearly define the lofty mountains of Sumatra away in the distance, dancing on the horizon aided by refraction and the higher humidity. Eventually a smudge appeared fine off the starboard bow. It was my old friend Pulau Weh with the port of Sabang just visible through binoculars as a tiny white spec. We must have sighted it a considerable distance off because it was 3 more hours before we covered the distance and passed it, thereby entering the Malacca Straits. Three hours at 16 knots, converted into distance equates to about 48 miles away when we first sighted the island. Again, probably assisted by refraction, which is a frequent phenomenon in the region. Often, in the heat of the day, islands or far off coastlines are seen floating and shimmering above the horizon. The best example of a visual sighting caused by refraction that I had experienced during my time at sea thus far, was seeing Table Mountain in Cape Town at a distance of 98 nautical miles.

It was early but the sun poured down upon us already burning hot. No sooner had we passed Pulau Weh before we encountered the usual fishing fleet, masses of small boats dotted all about from horizon to horizon as far as the eye could see, with the odd cargo ship here and there amongst them. The sea was absolutely placid and like a plate of dark glass with no wind, so much so that the funnel smoke from the distant vessels rose vertically like dark fingers reaching for the sky. One had to be weary when in amongst these fishing boats as they were frequently used as a means of a decoy for pirates who lurked in their midst, masquerading as fishermen but ready to pounce if any unsuspecting vessel came close enough. We were on heightened alert and passed thru the convoys of small craft, unscathed. As night fell upon us we were clear of the pesky fishermen and set direct course to pass two miles off the One Fathom Bank, which signaled our approach to the Pilot Boarding Ground at the start of the Port Swettenham channel.

I was excited at being back "home" again and that my training would be completed in a relatively short time, now only a matter of weeks, rather than months. The future seemed assured for me and I was about to complete the biggest test of my life but nevertheless I forced myself to focus on what little time that I had remaining to complete my Indentures. I think this was one of the happiest periods for me as I sat in my usual spot on the monkey island after completion of my 4-8 watch, savoring the balmy conditions and sweet landward smells wafting on the sea breeze coming from the shoreline and hinterland, so typical of Asia.

25 Home Waters Again

It was great to have returned to my own back yard once again. We majestically transited the meandering buoyed channel taking us towards Port Swettenham. It was early morning and a joy to be about. En route upstream we pass a couple of Straits Steamship short sea traders heading downstream towards the Malacca Straits, no doubt bound for tropical and exciting ports somewhere in Indonesia, Malaysia or similar areas close to hand. We always came across them between Port Swettenham and Singapore. These beautiful little ships often acted as "feeders" carrying cargo from smaller inaccessible ports to the major hubs of Port Swettenham, Singapore, etc.

We had a busy time in Port Swettenham sorting and collecting dunnage from the tweendecks after we had discharged several parcels of Baled Cotton, Bagged Coffee and Cases of Tea and Cloves. Even though, if otherwise sound, any dunnage that was stained or tainted was discarded along with broken or splintered planks. We pre slung all the condemned wood and placed the large bundles on deck ready to be loaded into an empty lighter for transport and disposal ashore. No doubt much of what we sent ashore would be resorted, salvaged and resold to the unwary inb true Asian style. It was usual practice for us to replenish our discarded dunnage with new at Port Swettenham, in preparation for use on our southbound voyage.

As it had been confirmed by the company I would sign off in Hong Kong, I took the opportunity to venture ashore the night before we departed. I had intended to buy some gifts but, alas, being in a buoyant mood I got no further than a bar close outside the dock gate and spent the evening in the company of a couple of expatriate officers from Straits Steamships. As usual I was mesmerized by their intriguing tales of life style tramping about Asia in their uniquely handsome little ships, I was so stimulated by the fact that the same may be just around the corner for me, hopefully! I was seriously stoked.

We slipped from the buoys early in the morning. It was overcast with a constant drizzle. Visibility was not that good and for some reason I was overcome with a feeling of gloom wondering when I should next return to Port Swettenham. If I had my way it would be sooner rather than later.

It was not long before our engines were pounding away working up to full speed as we said goodbye to the pilot and cleared the fairway buoy, leaving One Fathom Bank distant to starboard and heading on a southerly course towards Singapore, a perfectly straight wake astern, as we cut through the water at our usual 16 knots. The "Walker's Log" was streamed, the brass "fish" just visible at the end of the line as it rotated endlessly, catching the occasional ray of what little sun light there was. I expect it must still have been the squid season (which never seemed to end) going by the number of small fishing sampans that littered the area a few miles offshore. It was not long before we cleared the gaggle of small craft and continued our race down the coast towards the Singapore Straits.

The rain squalls and associated electric storms increased in frequency as we edged further southward. At one stage the rain was so heavy and the visibility so restricted our radar was a complete clutter and ineffective, so it became necessary to reduce speed to dead slow whilst dodging our way between a fleet of becalmed junks and sampans that wallowed becalmed in the low swell.

We passed close quarters to an old Indonesian steamer that emerged from the murk, an absolute floating wreck complete with counter stern and her partially submerged propeller creating a plume of white spray as it thrashed furiously to gain a grip of the water in order to make headway, no doubt towards some backwater Indonesian port. Her faded multi-colored cigarette funnel belching dense black smoke and rust streaked hull, which looked as if it had at one time been painted grey, made her appear almost derelict and ghost like. Even her ensign drooping motionless at the stern was dirty and tattered. One wondered what enticed anyone to sail on such a ship and how a vessel so obviously rundown was even allowed to sail the seas.

By early evening the weather and visibility improved and we once again resumed normal navigation but the heavens ahead remained menacing for the last few hours of our short passage. We passed the "Brothers" and once abeam of Raffles Lighthouse the weather became more acceptable and made for a nice landfall. Upon arrival at Singapore we remained at Western Anchorage for half a day whilst awaiting a berth at Keppel. Eventually we weighed anchor and proceeded towards Keppel Harbor, passing the dry dock to port on the way. It was interesting to see it occupied by an RFA vessel "Resurgent". I believe (the RFA and RN far east squadron still had quite a presence in Singapore and Hong Kong at this point in time). Finally, we slid into the vacant berth allocated to us and as soon as the gangway was in place the stevedores swarmed aboard and set about their work. It was only a short time before our union purchase gear was working all hatches at full capacity. I waited eagerly for our agent to come aboard as he would bring all the crew mail with him.

Our ship's agent, Mr. Dominic Leung arrived on board with a stack of mail; I was waiting for him at the top of the gangway. He handed me the crew mail (which was usual practice for me to distribute). I quickly flipped thru the two thick piles and was delighted to find exactly what I was looking for; no fewer than 4 envelopes bearing various company house flags, in response to my letters of application. I was overcome with a flush of excitement and hurried to distribute the mail to the officers and crew before going to my cabin to open my long awaited replies. Now I would know what the future held.

The first I letter opened was a shock to my system and much better than I could have ever hoped for. It was simple and to the point. I should make contact upon my arrival in Hong Kong to arrange an appointment for an interview; if successful and once I had obtained my second mates certificate they would offer me a post as 2nd Mate. The usual terms and conditions of service followed. The second and third letters were almost identical in content and offer. The only difference being a slight variance in salary (one was somewhat higher than the others but it was a 3 yr expatriate contract). The fourth letter simply asked me to make contact to arrange an early interview and that they did anticipated having suitable vacancies for qualified 3rd and 2nd Mates around the time I expected to obtain my certificate of competency. Naturally I was elated and walked around the ship for the rest of the day with a Cheshire cat grin on my face. All I had to do now was pass the interviews but most importantly, pass my exams.

Now that I more or less knew my fate, life took on a new meaning for me; I suddenly realized it was only weeks away and I would be released from my indentures, having satisfactorily completed the period at sea, set out within. I had no regrets at having seen it through, although there had been the occasional period when I had become a bit depressed and considered throwing in the towel. It was with a sense of achievement that I turned in that night, having read my letters from prospective employers once (or twice) again. I slept soundly.

Our stay in Singapore totaled 5 days, mostly discharging crates of Tea, Cotton and Coffee amongst the assorted generals. Some heavy machinery was landed. This was awkward for the stevedores to handle, not so much the unloading but the lifting and landing on specially fitted trailers that were purpose built for the task. By the time we had completed are draft had reduced quite noticeably, this was good because as our next port of call was Bangkok so it meant we would not have to lighten at Koh Si Chang.

I managed a night ashore in Singapore, spent mooching around with visits to the Cellar Bar and Connell House. I was surprised to find that both the Pubs were almost empty with little atmosphere, so I did not stay long and wandered towards Change Alley where I bought a few odds and sods to take home to Hong Kong before heading back to the ship.

Having secured the vessel for sea the Pilot Boarded and we cast off from the wharf and headed seawards into the Singapore Strait. Calm sea and light airs with a slight haze as we pierced our way thru the placid conditions. I do recall there was a large Dhow close in towards Batam Island, an unusual sight for the Singapore Strait, more often seen in the Java Sea or the northern part of Sumatra Island. Some of these Dhows made long voyages and were superb sailing vessels. This was one of the largest I had seen and was obviously built for ocean voyages. The rest of the transit to the Horsburgh Light was run-of-the-mill and once clear we altered to the North into the Gulf of Thailand.

What luck, my last port of call before signing off in Hong Kong being Bangkok, where we were to load a larger than usual amount of bagged rice. This was expected to take almost two weeks once we had discharged all our generals and shifted to mid-stream to load the rice from barges. It took us just over two days to reach the Bangkok Bar where we anchored to await our designated time to proceed upstream towards Pak Nam thence Bangkok itself. Our Pilot arrived before sunrise the next morning and we weighed anchor and started to move up river. The rising sun caused the winding river to glimmer and produce a golden sheen on the water. The low laying banks looked especially serene in the early morning calm as we progressed, the tranquility aided by distant statues of Buda's and Temples. Only the occasional tug and barge or ship racing downstream towards the open sea, shouldering aside large weed rafts, broke the almost hypnotic calm. As we closed on our destination the volume of river traffic increased with the usual array of "longtail" boats scooting in all directions in and out of the numerous Klongs feeding off the river like lanes leading to townships, small communities or even Watts (the local name for Temples).

Soon we arrived at Pak Nam where we anchored for a short while to undergo port and immigration formalities; then it was a continuation upstream to our designated berth at Klong Toei. It came as no surprise to see our lady friends again, Tasanee was there as usual and the remaining females climbed on board, from small boats, before we had even completed tying up alongside.

At the adjacent wharf was a rather ramshackle Hong Kong registered tramp steamer with the romantic name of "Diamond Fortune". Her crew were busy painting out the slogans that were plastered all over her black hull, the usual "Go home Imperial Dogs" and "Down with British Imperialism" Obviously the ship had sailed directly to Bangkok from China, where during this era it was not uncommon for radicals and other communist

278

incited groups to paint such things on the side of visiting foreign ships. They held no respect for the property of others and were a law unto themselves. It was very unwise to intervene or try and remove this artistry from the ship until after departure for fear of recrimination from these swarming hoards. The situation became even worse a few years later during the infamous "Cultural Revolution" when so called "Red Guards" ran amok throughout China. It was also the time when sailors from every foreign ship were presented with a little red book "The thoughts and sayings of Chairman Mau". All in all it was the beginnings of the very unstable and volatile period in China's modern day history which eventually triggered the Cultural Revolution.

It was not uncommon I am told, when in China, for crews to be mustered on the boat deck at midnight or 2am and be subjected to a rambling lecture focused on the little "Red" book. In fact this political unrest was not only restricted to China but also the northern Ports of Vietnam where there seemed to be a very strong communist influence brewing about this time. High tension still remained in Korea and Taiwan (then still known as Formosa). We simple seafarers working in Asia more or less shrugged it off and went about our business as usual. What else could we do?

Being my final port of call before I left the vessel, the officers decided that they should send me on my way with a real sailor's night ashore. I was very apprehensive about participating but knew it was all well intended and if I did not follow it would offend. Having assured Tasanee I would be fine, a group of us headed ashore one evening all ready for whatever Bangkok could offer. Privately, I knew the group would soon break up once some of the more sexually motivated types were embraced in the arms of the local female persuasion. I was not wrong.

We crowded into a couple of Tuk Tuk taxis which became grossly overloaded and headed towards the Pat Pong area, even then notorious for its girly bars and short time hotels. Our first stop was the "Falang Bar" (one of many so named)), we drank a few beers and were entertained by the ladies and the lightly clad go go dancers, openly selling their sexual favors. We stayed about an hour before moving on to new surrounds, all more or less offering identical entertainment, then it was the "Crystal Bar", followed by "Jennie's Place" and the classier "Cleopatra's". By this time we had lost about half of the team who had succumbed to other activities. By eleven o'clock there was only the "Sparks" and myself remaining so we decided to go to one of the more respectable hotels for a late feed before going back to the ship. We later heard that one of the groups had become unknowingly entangled with a "Lady Boy" (transvestites who were numerous and regularly infiltrated the bars passing themselves off as women). The resulting antics were hilarious going by what we later heard. From the description I think that particular "Lady Boy" would remember his encounter with our crewmate for a long time.

Walking through the lobby of the hotel heading in the direction of the 24 hour Coffee Shop, I was suddenly confronted by someone calling my name rather loudly; I looked in the direction of the caller and was amazed to see one of my old school friends…an American. We greeted each other like long lost pals, then he dropped a bombshell…he introduced me to his wife. I could not believe what I was seeing and hearing because they were only just 21 years of age. Nevertheless, I was envious because his wife, whose name was Adel, was one of the most gorgeous women I have ever seen, being of mixed blood with olive skin, tall and slim, beautiful features and glistening long dark hair as well as being highly charming with an elegant sophistication.

We sat for a while during which Greg (my pal) explained that he had just started working as a trainee executive for one of the international Banks in Hong Kong and got married only weeks before being transferred to Thailand on a 5 year contract. Greg and his wife were staying at the hotel whilst waiting for their apartment to be decorated. We sat for a while reminiscing over our school days, other old friends and the latest Hong Kong gossip, then we said our goodbyes and I headed back to my ship. I never did see Greg again although I do believe he still lives in Thailand until this day. However, I later heard from other reliable sources that the marriage did not last long and broke up. He has long since remarried according to local chin wag.

It was about 1am when I arrived back on board and strode into my cabin. Tasanee was asleep on my settee, I looked at her sleeping soundly and my heart went out to the poor girl who was the sole supporter of her family and whom I had now known for quite some time. I felt I needed to do something to help her best I could as I did not know if and when I would see her again.

Next morning I asked the Chief Steward for a small carton of Lux Toilet Soap and 6 cartons of Lucky Strike cigarettes. The Chief Steward owed me many favors but I naturally did pay for the fags… I then went to see our Captain and asked for a 5 Pound cash advance, explaining why I needed it. He obliged but did try to caution me over being too generous to the likes of Tasanee…I suppose he thought he was offering sound advice but I relied on my own intuition, believing I knew better than anyone how sincere the poor girl was. Poverty was very prevalent in Thailand, people worked at whatever job they could find most of which paid almost nothing, or begged for whatever scraps they could get. Tasanee was a very proud young girl and had never asked me for anything, always being so grateful for what little I gave her. This was the least I could do. I left all the goodies in the care of the Chief Steward until the time was right to convey the gifts to Tasanee. I suddenly remembered a giant box of chocolates my Mom had given me last call in Hong Kong, so I added them to the pile of gifts.

That afternoon we shifted to mid stream to start loading the various parcels of rice. It rained solid for almost two days during which we did not load anything, finally it dried out enough for us to start. There were literally dozens of stevedores in each hatch preparing the foundations for what was to become a perfect stow, which steadily grew. They meticulously laid their rush mats to keep the bags of rice clear of any steel work as well as their wooden air ducts in rows every couple of tiers amongst the stow; they were all perfectionists in their own right – the cargo stow ended up being immaculate, as usual.

After about a week I decided to give Tasanee her presents and told her to go see her family for a few days before coming back to say goodbye. I passed over the gifts and 5 Pound Note; she immediately broke down sobbing and clutching on to me for dear life. I reluctantly sent her on her way and I did miss her but she would be back before we sailed; I hoped.

I spent the ensuing few days sorting out my belongings and memorabilia ready for packing and my signing off, most of which I had collected over the past 20 months I had served on this vessel. In my off duty hours I lay on my settee going over my experiences since I first joined my first ship and trying to map out some kind of plan for the future. It must have been 9pm one evening about 2 days before we were due to sail, when there was a knock on my cabin door. I opened it to find Tasanee standing there with that lovely open smile on her beautiful face. She looked stunning in her Thai national dress. I hurried her inside as I was so pleased to see her again. The day finally came when we had completed our loading and I had to say my goodbyes to Tasanee, it was a sad occasion and there were tears on both sides but we did promise to keep in contact and see each other again as soon as I returned to Bangkok. I had her phone number and address and she had mine. We parted with sadness but our promises to each other were kept over ensuing years.

Our passage down the river was speedy and it was only a couple of hours before we had disembarked the Pilot and we were heading south down the Gulf of Thailand, leaving Cambodia and Vietnam to port. I again was overcome with a sense of emptiness wondering when I would next return. I sat on deck just looking at the horizon and the endless sea – and being cruel in the sense one never knew what to expect from it. I always held the view that the sea was the most least understood and underestimated form of natural energy on our planet. One wave crest merged into the next and my mind wandered but eventually refocused on my future.

26 The End of the Road

During the past years as an apprentice, I had kept a rough diary, whilst very basic, briefly outlined daily proceedings. Over the ensuing couple of days, I read thru it and relived the nostalgia, finding it difficult to read my own scribble at times. I packed it away in my suitcase with my other belongings ready to be taken ashore in Hong Kong. It did little to help me shake off the growing apprehension I had regarding my future. Once I signed off in Hong Kong I would be on my own and my destiny in my own hands. Since going to sea I had always had someone to turn to, support me and indeed look after me, but now I would effectively be unemployed and very much on my own until I passed my exams and became re-employed with one of my favored shipping companies. This was a little unnerving and most certainly stimulated me to get to college and prove my ability to the Board of Trade (now MCA) examiners and become qualified.

I did not do much during the last two days of our passage to Hong Kong. In fact most of the officers offered me plenty of beers to celebrate the completion of my indentures. After all it was like coming of age and something that only ever occurred once.

I kept watches but was very quiet and subdued. On the afternoon before we arrived in Hong Kong I was called to see the Captain. He sat me down and he also offered me a beer!! This was much unexpected. I think, he along with several of the other senior officers had noticed my becoming a bit reclusive over the past weeks and he wanted to talk to me about the future. He started by telling me that he had given me a very good reference to the Company and there was no doubt I would be reemployed (I did not dare to mention my own plans).

He went on to inform me that he, and many others, whom he knew suffered the same sort of uncertainty when about to complete their Indentures. He explained this was part of growing up, the end of a chapter and the opening of new horizons and professional challenges for me. I should look at it this way and not feel depressed but rather, elated. After all I had achieved a lot over the past years. He wished me well and after about an hour I left his cabin and went about my duties. I had to say, the talk had lifted a huge burden off my shoulders and done much to improve my spirits. It made me start to view the future in a different light. I suddenly realized I had become my own man and was responsible to myself for my future success, or failures.

The night prior arrival in Hong Kong it was blowing a little from the North East, not too strong but enough to cause the sea to rise marginally and create the odd spray on deck. I was on the bridge and after my watch with the Chief Mate; I remained to talk with the Third Mate. It was past midnight when we finished – he had, amongst other things given me some valuable tips about preparing for my exams. I stayed on a while to talk with my pall the 2nd Mate but sleep finally got the better of me so I went to bed. We were due to arrive in Hong Kong about 11am and it must have been a good hour before I dropped off to sleep - I lay there mulling over my chat with the Captain, cabin window wide open listening to the sound of the wash rushing past the ship's side as we sped onwards at full speed towards Hong Kong.

Having been through the ritual of disconnecting one of our anchors and preparing the anchor chain for securing to the Typhoon Buoys, I went aft for smoko before the Pilot arrived. We were just coming up abeam of Shek O, so not far to go. I stood on the port side of the boat deck watching Hong Kong Island glide past as I sipped my coffee, then I shifted to starboard and was behold with a clear view of Waglan Island in the distance, a member of the Poi Toi group of islands, with its lighthouse and metrological station clearly visible. Far beyond to the northeast I could see the definitive outline of the Ninepin Group which marked the easternmost boundaries of Hong Kong waters. Finally, ahead I sighted the Pilot Boat and Lye Ye Mun pass. It dawned on me suddenly; in a few hours my safe little life for the past 3 and a bit years would soon come abruptly to an end and I would be unemployed.

I reflected it was 6 October 1964; I was still only 19 years of age (still 5 months to my 20th birthday, the minimum age at which one was eligible to sit for Second Mates exams). I had sailed around the world and seen more places than many would see in a lifetime. I had become worldly in my outlook on life and mature for my age, and, I had a thousand stories to tell. I held an inner sense of disappointed, not in my experiences, but only because it was soon to end for a while.

We entered Lye Ye Mun and the magnificent panorama of Victoria Harbor unfurled in front of our eyes. As usual the harbor was busy, Junks, ferries, walla wallas, launches, utility boats, tugs, cargo barges, you name it all scurrying about in every direction, going about their business. Most of the mooring buoys were occupied and the harbor was quite full. Victoria Peak was shrouded in mist and the many buildings that encroached up its slopes seemed eerie in the light of day. Nevertheless it was a magnificent sight to witness and I was overcome by the feeling of excitement Hong Kong always generated within me

Having tied up to the Typhoon Buoy at a central position in Hong Kong Harbor it was not long before the family arrived on board. After the usual greetings they left as I was to go ashore later. Soon after I left the Captain called me to see him. He enquired that I had completed my time successfully, customary shake of the hand, but he wanted to know if I was prepared to remain on board 2 days to assist with some new joiners (two more apprentices), I willingly agreed and went on my way.

My mother and father looked a little worried when they had been on board, it happens that they were to again due to proceed to England in a few weeks on their regular leave and were concerned about leaving a 19 year old on the loose in Hong Kong. I shrugged this off as I had already devised a plan of action to put them out of their concerns. Within the next days I would hopefully be attending interviews with prospective shipping companies, I figured I did not need 5 months at college before sitting my exams so I would seek an uncertified 3rd Mates vacancy for a few months beforehand if it was possible. I would just take a week off to sort myself out then try to go back to sea. If successful, my parents would be back by the time I returned from the voyage.

At 5pm two days later, I departed my home for the past 21 months. There were sad farewells and suddenly it was all over as my company launch sped towards Queens Pier. I felt both sad and happy but most of all a sense of forlornness. As if I had lost something important to me but couldn't figure out quite what. Little did I know the influence the past 3 years or so would have on me during the next 40 odd years I was to spend in the shipping industry?

That evening, at home, I explained to my parents what I had in mind and after a good dinner, a few Lucky Strikes and numerous cold San Miguel beers, I could see the relief on their faces. The next morning I would set about contacting those companies that had expressed interest in me.

27 Reflections and New Doors Open

Upon opening of business the next morning I started to make my phone calls. I thought if I could arrange interviews over the next week it would be great. I was shocked – first company I called was John Manners. I spoke with the Marine Superintendent who recalled my letter of application immediately. He took me by surprise asking if I was available for an interview at 2 pm that same afternoon. You can imagine my response.

I dressed in a light grey tropical suit and wore casual brown suede shoes. A cream raw silk shirt and nautical tie. I looked the part. John Manners' office at that time was in Union House in the central district of Hong Kong, just across the road from Lane Crawford's. I took the elevator to the designated floor and walked in on the stroke of two. I enquired of the receptionist, a middle aged Portuguese lady who was very softly spoken. I sat waiting to be called, albeit somewhat nervously.

Soon a tall gent with horn rimmed glasses, very well presented and obviously, a Scot, approached me. Ah! young man, pleased to see you, do come thru to my office; I followed like a lap dog.

I entered his office whereupon he introduced himself formally, presenting me with his business card. Then the phone rang and he answered. The conversation took several minutes during which time my eyes took in everything. It was a large well furnished office which commanded a superb harbor view (I observed my old ship still at the buoy). Several nice paintings of company ships hung on the walls and against one stood a wonderful model encased in a glass cabinet of one of their vessels. Having completed the telephone conversation he apologized for the interruption and we began to talk.

He started the conversation by asking all sorts of questions about my background, apprenticeship, experience, trades, various cargoes carried and ports visited. Then after about 20 minutes, out of the blue he popped the question. I note you have 5 months until you can sit 2nd Mates; I can offer you a firm job as 2nd Mate as soon as you obtain your certificate he said but I was wondering if you could help me out in the meantime, he went on. I thought to myself Uh Uh! Here it comes. I was not prepared for what followed.

We have a ship due here next week called the "Asia Fir" (later renamed "Asia Breeze"), the 3rd Mate needs to be relieved as he has some family issues; would you be prepared to join her as uncertified 3rd Mate? I can assure you the maximum time away would be 3 months then be relieved in order to go to college here in Hong Kong and return to the company as 2nd Mate once having passed the exams. You could have blown me over like a feather. I couldn't believe my luck. I accepted without hesitation. Good that's settled then he said.

The Superintendent went on to advise me the ship would be spending a month around the Philippines coast loading bagged Copra nuts for Japan, after which she would return to Hong Kong for dry docking. It was all too good to be true. He would ensure I was relieved upon arrival. He went on to discuss pay scales, terms and conditions, all subject to Hong Kong Shipping Act, as the ship was Hong Kong flag. I was then taken to another office where I was handed over to some crewing official to complete the necessary documentation, the deal had been done and I was in.

I left the building with a spring in my step and walked across the road to the Gloucester Hotel where I sat drinking an expensive glass of beer to celebrate and reflecting on my good fortune. I was no longer unemployed. I was about to fulfill my ambition; I pinched myself to make certain I wasn't dreaming.

My mother and father were delighted at the news and though it was a very sound move. I did some research into the vessel and ascertained she had been launched originally as the "Carronpark". I went to bed that night drunk with happiness.

The next week was mainly spent preparing for my new job. I could now shed all my working gear and replace it with khakis and some whites. I bought some epaulettes with a single gold stripe and half diamond (half diamond indicating uncertified).

A couple of evenings later I was sitting at home with my folks when I suddenly remembered. I went to my room and took a tattered envelope from my drawer. I gave it to my father who hesitated. It's OK I said please open it. He did so and I saw a sign of a tear in his eye. The envelope contained the 200 pounds he had given me for emergencies, that long gone morning at Hayward's Heath railway station. He passed me back the envelope complete with money. No son he said, you have earned it.

During this time I did not see my brother as he was at boarding school in the UK. I think he had become a handful for my folks living in Hong Kong as a teenager and been shipped off to learn some discipline. Hence the house was quiet without him but whilst my dear ones were at work I had the two "A's" to keep me on the straight and narrow.

The next week I spent preparing for my new role at sea, I was very calm but quietly excited. When the day finally came I said my goodbyes and set off to Queens

Pier to board a walla walla to take me the mile or so to the "Asia Breeze" which was moored at a buoy not far from Stonecutters Island. As I approached I noted her pleasing lines and well painted hull and superstructure. Eventually the boat came alongside and I was helped up the accommodation ladder by the duty quartermaster who carried my case. I had arrived just in time for lunch, the aromas of which I could detect drifting from the galley.

This was the start of a new adventure for me, but that was a story for another day I thought!

Part Two – East of PulauWeh
MV. Kaethe Jebsen

Photo KP ©

"Kaethe Jebsen" was a very handsome Danish general cargo ship, a regular caller at Hong Kong which operated mainly within the S.E Asia region, with the occasional visit to Australia for good measure. Always immaculately presented she was a superb vessel and somewhat typical of the era; she was subsequently sold to Singapore owners. It was sad to see the demise of such iconic vessels in the late 1970s. Kaethe Jebsen was one of a group of similar vessels operated by the same Danish group, servicing the Asian region, namely: Clara Jebsen (sister to Kaethe Jebsen), Michael Jebsen, Jacob Jebsen, and Carl Offersen. They later supplemented their fleet with two newer Container-Multi Purpose ships, Emma Jebsen and Heinrich Jessen, replacing the former Heinrich Jessen which was sold in 1964 and renamed Aru Mariner, later scrapped at Hong Kong in1970.

Photo KP ©

A fine study of **"Waheng"** ex "Kathe Jebsen" showing a nice profile of her classic lines. Looking almost as good as the day she was built. Her simple lines make her design seem ageless. Photo taken some years later in Singapore Straits, after being sold to Singapore interests in 1977 for continued trading. Built in 1959 she served some 30 years until 1990, when broken up in China

Photo KP ©

Another stylish, full blooded Dane, from the Jebsen's fleet **"Carl Offersen"**, at Yokohama in 1974. Said by many to be the best looking of all the Jebsen ships.

All these wonderful ships were only to be replaced by the "Boxships" of today, which, whilst functional, completely lack any kind of style or character and which bare no comparison to the beautiful sleek ladies of yesteryear.

It became apparent to many ship owners in the 1970's that retrofitting the world's existing fleet of cargo ships to meet the demands of rapidly expanding containerization was not only impractical but also far too costly, and as a result, an entirely new international fleet needed to be constructed to meet world demand for containers. This caused many traditional shipping lines to suspend operating, unable to bear the expense of building complete new fleets. Another factor was of course the increases in cost of marine diesel fuel during this period.

The dilemma of rapid containerization, whilst difficult for existing shipping companies became catastrophic for many world ports and the cities reliant upon them. Such renowned international ports like London, Liverpool and Glasgow suffered as a consequence and became a mere speck on the world stage in comparison to what they had been in years prior to containerization. Some may claim these ports, and they were by no means unique in this regard, were too slow to latch on to trending changes and port managers lacked foresight, but I don't think that is entirely true, rather it was the unanticipated pace at which the transition to total containerization actually developed internationally. It took most by surprise.

The ship owner was only part of the equation. Port Authorities had to completely rethink their method of operations. Many started to convert existing docks and improving the number of container handling wharves but this proved not to be the total solution as completely new ports were needed with space to develop new deepwater berths and specialist terminals to accommodate the increasing number of container vessels that were arriving with their modules. Ports began to completely relocate from their traditional docks close to the cities they had hitherto served. Completely new infrastructure was needed in the majority of world Ports. In Europe and the Americas this was not that easy a task as it may seem due to the need to decentralize large workforces. In actuality, it proved much easier for developing countries to establish completely new Port facilities focused almost entirely on container traffic, many of which became Container Hubs, depending on their geographical location, specializing in transshipment with containers brought from smaller regional ports.

Seafarers on ships were similarly affected. Containerization completely changed the lives of sailors forever. The majority of the world's fleet was owned and operated by Western and European shipping companies based in the worlds shipping mega-centers, in particular London, Liverpool, Glasgow, Bristol, Amsterdam, Oslo, Copenhagen, Piraeus and New York to name but a few. A large portion of Sailors originated from these locations and found fewer and fewer jobs at the terms and conditions previously expected as the fleets decreased in number or ceased to exist. This caused employment hardship and triggered many into giving up the profession and seeking alternative employment, which in turn created a critical shortage of qualified seagoing personnel in later years as the source and continuation of trainees through the system dried up. Hence, many ship-owners took the opportunity to adopt a more cost effective route, replacing traditional crews on their vessels with cheaper mariners from Asian countries, (also later East European States) which created new opportunities for them, at the expense of western crews. Hence it became the last of an era for many a sailor who now only lives on in nostalgia.

Part Two - "East of Pulau Weh" covers the early voyages the author spent as a newly promoted Captain on general cargo and container vessels sailing throughout South East Asia and Oceania, in those golden transition years from break bulk and general cargo to containerization during the 1970s, which nowadays has become the world's preferred mode of shipping transportation.

Some terms used are from a bygone era but were common during the period depicted and may not necessarily be used nowadays from the point of view of politeness or political correctness.

The 1960-70s saw the pinnacle of change in Hong Kong and its establishment as the financial centre of Asia. It seemed no matter what venture Hong Kong embarked upon the outcome turned into pure gold for the colony. During this period there were many new developments such as Ocean Terminal, Extension of Kai Tak Airport and Cross Harbor Tunnels, significant increases in local manufacturing and exports, massive low cost housing projects together with new skyscraper buildings erected at a rapid pace not to mention a boom in tourism as Hong Kong had suddenly become more accessible by air with an abundance of world class hotels. The Hong Kong skyline was in a state of continuous motion – buildings that had been around for ages were suddenly demolished and immediately replaced by high rise structures. The shanty huts and squatter areas were cleared and their residents rehoused. This prosperity created wealth the likes of which Hong Kong had hitherto never experienced, society was becoming more affluent, which was a marked contrast to the previous decade.

Meanwhile, time had passed quickly for me and the 1970s had arrived. During the past 8 years years I had continued to reside in Hong Kong and roam the oceans on a variety of ships whilst consolidating my sea service in order to finally qualify to present myself for examination to the Board of Trade for my Masters Certificate. Most of the time was engaged sailing between East and South Africa to the Orient. I steadily progressed through the various ranks of 3rd Mate, 2nd Mate and Chief Officer. Once the ink was dry on my Master's Certificate and safely in my pocket I concentrated once again on sailing exclusively within the Asian region for reputable regional owners.

Vacancies for qualified deck officers during these times throughout Asia were plentiful and to a degree one could pick and choose on which trades and ships one sailed so one became very selective as for whom one was working. This was an important issue because with the expansion in shipping during this era, Asia had amassed its share of clapped out or decrepit tonnage. Also emerged a number of very shonky operators who usually placed their vessels under the Panama, Liberia, Somali or similar non descript Flags of Convenience (FOC) as it was much cheaper to do so. It would be true to say that many of the new ship owners were only interested in the cheapest of the cheap operating costs for their ships and mainly in turning a quick buck, thus avoiding as much as possible operating their ships to decent international standards. However, this did not prevent them from trying to entice good officers and crews with the promise of highly inflated salaries – unfortunately there were the gullible resulting in many instances of crews being owed wages or not getting paid at all. For owners who fell into this category it was not uncommon seeing their ships under admiralty arrest rotting in some Asian backwater whilst the crews desperately attempted to recover what they were rightfully due, be repatriated or in extreme cases even get victuals on which to survive. It was not unheard of that some of the less trustworthy FOC operators emptied bank accounts and closed up shop overnight leaving their ships and crews stranded, the owners having absconded with the funds, never to be heard of again. Such was the sad lot of some seafarers about this period.

A good percentage of the newly established owners operating under Flags of Convenience were front companies for Communist countries such as Mainland

China, Indonesia (Communist regime at that time), North Korea as well as Formosa (Taiwan) because of its conflict and trading restrictions with China. This enabled these operators to earn foreign exchange as most shipping transactions were conducted in USD. Needless to say, the shady and less scrupulous outfits did not last long and soon collapsed – besides the word soon got about and well qualified crews refused to sail on their ships.

I had been very fortunate and had landed on my feet as I worked for a very well established Hong Kong ship owner that had been around a good number of years and had built an excellent reputation. They owned about twelve ships and managed about 20 on behalf of other owners. Ship management as opposed to outright owning was becoming a lucrative business. Those who owned ships soon found that the management of additional tonnage on behalf of others could be done with more or less the same technical and support staff so ship management soon became an excellent source of supplementary income. Besides, many of the new ship owners of the period were very naive and were therefore more than happy to pay a decent manager to operate the vessels on their behalf as an economically viable investment. Basically, all that the new owners wanted was their logo on the ship's funnel and select a name and make money, the rest they left to the managers. There were some imaginative names, Golden Dollar, World Pink, Lady Luck, Hot Spice, New Jumbo Enterprise, Eastern Empress, Asia Plenty, etc, etc., to name but a few. Most of those with the grandest names were more often than not, the worst.

29 Call me Captain

My ship was secured at the Typhoon Buoys in Victoria Harbor, Hong Kong. We had only just commenced loading a combination of general cargoes for Bangkok, Singapore and Rangoon.

 After having been on deck most of the day I was sitting in my cabin late in the afternoon enjoying a cold beer. Suddenly there was a knock on the door – "hello Mr. Mate" a voice said from behind the drawn door curtain. It was the Master. I quietly greeted him with the respect his position required and gestured for him to take a seat, at the same time offering him a beer – which he readily accepted.

I had been Chief Officer on the "Hoi Wing" for eighteen months, having joined soon after obtaining my Master's Certificate. The ship was an ex-British tramp, previously owned by a Newcastle outfit, twenty years old but as stout as a drum, she had no vices and was a typical old "Hong Kong Dustbin". Dustbin referring to the all black funnel sported by most Hong Kong registered tramp vessels of the era.

I had joined because of the trade in which the ship was engaged - mostly tramping throughout the Far East - Philippines, Indonesia, Malaysia, Singapore, Thailand, Borneo, Japan, Korea and Taiwan with occasional calls to mainland China. A very rewarding employment package also sweetened the pie. I had lived in Hong Kong most of my life, considered it to be my home and really knew no other abode so I guess it was natural that I followed a career path in my own back yard so to speak. The shipboard conditions were good and the owner's professionals, who knew what they were doing

in comparison to many other Far Eastern shipping
concerns around at this period in time

The Bank Line Ltd - London

A magnificent photo of a Bank Line ship of the 1960s
era at anchor. Capturing absolute tranquility, I presume
during that period of calm just as a tropic dawn is about
to break. I suspect this was taken whilst at anchor off
some small port in the Solomon's or Pacific Islands
whilst engaged on the "Copra Run". The start of another
beautiful day ahead, with the cargo barge already
alongside and derricks topped, whilst no doubt the cook
prepares a delicious Kedgeree for the crew's breakfast.

The 1960s and 1970s was a time when old tonnage was
cheap and readily available on the market. Many rich
Asian businessmen were very astute and wished to
become ship owners so they bought these ships in
abundance and became ship operators overnight. Some
were good but most of them not so, with the vast
majority of their ships being placed under a FOC but
operated from Hong Kong or Singapore by a specialist
ship manager. Anyway, in my case I was fortunate as
our management was sound with mostly expatriates in

senior positions who were well experienced and acquainted with shipping operations and management. All twelve of our ships were well maintained and manned by properly experienced officers and crew and operated to what was considered an above average standard for the time.

The "Old Man" came straight to the point – The Owners think you have done a reasonably good job so far and they are enquiring how you would feel about being promoted to Master. I was taken aback – I had expected this in about a year or so but not quite so soon. I instantly gathered my thoughts and knew what my response must be – one seldom gets asked or offered this type of opportunity twice at such a young age as I was still only in my early 30s. I took a deep breath and long swig of my beer, and responded "fine when do I start". The "Old Man" grinned and shook my hand. He explained that the Marine Superintendent would like me to go to the office the following morning, when I would receive all the details. The Agents launch would be at the ships gangway about 9am so I could take that ashore and whilst I was away the Captain would keep an eye on the cargo operations.

The Captain finished his beer and went about his business, leaving me alone in my cabin to reflect. Frankly, I was stoked at the prospect of my own command and tried hard not to show my happiness too outwardly. I decided not to say anything until it had all been officially confirmed by the Marine Superintendent and I was privy to all the details.

I found it hard to sleep that night with all sorts of strange ideas going through my head – what if I ran the ship aground, or got lost! If I had a collision or the like! Maybe they would change their mind! I soon dismissed all these follies as I had confidence in myself and drifted off to sleep.

The following morning, I briefed the 3rd and 2nd Mates on the day's cargo operations and what I expected of them. I explained I needed to go ashore to the office urgently but did not expand on the reason why. I hurriedly donned a suit and tie, clambered aboard the Agent's launch and headed off towards Hong Kong Island and Queen's Pier.

I was somewhat apprehensive, arriving at the Company's 10th floor offices at 9.45am. I was expected and greeted by the Marine Superintendent – an Irishman with a very strong accent who was an ex Irish Shipping Company Master. He wore a white long sleeve shirt and a blue tie with some kind of club or society motifs on it – I knew him already so the atmosphere was quite relaxed and cordial considering the matter at hand. He commenced the conversation by telling me that I had done a good job on the "Hoi Wing" and received good reports and recommendations for promotion from the Master.

He informed me the Company had just acquired an ex Australian cargo vessel of about 8,000 Goss Tons and were about to take delivery in Hong Kong with the intention to introduce her in support of the "Hoi Wing" in regional trading. The ship was being delivered with an Australian crew, (who would sign off and be repatriated immediately upon arrival) and be manned with Hong Kong Chinese crew. The ship was expected to arrive in Hong Kong in about 3 weeks time. She was to be renamed "Hoi Hing" (loosely translated means Sea Prosperity) and placed under the Panama Flag. Therefore, I would need to apply for a Panama License (a formality) which would be issued on the strength of my own British Master's Certificate. I would have

European senior officers; the Junior Officers would be either Hong Kong Chinese or from the Philippines. This satisfied me totally as I had no concern about the vessel being placed under Panama flag because I knew and trusted the owners and their high standards of ship management.

During the lead up to the ship's arrival I was to prepare a good handover for the new Chief Mate on the "Hoi Wing" and stay with him a few days once he had arrived until he was fully familiar with everything. The 2nd Mate on the "Hoi Wing" had not been promoted on this occasion even though he held a brand spanking new Mate's Certificate. He was highly regarded by the Company but was considered a little too young for the role of Chief Mate at only just 24 years of age – his time would come in about a year or so. My replacement as Chief Officer was about 28 years of age, a Portuguese Chinese from Macau and going by his resume reasonably well experienced for the task. It was expected he would join in 2-3 days time.

Prior to her first voyage the "Hoi Hing" would go into Dry Dock for pre-purchase survey and maintenance, she being no stranger to the shipyard as she has been re-engined there some years earlier when her main engine had been converted from steam to motor, with steam auxiliaries. This all sounded great to me and as soon as the conversation ended with the Marine Superintendent I was taken around the office to meet everyone and introduced as the new Captain of "Hoi Hing" – I felt elated and much elevated indeed. Obviously, never having been called "Captain" before, it would take some getting used to it.

Upon my arrival back at the "Hoi Wing" the news of my promotion had spread like wildfire – I was congratulated by everyone and must admit to feeling a little embarrassed by it all. The ensuing days were busy for me preparing the handover particulars for my relief and at the same time watching cargo proceedings.

A few days later my relief, Tony Roberio, arrived on board and the handover began in earnest. Tony was a nice chap with a good sense of humor, he lived in Macau although he had been born in Hong Kong and taken all his qualifying examinations in Hong Kong. He soon settled in and took control of daily management of the ship, at which time I bowed out and went ashore to my home to visit my parents and convey my good news.

After a week or so at home my new command arrived in Hong Kong and went straight into the dry dock. I joined soon after and was welcomed by the outgoing Australian Master who signed off the same day along with all his fellow Australians. I suddenly realized the responsibility of command – I was on my own and it was up to me to properly manage and operate the vessel in all respects. At least I would have a little time to settle in as the ship was scheduled to be in dry dock about one week during which time the remainder of my officers and crew would join. I was accommodated ashore close to the shipyard whilst awaiting my crew to arrive, although I did manage most evenings at home.

A day or so later the vessel was refloated and shifted from the dry dock to a lay by berth at the same ship yard. It was then that I, along with all officers and crew signed on ship's articles.

My Chief Officer, Les Barnes was English, from Liverpool minus the accent. An energetic little man, and a newcomer to our company. Les had been sailing as Chief Mate for just over two years. He was a couple of years my senior but that was of no consequence and he held a Masters Certificate. The 2nd Mate was from Newcastle and an ex Bank Line man, whilst the 3rd mate was a young Filipino who went by the flowery name of Jesus Jose Catalan Empleto.

On the engineering side, the Chief Engineer was a New Zealander, as was the 2nd Engineer, both heralding from Taranaki, whilst the 3rd and 4th Engineers were Geordies from the Northeast part of the UK. The remaining Junior Engineers being Hong Kong Chinese. Our Radio Officer was a very brogue Irishman from Belfast. This was his first trip to the Far East and it was not difficult to ascertain his sense of excitement and awe at being in new and unfamiliar pastures. He was very industrious and even before unpacking his bags he set about testing his Radio equipment and monitoring the installation of a newer model Radar unit which was in the process of being fitted by the shipyard technicians. We would end up with two as the older one was still in good working order and usable so was not being removed.

Our Chinese crews were all experienced and a thoroughly reliable crowd, some of whom had sailed with me previously on other vessels. Hence, this was my ship's complement and I was determined to make it all work and not let down the Owner's (or indeed myself) at having been given this opportunity.

30 My Pride and Joy

The "Hoi Hing" lay at the shipyard for another few days during which time everyone was kept very busy settling in and taking over the ship. She was given a fresh paint job and new names painted on bow and stern with port of registry "Panama" also featuring prominently on the stern, below the name. She looked very trim indeed and I was quietly satisfied by the entire chain of events since my unexpected promotion only a few weeks earlier.

It was only now that I had time to truly discover the ship. She was a 15 year old lady but had reasonably flowing lines, streamlined accommodation and upper works, a standard tweendecker with the usual five holds and five hatches along with a set of twin deep tanks. The funnel was slightly raked and painted the usual black as was the hull, whilst Masts, Sampson Posts and Derricks were all Buff in color. The accommodation was spacious and comfortable and had obviously been well cared for by previous Australian crews.

My quarters were large and occupied an entire deck below the Bridge deck. I had a Day Room, adjoining Office (complete with large desk and conference table with six chairs), Bedroom and en-suite Toilet, Bath and Shower facilities. The bulkheads were a darkish veneer and the curtains and seat coverings throughout were nicely color coordinated to afford an appearance of comfort. The decking consisted of beige vinyl tiles which had been buffed to a high gloss finish and added an air of grace and composure. There were four forward facing windows in my Dayroom and Office, two side windows in my Bedroom which overlooked the sea and a frosted window in the washroom. A short distance down the alleyway to starboard I had a private Pantry, large refrigerator and cooking hot plates (in case required). On the port side of my deck was situated a small single berth Pilot's Cabin which had seldom if ever been used by the look of it, other than for storage space. All things considered, not a bad layout.

My Deck Officers, Radio Officer and senior Engineer Officers were housed on the deck below. All having similar style accommodations, albeit not quite as large and spacious as mine, but nevertheless quite comfortable. The junior Engineers and catering staff were located on the deck below that, whilst the deck and engine ratings were all situated aft in the Poop accommodation, which was also quite acceptable. The ship's complement was 32 all up which included 2 Chinese fitters for maintenance of the cargo winches.

Our Chief Steward Purser along with the catering crew set about scrubbing out all the galleys, fridge rooms and dining areas, public rooms and alleyways. An abundance of new stores and provisions arrived even though many of the provisions and stores were carried over from previous owners provided they were within the use by date. Similarly, our Bosun and his sailors attended to the array of deck stores that the company delivered on board, more or less standard issue for any new ships they purchased. Within a week we were ready to go when ever required.

Eventually, after a couple of days I was given order to shift from the dock yard to one of the Typhoon Buoys not too far distant from Stone Cutters Island. The harbor Pilot arrived on board at 7am and we cast off, moving slowly through the harbor traffic to the designated Compass Swinging area for periodic adjustment and check of our Magnetic Compass, followed by the issuance of an updated Deviation Card provided by the Compass Adjuster himself. Then on to our buoy where we moored using our anchor chain and slip wires. One of our anchors had been disconnected from the chain and hung off so that we could shackle the anchor chain direct to the buoy. It was a simple exercise to reconnect the anchor at a later date upon departure.

Soon after our arrival at the mooring buoy I received a visit from the Marine Superintendent. He was accompanied by the Engineer Superintendent who came to inspect the vessel and have discussions with my Chief Engineer. I received the usual "Pep Talk" from my Irish Boss, being a newly promoted Captain, along with a variety of instructions including details of our imminent cargo fixture. I recall very clearly his parting words to me "remember…obtaining command is easy …maintaining it is harder". Very sound advice for a fledgling Captain.

I learned that we were to take a cargo of semi-refined bagged sugar from Hong Kong to Singapore. The bagged sugar, in heavy duty paper bags, would be loaded ex lighter at the buoys rather than at the usual Taikoo Sugar Refinery wharf, situated quite close to the dock yard from which we had just shifted. It seemed the Sugar Wharf was booked already by an inbound ship arriving with a full cargo of raw sugar from Mauritius. Following discharging in Singapore it was likely that we would proceed to one of two destinations which was yet to be finalized, namely, some Indonesian river Port to load a cargo of dressed logs for Japan or Bangkok to load a cargo of bagged rice for China. I hoped for the latter rather than proceed to some upriver jungle logging camp to load logs – personally I dreaded the thought of anchoring in some desolate place like Paia Inlet or Umuda Island located in the steaming river estuaries at

311

the head of the Gulf of Papua. Loading logs into a tweendecker in locations like that could take weeks.

Our chartering department would pass on information to me once all had been decided. However, I had enough information to be going on with in order to ensure our 2nd Mate ordered all the required Admiralty Charts and Sailing Directions for the entire South East Asia region. The ship had only been delivered with limited chart folios for Asian waters, only sufficient to cover her delivery voyage to Hong Kong, as she had been engaged for many years operating around the Australian coast. In any event most of the charts remaining on board were either outdated or in desperate need of being replaced. It was recognized that correcting and updating the existing charts on board would be a mammoth task for the 2nd Mate, not to mention most of the charts looked as if they had been used as table cloths being full of coffee and tea stains, or torn. Hence it was agreed with Owners we purchase new charts and build our own chart folios afresh.

As it would be a day or two before we commenced loading, we were to bunker Fuel Oil and Lubricating Oils in drums. Soon after therefore, the Bunker Barge came alongside to replenish our tanks with 750 tons of bunkers as by now our reserves were quite low as the ship had been delivered to us with minimal quantities remaining on board.

We used the waiting time to check all the cargo winches and cargo gear. The ship, being steam auxiliary, was fitted with steam winches which could be operated very fast when handled by expert stevedore winch operators. Some replacements were made to cargo runners and derrick head and heel blocks as well as a few guy ropes. Eventually, I was able inform the Owners we were fully operational.

Cargo lighters and barges used in Hong Kong are frequently owned by the families that operate them – not only do they handle all the cargo, barge winches and derricks themselves but also live on board with their family members, including small children, dogs and cats etc. Occasionally large stevedoring concerns would own a fleet of barges but this was not the norm. Hence the cargo barges were immaculately maintained and expertly operated.

The time arrived when the barges were towed out to us in mid-stream and moored alongside, one for each hatch. Without delay our union purchase gear started the long task of transferring the slings of bagged sugar from barge to ship's cargo hold where stevedores set about stowing it in rows and tiers. Barges were replaced immediately once they were emptied. Fully laden barges promptly replaced them. This went on for seven days around the clock until the last sling of sugar was loaded. Hatches were full and were then battened down and the ship made ready for sea.

The agent came on board with the Cargo Manifest and Port Clearance, soon after the harbor Pilot who would guide us towards Green Island and the Sulphur Channel then towards Llama Channel as we were departing towards the South West. I gave my fist order "Stand by Engines" the telegraphs rang out and was instantly answered by the Engine Room indicating all was ready. Upon the advice of the Pilot I ordered that we disconnect the anchor chain from the buoy. Soon after (and having taken a deep breath) let go your slip wires….we were free and underway as we cleared the buoy I gave the order "slow ahead, port twenty" and slowly felt the vibration under foot as the engines worked up and the ship gained momentum. It was comforting to hear the slow "Thump, Thump, Thump" of our Doxford main engine as we glided slowly through the water towards the Pilot disembarkation point just clear of the Sulphur Channel. As soon as the pilot was clear I ordered a progressive increase in speed until some 15 or so minutes later when passing the fairway buoy and clear of conflicting traffic, I instructed the 3rd Mate to ring down to the Engine Room "FAOP – Full away on Passage" indicating to the duty Engineers they could now assume full sea speed.

I stood on the starboard bridge wing for a while with the sea breeze blowing through my hair, passing the occasional course adjustments until we were well clear of all other shipping and fishing boats. With the "Hoi Hing", well established on her course by this time, the auto pilot was then engaged. I remained on the bridge for a good half hour checking all was well and the courses were accurate and most importantly our young 3rd Mate was comfortable and ready to take over. Once I was satisfied we were on track and well clear of any potential hazards I left the Bridge and handed over to the 3rd Mate (trying as I may to make it sound as if I had done it a thousand times before…) making certain he fully understood he was to call me without hesitation if I was needed, he was ever in doubt or the traffic volume increased.

I went below to my cabin, trying to hide the slight tremor in my hands caused by the excitement of the moment. After about an hour, and not before numerous interim glances through my forward looking cabin windows, I returned to the Bridge to check all was well and we were on track. The 3rd Mate was doing the right thing by taking frequent Radar Fixes to check our position as the outlying Islands of Hong Kong slid into the haze over the distant horizon. We were dead on course – I expected nothing less. During this lapse in time Les, our Chief Mate, had reconnected the anchor to the anchor chain and housed it properly in the Hawse Pipe.

As Noon approached our 2nd Mate appeared on the bridge, he handed me the "Noon Chit" which indicated, Noon Position, Sea Speed, Course, Distances covered and remaining to destination, Propeller Slip, Daily fuel Consumption up till Noon since departing Hong Kong and tentative ETA Singapore Eastern Pilot Boarding Ground. I in turn extracted all the data, compiled a telegram with all the information and passed it to our Radio Officer for relay to our Owners. We were now truly on our way and the ship's destiny firmly in my hands.

31 My first Passage

I did not bother the 2nd Mate during the afternoon watch, as I wished to let the Officers know I had confidence in them so it was not until about 4.30pm that I again ventured to the Bridge to have a chat with Les Barnes. The weather was not bad and the visibility reasonably good. The weather forecasts, which I received twice daily from the Radio Officer, was not indicating any adverse conditions. Hopefully that would remain the case until arrival at Singapore.

My chat with Les was intended so I could get to know him better – we had both been busy since joining and had not hitherto had a suitable opportunity. Our chat was more social than anything else but we did both agree on one thing and that was how well the crew seemed to be bonding together into a team unit.

The next morning, as is my usual practice at sea, I rose very early and in this case was on the Bridge by 5am for my first coffee stimulant. It was difficult for me to get going for the day before downing several cups of good strong freshly brewed coffee. This set me up for the day. I checked the ship's position on the chart and the log book to check that my night order book had been properly signed by all the watch keepers. Looking at the details that had been recorded from the Walker's Log, we were maintaining a steady 11 knots. This was not surprising because the ship had only just come from dry dock and her underwater hull was freshly painted and absolutely clean. I watched the sunrise. It was one of those typical tropical sunrises, very quick and went from full darkness to full daylight in no time at all. My ship was starting to come to life with the Bosun and his crew wandering about the main deck commencing their daily duties and the ship's carpenter (referred to as the

"Chippy") doing his daily rounds of sounding all the Ballast Tanks and Double Bottoms. There were occasional wafts of cooking smells as our Chief Cook prepared breakfast for all.

By now we were approaching the northern extremities of the Paracel Islands where there were numerous fishing junks scattered about. These sailing or motorized fishing junks ventured hundreds of miles out into the South China Sea and could pop up from nowhere unexpectedly.

The Paracel Islands lie about 280 nautical miles South South West of Hong Kong and are mainly of low elevation and consist several groups; they lay to the West of the normal Hong Kong to Singapore route and can produce strong and unpredictable currents if one approaches too close as evidenced by several wrecks clearly visible on some of the outlying reefs. In general terms however, they are well charted and pose little danger to navigation provided a good visual and Radar look out is maintained. Nevertheless, in bad weather or poor visibility they should be given as wide a berth as practical.

Another danger not far distant is the Macclesfield Banks. These reefs are about 80 nautical miles South East from the Paracel Islands and about 35 nautical miles South East of the recommended Hong Kong to Singapore track which traverses between both these danger spots. Macclesfield Banks is a submerged atoll of about 75 nautical miles diameter and is best well avoided at any time particularly in view of the fact it had not been completely surveyed at this point in time. The associated reefs are peppered with numerous wrecks – both large and small.

With luck we should have passed through these dangerous shoals during daylight hours and be well clear by night fall. The weather remained nice and the ship in her loaded condition rolled lazily to the ocean swell in the late morning sunshine. We had the usual flocks of sea birds boldly following in our wake. I was very contented with my lot.

During the afternoon "Sparks" our Radio Officer passed me a cable just received from the Company Agents in Singapore. It seemed we would commence discharge at Eastern Working Anchorage and I was requested to apply for Radio Pratique 24 hours prior to our arrival. I acknowledged the message and passed the information on to Les Barnes and the Chief Engineer.

As we progressively closed on the Vietnam coast we started to observe more and more military activity. American aircraft and ships were popping up everywhere, quizzing everyone and everything as if they owned the oceans. The Vietnam War had passed its zenith and was approaching its closing chapters, and whilst the Americans did not have it all their own way in the conflict they still maintained a strong military presence in the neighboring seas. Aircraft would buzz us at bridge level and repeatedly call us on VHF channel 16. It all became a little repetitive and somewhat tiresome. Some of the language exchanges over the radio with the Americans were very colorful and descriptive; especially from ships they quizzed who had little sympathy with their cause in Asia. Believing there was no reason why this annoyance would not continue I suggested to the Chief Mate he have the ship's name and call sign painted on the Monkey Island deck atop of the Bridge in large white letters. This could only be seen from the air or Mast Head and hopefully would go some way to placating these pesky aviators.

Every time I had previously passed the southern cape of Vietnam the weather had turned sour, this time was no exception. As we sailed along our track towards the area the sky became overcast and the sea and wind increased causing us to roll and pitch a little more noticeably. Usually these conditions did not persist too long unless during the North East Monsoon months when weather could be blowing from the North East almost continually, often with associated Typhoons which originate in the Pacific Ocean then track towards the South China Sea, usually from the direction of the Philippines.

As predicted, the fresh weather soon passed as we distanced ourselves from Vietnam and by the time we made landfall on the Anambas Islands favorable conditions prevailed once again. The Anambas Islands, with the picturesque little township on Matak Island, are located about 150 nautical miles North East of Singapore so we knew we were nearing our destination when their mountainous terrain was observed on the distant horizon late during the 2nd Mate's afternoon watch

Early on our fifth morning at sea there appeared a loom of a light ahead fine on our Port bow, it looked very ghostly like a warning finger sweeping the horizon; this was the Horsburgh Lighthouse which marks the Eastern approaches to the Singapore Straits. We continued towards it at a steady 11 knots and within a couple of hours could clearly make out the lighthouse standing rigid guarding the entrance. Our Radar had detected this and the East coast of Singapore some hours earlier. At this point I was on the Bridge for the transit of the Straits and final approaches towards the Singapore Eastern Pilot Station. By 9am the lighthouse was abeam to Port, just over one nautical mile distant. We easily slotted into the line ahead formation along with the many other ships transiting the Straits towards the West. Singapore was now also clearly visible to Starboard. At this time I ordered the main engines to be placed on standby so they were prepared and immediately ready for any unexpected or imminent engine movements. Other than for the odd Tug and Barge crossing the traffic lanes our final approach to our destination was uneventful and by 12 o'clock local time I had started to slow down and maneuver the vessel towards the waiting Pilot launch.

It was a relatively short distance from the Pilot Boarding Ground to the Eastern Anchorage and our Singaporean Pilot guided us expertly to a vacant position within the very crowded Anchorage. We let go the Port Anchor which was brought-up with four shackles in the water. We had arrived and inwardly I sighed a sigh of relief, my first test had been completed. It boosted my confidence no end. From where we were anchored I could clearly see Amber Light Beacon and I was suddenly overcome with nostalgia and memories of the hours I had stood watches as a young Cadet, and on many other occasions in almost the same position. Nothing much had changed except for the blossoming skyline of Singapore and its growing number of skyscraper buildings. The sounds and smell remained unchanged as did that special Asian ambience and the scented light airs wafting from the shore, which added to the Island's special charm.

Our Port Agent soon arrived on board to see me. Mr. Chan was a middle aged Chinese with graying hair, he wore spectacles and walked with a slight stoop. Initially I think he was taken aback as to my youthful appearance but being a true Oriental gentleman he said nothing. We exchanged paper work and inward clearance. I was advised that discharge would commence at 6am the following morning and we were expected to remain in Singapore for about 7 or 8 days to complete the outturn of cargo. He brought me ships mail and asked if I had any requirements – I did not, other than handing him the ships arrival details for conveying to my Owners and a reminder for ship's cash, which I had requested a day or so earlier by ship's cablegram. This was so I could accommodate those crew members requesting a cash advance on their wages. Soon thereafter he departed in his launch, stating he would return the following morning. I had taken the opportunity of his visit to arrange a daily launch schedule so our crew could go ashore when not on duty.

Soon after Mr. Chan departed I asked Les Barnes and the Chief Engineer, who was named Ned Gates, to come to my cabin. They soon arrived and I briefed them as to the plan for our stay so they could organize the vessel. By this time the sun was above the yard arm so I offered them each a cold can of beer which they drank as we sat chatting in my Day Room. Ned Gates a tall lanky man, who exuded confidence, reported that so far the engines were running like clockwork and he was satisfied with their performance. This was music to my ears.

By mid afternoon the crew had topped all the derricks and removed the top canvas Tarpaulins from the hatch covers – leaving just a single Tarpaulin in case of rain. The ship was ready for the stevedores the following morning. Les had, as usual practice, placed the Quartermasters on Gangway watches and the Deck Officers on Anchor watches.

As Piracy was prevalent in the various Singapore Strait anchorages at this time, additional cargo lights (Cargo Clusters) were hung over the ships side at regular intervals, so no boats could sneak up un-noticed. The Quartermasters also conducted frequent deck patrols as an added means of security. There had been some cases of serious Piracy reported recently and we did not wish to fall victim. It seemed Piracy was becoming a growing menace in the coastal Ports of the South China Sea.

When I entered the Dining Saloon for dinner that evening it was full with all the officers except for those on duty. Duty Officers usually took their meals in a small Duty Mess situated adjacent to the Dining Room Pantry. The atmosphere in the Dining Saloon was lively and they all seemed a happy lot and why not…the food was quite good and the Chief Steward looked after us well as did our Chinese cooks. Fresh bread was baked every morning and the menu was comprehensive with quite a wide range of choices There were a few regular daily specials that always appeared, namely; Hainan Chicken Rice, Beef or Chicken Curry and for breakfast – Kedgeree or Eggs Bacon and Sausages. At lunch time we usually had a Soup followed by a Roast, Lamb or Pork Chops, Vegetables, Potatoes and there was always a fresh salad available from the buffet bar. Some favorites were Spaghetti Bolognaise, Shepherd's Pie and Fish and Chips usually served on Fridays. Other favorite dishes were Bubble and Squeak and Bangers and Mash. Once a week we had Chinese Chow which was always well received. We were always offered a wide range of deserts which was followed by biscuits and cheese selection and endless cups of freshly brewed coffee. At lunch time on Saturday and Sunday all officers were offered two cans of beer – courtesy of the Company. Our Chinese crew had their own cook to cater for them and going by the smiles on their faces so they obviously had no complaints

The ship had a small, but cozy, Officer's Bar located next to the Smoke Room. It had been decorated by previous crews over the years and featured flags, paintings, brassware and a variety of nautical memorabilia. The "piece de resistance" was a beautiful Brass Ship's Bell and a Brass Life Boat Compass complete with miniature Brass Binnacle which sat at the end of the highly polished wooden Bar.

As Captain I provided the alcohol, cigarettes and other essentials from the Captain's Bond - which was purchased with my own funds and managed on my behalf by the Purser Chief Steward (who received a small cut of the profits from sales in recognition of his services). Beer, Spirits, Cigarettes and Pipe Tobacco were sold to individual Officers and crew at duty free prices with a minimal mark-up. The Officers elected a Bar Committee (the Captain usually being the chairman) – this was good because it enabled me to discretely monitor alcohol consumption by the various individuals. The committee also set the Bar rules. The Bar was usually replenished from the Captains' Bond on a monthly basis unless it was a larger special order (for example Christmas or New Year). When on duty being caught in the Bar was strictly taboo.

That evening a number of my crew went ashore in the liberty boat which I had pre-arranged. At the head of the queue was our "Sparks" eager and ready to explore all that the Orient had to offer – I chuckled quietly to myself and wished him well. No doubt I would hear all about it from him in the passage of time.

I spent the remainder of that evening in my cabin reflecting on the events of the last month and writing up my voyage log, supplemented by the occasional Gin and Tonic just for good measure. At about 9pm I meandered up to the Bridge to make certain all was in order for the night and to update my Night Order Book. Then I went below and hit the sack.

32 Sulu Archipelago and Celebes Sea

Our stay in Singapore was just a week until the last bags of sugar were transferred to the lighters' The stevedores had worked fast, but they did have 4 gangs working in each hatch. The outturn had been good with only a few torn bags. Hatches were swept clean then quickly hosed down ready for our next cargo.

Despite what I was expecting we were not going to Bangkok for rice or indeed to some other port to load logs, instead I was instructed to proceed to the Port of Manado in the Celebes to load a cargo of Bagged Copra Chips for Kaohsiung in Formosa (now named Taiwan). The main Port of Manado lies on the northern tip of the Celebes Island in the Indonesian Archipelago and is situated in the Celebes Sea, only about one and half degrees North of the Equator. The Celebes is a funny shaped Island, rather like an inverted hook – Manado being at the extreme tip of the hook!

There were two routes available for me to consider namely; through the South China Sea following the North East coast of Borneo, transit the Balabac Strait then the Sulu Archipelago and into the Celebes Sea to the Celebes and Manado, or from Singapore via the Karamata Strait passing the Southern part of Borneo and then North East through the Makassar Straits. After discussing the route and respective distances as well as the pros and cons with our 2nd Mate, I opted for the Northern route through the Balabac Straits and Sulu Archipelago. The North East Monsoon was not prevalent during this period so the weather could be expected to be reasonable and the distance between Singapore and Manado was only 1900 nautical miles which would take us just a tad under 8 days at 11 knots sea speed. Another factor that swayed me in favor of this route was my familiarity with it from previous voyages on other ships.

Eventually we were all ready to depart from Singapore, but not before we had replenished a few hundred more tons of bunkers and our Fresh Water tanks were filled to capacity. When trading to some of these remote Asian Ports it was always wise to keep the vessel well topped up with these consumables as they may not always be readily available and it prevented the necessity to make intermediate bunker calls at other ports en route.

My crew had enjoyed their stay in Singapore and I sensed an air of sorrow when time to leave, especially amongst our Chinese crew, nevertheless depart we must, so at 6am amidst one of those wonderful tropical sunrises we weighed anchor, disembarked the Pilot then headed Eastbound along the Singapore Straits towards our trusted Horsburgh Lighthouse and the South China Sea. It was a very calm morning with not a breath of wind and as usual the sea was like molten glass. There was only the odd Arab Dhow groping to find a breeze, over towards the Indonesian side and Bintan Island, these sailing craft needed careful observation in such calm conditions as they could suddenly catch a breeze and attempt to cross the channel then become becalmed again right in front of your ship causing much embarrassment; otherwise there was surprisingly little traffic. A few ships were miles away, mainly hull down or dancing on the horizon due to refraction; their usual visible giveaway rising fingers of smoke being emitted from their funnels drifting endlessly skywards.

Most of my morning was spent on the Bridge with the 3rd Mate, as we continued our transit of the Straits. I also used the time to carefully check all the courses charted by our 2nd Mate for our voyage to Manado which I found to be in order.

Once having cleared the Singapore Straits and entered the South China Sea we altered course more towards the East to skirt the Borneo coast, passing the Ports of Kuching, Bintulu, Labuan and Kota Kinabalu distant on our starboard hand as we progressively sailed in a more northeasterly direction. We would then pass though the Balabac Straits which lies between Philippine Island of Palawan and northern most tip of Borneo. This passage serves as the conduit and principal route between the South China Sea and The Sulu Sea in this region.

Having navigated the Balabac Straits our intention was to alter course to the south, leaving the timber Port of Sandakan well to starboard and slip through the Sulu Archipelago, keeping to the West of the Tawi Tawi group of Islands and into the Celebes Sea, then on towards the Celebes (now called Sulawesi) and finally Manado.

The Sulu Archipelago is very serene and idyllic but is prone to Piracy so caution is required and it is always prudent to keep clear of fishing boat fleets or unidentified craft. The various islands which form the archipelago, like a chain between Borneo and the Philippines, are all extremely beautiful with their silver sand beaches, swaying palms and off lying coral reefs. They are frequently referred to as the "Paradise Islands" because of their pristine setting. No doubt many of their inhabitants being fishermen and perhaps part time Pirates! Or perhaps the reverse! The two principal islands are Jolo in the north with the southernmost being Tawi Tawi. In actuality, the Islands are a string of extinct volcanic cones and give rise to the surrounding waters being pristine with a wealth of sea life, including Whales at certain times of the year, as they migrate.

Some three days after departing Singapore we were approaching the northern part of Borneo and could quite clearly see Mount Kinabalu in the distance. The peak protruded through a layer of cloud or mist. It painted a wonderful picture in the afternoon sunshine and acted as a very good landmark and beacon for us. The 2nd Mate seized the advantage and set about taking compass bearings of the peak and charting them; even allowing for refraction and other atmospheric anomalies the various bearings all intersected reasonably well and confirmed our position. I made a practice of encouraging my junior Mates to take visual bearings and compass azimuths whenever possible as one never knew how quickly circumstances could change and they could become very useful indeed.

Being a Saturday I decided to call a random Boat and Fire Drill. These drills were mandatory and were usually conducted fortnightly on cargo ships. At 2pm I sounded the Emergency Signal on the ship's siren followed soon after by the Fire Alarm on the ship's Alarm Bells. As expected the crew donned their lifejackets and proceeded calmly and orderly to their Muster Stations. We had two life Boats, one each side, so we had two corresponding Muster Points. The Chief Mate was, along with the other Officers, kept busy ticking off names from the muster list as well as inspecting lifejackets. As the weather was good I ordered the boats be swung outboard to boat deck level. This was done without a hitch and the boats were soon recovered and housed in their respective Davits. During the recovery process the wire boat falls were inspected and greased. Both Life Boats had an engine so each was test run by the engineers to ensure proper functionality. Our Radio Officer thrived at the opportunity to test his emergency Radio which required cranking in order to operate and transmit effectively. I think he was reluctant to put it back in its waterproof box!

Upon completion of the Boat Drill we moved on to the Fire Drill. I had opted for a simulated Galley Fire. The fire Parties all went about their business efficiently. Fire hoses were run and Emergency Fire Pump operated. Fire Blankets were deployed and additional portable Fire Extinguishers were brought to the scene of the simulated fire and two discharged on deck just outside the Galley to make sure they worked – they were later recharged by our 3rd Mate and placed back into their designated positions. All these activities took about an hour to complete, at the conclusion of which the Chief Mate arrived at the Bridge to report a successful exercise. So ended our Emergency Drills for the day but not before I had made the appropriate entries in the ship's Official Log Book and had it countersigned by Les Barnes.

By this time all my officers and crew were starting to settle in well, particularly Les Barnes and Ned Gates. It was easy to detect they were both very competent at their jobs. I was very impressed with Les and the methodical manner in which he set about his work. He was a thinker and a planner and always created a solid course of action before having his deck crew commence any task. When we had taken over the vessel she was somewhat rusty and weather beaten about the decks, I suspect due to the busy trade in which she had been engaged around Australian coast. In the month he had been on board since joining in Hong Kong he had already scaled almost all the residual rust from the decks and hatchways. They had been primed and top coated and now looked like new. Les worked his crew effectively to maximum advantage. He shared his future plans with me concerning his proposed maintenance schedule, they were impressive. I believed when next we called at Hong Kong or received a visit from the

Superintendents I am sure they would not recognize the "Hoi Hing"

Similarly, Ned Gates ran an efficient and happy Engine Room. He was a perfectionist and watch out anyone who tried to short circuit his methods. During my weekly inspections I always went down into the Engine Room as part of that routine. I can say in only one month it had been transformed, so much one could eat a meal of the deck plates. It was also fair to say he was very ably assisted by his experience 2nd Engineer who was always busy maintaining machinery of one sort or another aided by his other engineers and Chinese engine room ratings.

Eventual we entered the western approaches of the Balabac Straits. At the entrance there is a Philippines Navy Coast Watch Station to which all transiting vessels must report, but once done ships can proceed and navigate unhindered. The Western approaches to the strait are relatively clear but as one nears the eastern end there are numerous small Islets. I had elected to use the Nasubata Passage which is the recommended route for vessels proceeding towards the Sulu Sea, it is deep and relatively free of dangers but we did observe many logs, large pieces of drift wood and the occasional uprooted Palm tree amongst other varieties of flotsam drifting along in the currents, which tend to be strong at times. At night this flotsam and jetsam debris can prove to be dangerous to ships, especially if large logs collide with the propeller they can cause serious damage and in extreme cases disable a ship by snapping off a propeller blade. Anyway we had timed our arrival at the western approaches for sunrise so our passage would predominantly be in daylight, thus minimizing these risks. Hence by nightfall we had passed all the danger marks and were close to the Sulu Sea and Open Ocean.

The crossing of the Sulu Sea was a dream, excellent calm and fine weather with only light variable winds, it was now only mid-May and therefore quite a calm period as the South West Monsoon only really starts to build towards the end of June, at this time one could almost mark the calendar as to the day the monsoons would likely begin – they were so predictable. These favorable conditions assisted us in making an average speed of 11.5 knots whilst forging on through the Sulu Sea.

The point at which we would slip through the Sulu Archipelago was towards the south west tip; south west of the Tawi Tawi Islands through the Sibutu Passage. Whilst heading towards the Sibutu Passage we could clearly observe the low lying and relatively flat Tawi Tawi Islands, to port. Numerous small white fishing boats dotted the horizon but we made certain we kept our distance – not knowing what hidden dangers from Pirates may lurk within the innocent looking fleet.

The Sibutu Passage which connects the Sulu and Celebes Seas is about 18-20 miles wide, deep and does not pose any navigational hazards or dangers. On this occasion it was absolutely tranquil and it was the place I had observed many Whales, Manta Rays and Blue Marlin during earlier voyages. By now we were well into the Celebes Sea and about to set course towards northern Celebes and Manado.

Being an important body of water in the region, the Celebes Sea carries a formidable amount of shipping traffic, especially engaged in the short sea trades between Borneo, Philippines and Indonesian Archipelago Ports. It spans about 550 nautical miles East to West and 450 nautical miles north to South, but sadly is one of the most Pirated areas in the World. Many of these Pirates originate in the Sulu Archipelago but additionally in the Ports bordering the Celebes Sea, such as Tawau, Sandakan, and Zamboanga, etc. and do not only terrorize legitimate fishing vessels and other small coastal ships but also ocean going vessels. These Pirates are equipped with fast surface craft and hence become very mobile, not to mention that they have a very sophisticated intelligence network which is highly organized. These brigands are generally run by criminal syndicates who know what they are seeking and when and where to look.

It is understandable therefore that I asked Les Barnes to arrange for additional lookouts to be placed, especially during the hours of darkness. We also rigged fire hoses along the decks both sides of the ship so if any uninvited boats did try to come alongside they would be met with the full force of our water hose jets. I had learned this technique in the Malacca Straits, using it years before when still an Apprentice. It worked very effectively. Being a merchant vessel we had to improvise and use our heads as we carried no defensive weaponry of any kind. Fortunately, this trip passed without incident.

Some 7.5 days after departing Singapore the mountainous terrain of the northern Celebes could be seen ahead at some distance. An hour or so later we could just make out the township of Manado, as a white smudge seen through our binoculars. The mountains and volcanoes as well as off lying volcanic Islands characterize this region of the Celebes. By the time we closed the Port it was mid afternoon. I had been informed by radio that no Pilot was required and I was to anchor as close as was possible off the Port. Loading would be ex-lighter.

The anchorage at Manado is quite deep and therefore it is necessary to pay out a good amount of anchor cable and slowly kedge inwards towards the shore until the anchor finds the bottom and good holding ground. Great care is needed when carrying out this type of maneuver. The anchor eventually took hold but we ended up with a good number of shackles in the water. This had taken almost an hour to achieve because we needed to be certain the anchor was well embedded and holding; it was almost tea time before I was satisfied and ring down "Finished with Engines" on the bridge telegraph.

Our Port Agent was soon aboard and informed me that loading would commence at 1800 Hrs with 4 gangs, being increased to 6 gangs on the following day shifts. Cargo Cluster lights were rigged in all hatches and overboard to illuminate things for the stevedores and Lighters. Our Bosun being true to form had topped all the derricks and rigged the cargo gear about an hour prior to our arrival. Likewise hatch tarpaulins and hatch boards removed and stowed. Hatch tents were deployed on deck beside respective hatches to facilitate closing of hatches quickly, particularly in cases of sudden heavy rain.

Copra is the residuals of coconut shell and husks. Despite being fumigated prior to shipment it still carries its own passengers by way Copra Bugs These are small beetle like insects that penetrate everywhere. Copra is also subject to Spontaneous Combustion and is therefore classified as a dangerous cargo and which must be kept dry and well ventilated at all times. It also has a distinctly sickly odor. In this case the shippers were professionals and the jute bags containing the product were expertly stowed leaving narrow ventilation channels, with rope nets used for securing purposes in order to bind the stow. During the hours cargo was not being worked "Hatch Tents" were rigged to cover the hatches in case of rain showers and to allow suitable ventilation of the cargo.

In an attempt to minimize the inconvenience caused by the insects Les Barnes had engaged the crew in securing hessian and loin cloth over all ventilators leading into the accommodation areas. Also, he had posted temporary signs reminding everyone to keep doors and hatchways closed. Not that they needed reminding. Soon after the lighters arrived so did the Copra Bugs! That put an end to the prospect of sitting on deck enjoying a libation and watching the world go by, the magnificent sunsets and dancing stars above for which this part of the world was reputed.

I had been to Manado on one previous occasion but never had the opportunity to go ashore to see what it was like, so I hoped this call would be different, especially since our loading was expected to be quite slow taking a couple of weeks, so time was not an element. Our indomitable Radio Office would undoubtedly be one of the first ashore to survey the local scene and report back, usually at meal time when in the Dinning Saloon. I decided to wait and see as I was in no hurry for an excursion!

The milling Copra Bugs continued to be a menace even though stevedores were diligent fumigating the bags prior to loading. The stevedore laborers loading the bags into our cargo holds seemed to just ignore them and went about their business unperturbed. The lower holds were filled relatively quickly after only about a week then loading in the tweendecks commenced. This could be expected to be a little slower at the outset because the slings of bags were first landed in the square of the hatchway then bags needed to be carried into the wings for stowing. Our steam winches never missed a beat and worked endlessly throughout, their constant rattling and hissing not being of any annoyance since one became immune to the noise after the first few hours. It always amazed me how fast cargo could be handled using well rigged derricks and union purchase gear with the winches in the hands of skilled operators.

True to form, at breakfast time a day or so after our arrival in Manado our illustrious explorer, "Sparks" gave us all an assessment of his run ashore. Even allowing for his inexperience in Asia, nevertheless Manado appeared to be an interesting venue to which to pay a visit, according to his accounts. That same afternoon I talked him into accompanying me ashore to act as my guide. I was not so interested in the night life as I was familiar with the spoils of the "Far East" where I had spent most of my life living and working; one place was much the same as the other in that regard. After lunch we boarded a rather rickety launch for the short trip ashore.

I was immediately charmed by the old township of Manado with its captivating buildings, temples and shrines but above all by its thriving China Town and markets. These markets never failed to fascinate me and I could spend hours literally wandering about looking at the wide range of goods for sale. This was no exception and I bought a number of items, including several wonderful Batiks, a few small carvings with exquisite workmanship and some other cultural memorabilia. I could have spent many more hours just browsing and pottering about but I sensed our Radio Officer was getting bored and was starting to hint we should move on.

We had a quite excellent meal at one of the local restaurants; a mixture of Indonesian and Chinese food then went to have a look at the old Bon Hing Kiong Temple and soaked up the exuding culture of the place. By 6pm I was heading back to my ship, our "Sparks" having decided to stay ashore for further exploration; I suspect to evaluate what the night life had to offer! On the quick trip to the anchorage I was blessed by witnessing another magnificent sunset with the sky absolutely ablaze with colors as the Sun signaled its goodbyes for the day and dipped below the horizon in an instant, then it was time to be invaded by Copra Bugs once again.

Thereafter the days dragged a little as we progressed towards completion of loading. In the meantime the duty officers remained vigilant to make certain the bags of cargo were dry, properly stowed and well ventilated to prevent the possibility of spontaneous combustion. The derricks were finally lowered and secured and the hatches battened down. Upon completion of immigration formalities our agent passed me the usual Cargo Papers and Manifest together with the ship's Outward Port Clearance. I in turn handed over several cartons of "Lucky Strike" cigarettes and 2 bottles of Scotch Whiskey to signify appreciation for all their cooperation, this was customary. Now we were ready to depart for Kaohsiung.

Our route would take us back across the Celebes Sea, through the Sibutu Passage and Balabac Straits before turning to the North tracking up the West coast of the Philippine Islands direct towards our destination Kaoshiung. The Port of Kaohsiung is located in the south west sector of Formosa, facing the Strait that separates the Island from the Chinese mainland. The Formosa Strait was always a contentious area and the scene of much politicking between the two Chinese governments. Although tensions between Peking (now Beijing) and Taipei (now capital of modern Taiwan) were starting to wane a little, ships trading through the Formosa Straits on a regular basis still displayed their national flags painted conspicuously on each side of the hull.

Being a deep anchorage it took a little longer than usual to weigh our anchor but once it was secured in the hawse pipe we wasted no time in getting underway. We had about a 7 day passage ahead of us to Kaohsiung

Several thermometers had been placed in each hatch so it became the 3rd Mates job to record and log the cargo temperatures morning and evening. Typically, several hatch boards were lifted in each corner of respective hatchways to assist with better ventilation for the cargo. Of course this could only be done in fine dry conditions but we were always ready to close them in an instant if circumstances demanded.

Once again our passage through the Celebes and Sulu Seas was blessed with perfect weather. We encountered a few rain showers passing the Balabac Straits just to the south of Balabac Island but once clear into the South China Sea and having adopting a more northerly course to parallel Palawan Island and head towards the west coast of the Philippines, conditions became ideal once again, with calm seas and light airs. At night, standing on the bridge wing gazing up at the heavens, tempted to almost reach and touch the stars and planets above. Looking over the ships side our wash was alive with the luminescence and ghostly appearance of the plankton disturbed by our ship's movement through the water. Unfortunately we still had some non-paying passengers by way of Copra Bugs!

My usual habit as an early riser heralded from my nautical training so I made it my practice to be on the bridge at about 5am every morning, not only to check the vessel's progress during night but also reap the benefits of our cook who baked fresh bread early every morning causing the smell to drift upwards towards the bridge deck stimulating a craving. Hence every morning about 5.30 am our pantry boy arrived on the Bridge with a pot of freshly brewed coffee and a large plate of hot bread roles and knobs of butter. It did not take Les Barnes and I long I to scoff the lot every morning. My early morning chats with Les consisted part social and part work and became a morning ritual and something I looked forward to, it was a most agreeable way to start the day.

Early morning in the tropics is the best time of day, especially around the equatorial latitudes. The quick breaking dawn is a sheer delight to witness. The sky lights up long before the Sun rises above the eastern horizon, offering the most brilliant and spectacular display of color; creating a strange sense of stillness and tranquility during those few moments before the Sun actually gains sufficient amplitude to announce the start of another day and bursts forth. I considered myself to be very lucky and felt like a paid tourist on many occasions.

As we forged ahead through the pristine waters well to seaward of Palawan; the sea was a brilliant turquoise in color and through our binoculars to starboard we were just able to make out the silver stranded coastline and distant lofty mountains, this scene of serenity only disturbed by the never ending fleets of inshore fishing boats that frequented the area. We soon traversed the west coast of Luzon Island which was the largest of the Philippine Islands and then adjusted course to cross the Luzon Straits towards Formosa.

33 Goodbye Copra Bugs and Hello Land of Smiles

Arrival at Kaohsiung Pilot Station was timely, about 5am just as the daylight was breaking. Our Pilot was a very smooth Chinese character and spoke with a carefully groomed American accent; nevertheless he was quite proficient in the handling of our ship and by 6.45am we were all secured alongside the jetty which appeared to be quite remote from the City. Very serious looking Immigration and Customs officials soon came on board. Their first act to make certain the Republic of China courtesy flag was correctly displayed at the foremast. Once on board they were no problem except for some of our Chinese crew who had restrictions placed on their shore passes and some being prevented from going ashore at all. I guess the local Government had a phobia about Communist instigators. As far as I was concerned my crew was not politically motivated in any way and was only interested in good food, attractive ladies and a good night ashore, typical of any universal sailor arriving in any foreign Port.

There was also a curfew in place which was strictly policed by authorities and required all to be back on board by midnight, this was without exception. The ship's Radio Station was sealed and use strictly prohibited, under any circumstances, until after departure and 12 miles offshore. The usual armed sentries were placed at the foot of our gangway. It was all a bit intimidating but I had experienced it all before, especially in Mainland China and North Korea which could be even worse. In fairness to Formosa, one must realize the Cultural Revolution was still brewing just across the straits on the mainland, so perhaps their phobia was well founded at the time.

Kaohsiung lies at the mouth of the Ai River (sometimes referred to as the Lov River), a sort of a Canal River that flows through the City of Kaohsiung which lies close to hand. During this period Kaohsiung was heavily committed to ship breaking and demolition and was in fact the leading port in Asia for this type of activity. As one entered the Port the river banks were strewn with dozens of ships, both large and small, at the numerous breakers' yards, in various stages of demolition. It was a somewhat chaotic scene and polluted as a consequence. The Port had several major projects underway at this time, namely, a large shipbuilding complex and multiple container berths under construction. This was the beginning of the era when a move towards containerization within the shipping industry was inevitable and gaining momentum, but which had not yet fully impacted on general cargo ships such as mine. However it was forthcoming and only a matter of time before most cargoes would become fully containerized

The Copra berth was a little upstream from the breakers yards, well enough away from anything the Copra Bugs may annoy, although it must be said their numbers had dwindled considerably during our sea passage from Manado. As usual the stevedores wasted no time in boarding and setting about their work. Cargo was offloaded in slings and landed directly on flat top lorries, roughly stacked then driven to the processing plant a short distance away somewhere in the yard behind the wharf. It was a very smelly place as the rancid odor of past and present Copra cargoes always lingered in one's nostrils. However, discharging was a fast process as was evident to the eye so all going well we would quickly rid ourselves of this shipment.

Having visited Formosan Ports many times previously I did not venture ashore this call, not even to escape the remaining Copra Bugs that had been stirred up by the cargo being landed ashore. Although not a requirement, I volunteered for occasional nights on board so the Chief Mate and the other Officers could go ashore. Needless to say, our Radio Officer (who did not keep watches whilst in Port), acted as the main "Radar" for the others, ferreting out the best Bars, Restaurants, Ladies and night life, plus other places of interest.

It was about 2 days before completion of discharge that I received news from my Port Agents regarding our next deployment. The ship had been fixed to load another bagged cargo; Rice, from Bangkok to Hong Kong. This sounded fine as I was very familiar with Bangkok. I was also informed that a subsequent cargo of dressed round logs from Papua New Guinea or the Solomon Islands was still a distinct possibility and currently under negotiation by our Chartering Department. Details would follow but first I focused on our bagged Rice.

Our Departure from Kaohsiung followed a few days later. It was uneventful and we soon found ourselves heading off down the South China Sea once again. As I sat on the bridge wing one afternoon, drinking my coffee, my mind drifted back many years to when I had first visited Bangkok. I had met a young lady called Tasanee. She was a young "Sew Sew" lady who did my washing and ironing and generally cleaned my cabin and looked after me when the ship was in Bangkok. I had maintained loose contact with Tasanee over the years but I had not spoken to her now for almost three years. I knew she had married and I was therefore reluctant to suddenly pop up being a Falang (foreigner) and a "Blast from the Past" in case it caused a domestic row with her family. Jealousy was a rampant part of Asian culture. Anyway, if I had time this Port call I decided to discreetly try to contact her just to say hello. I still had her phone number but did not know if it was still valid. We were almost identical in age.

Time passed quickly as we headed south towards the southern tip of Vietnam then into the Gulf of Thailand. All our cargo holds had been hosed by this time to get rid of the final remnants of the Beetles and then well ventilated to dry out thoroughly. Rice was a cargo subject to taint and could easily spoil so we made certain all traces of the past cargo were well and truly eradicated and our cargo holds spotless.

As usual when passing the southern cape of Vietnam the weather was choppy but it soon diminished and resumed a more placid nature by the time we had entered the southern mouth of the Gulf of Thailand. The Gulf of Thailand is one of the major Gulfs within Asia being about 400 nautical miles north to south and about 200 nautical miles east to west. The Gulf, bordered by Vietnam, Cambodia, and Thailand as well as Malaysia, encompasses some of the region's most important Ports.

We sailed north passing Cambodia and leaving the Thai Ports of Rayong and Sattahip to starboard, then onwards passing Ko Si Chang Island and new Port development of Laem Krabang (now Laem Chabang) towards the Bangkok general purpose anchorage to await the Pilot for crossing the Chao Phraya River Bar, thence upstream and finally to Bangkok (Krungthrep) and the Port area of Klong Toei. The anchorage was about 2 nautical miles south east of the Pilot Station. From the outer entrance of the Chao Phraya River to Klong Toei is about 25 miles.

The Thai Pilots are all from an elite class, well educated and very capable, most being graduates of the Royal Thai Navy Academy located at Pak Nam on the shores of the Chao Phraya River. Our Pilot fitted this description exactly. We weighed anchor and cautiously crossed the River Bar which extends several nautical miles seaward of the river estuary and is littered with hundreds of fish traps each side of the channel. Once across the River Bar the trip is clear until arriving off the district of Samut Prakarn Watt where the Customs and Immigration officials board. Transit up the Chao Phraya is interesting; passing numerous Temples (Watts) on the way, all beautifully maintained and adorned in white, red and gold. Rickety wooden shacks on stilts located over the rushing brown waters and Long Tail boats with their "put put" engines darting in and out of the numerous Klongs which branch off the river carrying their passenger loads, to wherever; most of whom give a welcoming wave as ships pass them. In comparison to other river transits it is well organized. Especially in the rainy season, large rafts of Lotus weed (like small islands) float downstream as the river flows predominantly to seaward. When inbound, passing river traffic heading towards the estuary and sea seemed to flash by at great speed being assisted by the fast flowing downstream river flow.

On the occasion of our arrival we were required to wait for a vacant berth so we anchored mid stream not far from the area of Pak Nam. We remained there for 24 hours until our wharf became vacant, a private wharf owned by the rice exporting company, but still within the Klong Toei area. Our anchorage was surrounded by the Buddhist temples and shrines and on the starboard bank the prestigious Navy Academy. Even as a seasoned visitor to Bangkok the surrounds never ceased to interest me. It was vibrant and lively place but at the same time was steeped in culture and tradition; of course the predominant religion was Buddhism. However, at this time poverty was still prevalent amongst many Thais.

Soon after anchoring, the "Old Bangkok" once again came to life, with hoards of girls clamoring on board from boats, arriving from every direction. It was pointless trying to stop the flow so one just made gestures but inwardly gave up and acted discretely. Once again my memories of Tasanee came flooding back from all those years long gone, when I was a novice apprentice and she was one of the young girl domestics that came aboard to do my laundry, ironing and cabin cleaning. I clearly remember that in those days the going rate was either one bar of LUX toilet soap or one pack of LUCKY STRIKE cigarettes per day, or 6 bars of soap or one carton of cigarettes per week, (or as long as the ship was in port) which seldom exceeded a week unless loading rice).

Our Radio Officer was aghast with delight at all this feminine activity and participated whole heartedly, as did our junior engineers and younger Chinese crew. Officially I forbade these people on board but in reality the best I could do was to prevent these people wandering around the decks and ensure they observed some form of safety code, not to mention warning our Chief Steward to impress upon everyone to make certain their cabins were kept locked at all times and portholes closed. The security guards engaged in patrolled the decks and whom stood watch at the head of the gangway were in the overall scheme of things, of absolutely no use whatsoever in stemming the influx of females and would be thieves, with whom I suspect they had some kind of financial arrangement.

At last we were safely berthed alongside the wharf where we would load our rice. It was a relatively short jetty only sufficient to allow our union purchase gear to have access to the wharf to lift the cargo. This arrangement caused the ship to overhang a little at each end. Our bow and stern ropes were secured to Dolphins forward and aft. Our cargo was to be loaded in the traditional method of perfect stows and interconnecting ventilation shafts made of light timber placed between every couple of tiers, in amongst the stow, to assist in the through ventilation. The method of Random Stowing for rice had not caught on in Thailand at this time. In any event that method was best suited to bulk carriers with wide open cargo holds – not a tweendecker like "Hoi Hing" as stowage factors could be critical when lifting a full cargo.

Lots of dunnage, brown paper and rush mats were laid in cargo holds on the wooden tank top ceiling and ship's frames to keep the bags of rice away from steelwork. The standard "Spar Ceiling" that was provided was really inadequate as the sole means of preventing the rice contacting steelwork. Then the loading commenced.

Dozens and dozens of laborers carried heavy bags of rice on their heads to a point on the wharf where they were made up into rope slings, each sling weighing about one ton, ready for loading into the cargo holds. It was a very labor intensive system of loading and the stream of laborers carrying the bags was endless. As our steam cargo winches rattled away, below decks the stowed cargo grew steadily in size and in perfect formation, with not a single bag out of place. Each hatch had about 20 stevedores below handling and stowing the bags. In all my years of carrying rice stowed in this fashion I had never once experienced a bad outturn due to sweating, taint or similar damage.

Next morning after the Port Agent's customary visit I made a phone call from the Stevedore's office located on the wharf. It was really a half hearted attempt as I did not really expect to track down Tasanee. The phone rang twice and was answered by a Thai lady…."Sawasdee Kar". Do you remember me I said, which was followed by a moment's silence during which I expected the phone to hang up… then a scream of delight as she recognized my voice, I could not believe how easy it

344

had been to find Tasanee. We chatted away excitedly for the next 10 minutes during which time I discovered that her husband had been tragically killed in a motor cycle accident only a few months earlier soon after they had married. She was still living with her sister in the same place at Bang Na, her parents long since having deceased. We arranged a meeting for that same evening at one of the nicer local hotels. I hung up and went about my daily work feeling very satisfied with the outcome.

That evening I showered and put on a dark blue suit, white shirt and striped tie. After telling the Chief Mate my intention I descended the gangway, walked through the rice warehouse on the wharf and into the busy street where I hailed a taxi. I had been careful to have my Agent write down the location of the wharf in Thai so I would have no difficulty getting back that night. It was a 15 minute ride to the hotel venue, during which it became absolutely obvious to me as to how easy it would be to get knocked over whilst riding a motorcycle in Bangkok – road rules appeared not to exist or if they did they were made up on the spot!

Arriving at the hotel, a little early, I took a seat in the lobby out of sight of the main entrance but from where I nevertheless had a good view. Soon, in walked Tasanee looking as beautiful as ever in a long dress, I recognized her at once, her dark brown hair in a loose bun and looking absolutely stunning. She had not yet seen me, sitting a little secluded in a corner. I slowly ambled over and soon was standing behind her. Hello Tasanee, I said…she instantly swung around and in a single movement greeted me with a huge hug and kiss. We were both delighted to see each other and moved into the hotel restaurant so we could chat more freely. The more I looked at her the more I saw beauty and radiance and the sweetest of sweetest smiles. She had not changed at all. In fact her beauty had become so much more evident since I last met with her.

We chatted away telling each other our own stories. We had a nice dinner followed by a few drinks and still I could not get over how little she had aged since our first meeting almost 10 years earlier. She opened her hand bag and took out a small gold medallion of St Christopher which I had given her soon after we met years ago. I had long since forgotten and I was amazed she still had it. I always keep this she said, it reminds me of you and your kindness towards me long ago, I always knew you would come back to me! I was a bit chocked and hurriedly ordered another drink. Time was passing and it was getting a bit late, I did not ask if we could meet again, it was not necessary, the suggestion came from her. I arranged a taxi for her and one for myself. We said our emotional goodbyes then went our separate ways until tomorrow, when we would meet again. I was as emotionally confused as ever and found it difficult to sleep that night.

Sitting at my desk drinking my morning tea, having completed my daily paperwork, there was a knock on the door. It was the Chief Mate who had Tasanee with him. He was a bit embarrassed but said that the lady wished to see me and did I know her. I ushered them both into my day room and sat them down. I explained to Les Barnes who Tasanee was and our long standing relationship; he seemed relieved and soon departed. I believe he thought she was just some tart I picked up in a bar looking to get an extra payout. He was absolutely wrong, but I can't blame him for thinking that way.

Tasanee and I talked a long time; she was pleasantly surprised to learn I was now Captain. I talked her into taking me to visit the floating markets and the Grand

Palace if time allowed. That afternoon soon after lunch we set off on our day trip together.

She knew I was still single and during our excursion she suddenly looked me in the eye and asked me outright, if we could join together because she did not want to lose me again! I was shocked and taken aback but after a while I realized the amount of moral fiber and courage it had taken Tasanee, being a highly cultured Asian woman, to ask me such a forthright question. She looked so beautiful, refined and sophisticated as she sat in our little boat meandering between the mass of floating stalls. I explained that there was a special place in my heart for her but the relationship that once was could not be re-kindled so quickly. However, whilst I was not yet ready to get hitched, I was happy to let us continue our special friendship and see what transpired. She was happy with that response and rendered one of her unforgettable smiles, that only she could give and pressed her hand into mine. I knew I was facing a losing battle. To cut a long story short, over ensuing years Tasanee became my most trusted, loving and faithful partner; she moved to Hong Kong and we are still going strong today. She sailed with me on many voyages and was the best investment I ever made. Many people still ask me how I landed such a beautiful, elegant and charming wife. All I do is smile when asked. We now live in our home in Melbourne dividing our time between Bangkok, Hong Kong and Melbourne.

I received a cable from the owners informing me that when in Hong Kong to expect an inspection from top management as many had not seen the ship since she was purchased from the Australians. This was no issue at all because the ship was spotless both above and below; Les Barnes and Ned Gates having done a brilliant job. I was certain we would pass with flying colors. The only disturbing part of the message was a request for me to comment confidentially on the Chief Mate's suitability for Command; this I thought a bit embarrassing since I was only a recently appointed Captain myself. Anyway I considered the Company must value my opinions otherwise they would not have asked.

I carefully pondered over my response to owners regarding Les Barnes – he was a great Chief Mate, very capable, experienced and mature and managed the crew well and therefore well suited for command – there was never any doubt Les would receive my fullest support. It was just a matter of how I presented it to company management. Inwardly I wished him well and realized what a loss it would be to me if he was transferred away. I did not respond to the cable via the ship as it was strictly confidential, instead I telephoned the Office in Hong Kong and spoke personally to the Marine Superintendent. Naturally I did not mention anything to anyone aboard ship but during my call to the Hong Kong office I did glean there would be an acquisition of four new multipurpose additions to our fleet in the near future and we were soon to include Australia in our scope of operations.

We completed loading just in time, as the heavens opened and we were engulfed in a torrential down pour lasting half a day. Nevertheless, it cleared just as quickly as it had started. Soon thereafter we departed downstream heading towards the open sea. In usual fashion we sped down the river at a fast rate and once having crossed the bar (our departure from Klong Toei being timed so we would arrive at the river Bar on a rising tide close to High Water) and disembarked our River Pilot, we set course towards the south.

From Bangkok to Hong Kong is only about 1500 nautical miles which at our sea speed would take us around 6 days. We experienced consistent light rain for most of the passage across the South China Sea, at least the rain kept the seas low so we were able to maintain our sea speed of 11 knots as the visibility was not unduly affected. On the afternoon of our 5th day at sea we were in the Lamma Channel making towards the western approaches to Victoria Harbor, the Chief Mate already having disconnected one of our anchors from the anchor chain in the customary way ready for our arrival. There was no delay in the boarding of our harbor Pilot and we were secured at our designated Typhoon Buoy well before evening. That night the ship swung around the buoy to wind and current waiting for daylight and things to happen. The only people that went ashore that evening were some members of our Hong Kong Chinese crew.

Next morning all signs of the rain had gone and soon after daylight the cargo lighters were towed out to us and placed alongside ready to receive our cargo of rice. Cargo work commenced once the hatch covers had been removed, our union purchase gear working like a charm ably supported by our trusty steam winches. Not long after breakfast was over our Irish Marine Superintendent and other senior management arrived on board. He had a good look around the ship escorted by Les Barnes and Ned Gates. About an hour later my boss arrived in my cabin whilst the others were having morning coffee in the dining saloon. He commenced by saying how impressed he was with the work and maintenance done on the ship since I had assumed command just over 3 months ago. There followed details of our company's expansion program. Two of our older ships were to be sold to other Far East interests and the four newer vessels were scheduled to enter service with us over the coming months. They would be engaged on a semi-liner service between Hong Kong, Bangkok, Singapore and

Australian East Coast Ports. It was to be a part of a developing break bulk and container service.

Two cups of coffee later, I received the shock I was half expecting. I had anticipated Les Barnes was to be transferred, perhaps promoted to Master. This was not to be, it was I that was the guy going to be transferred, to one of the newer ships and Les was to take over from me in Hong Kong, with the 2nd Mate being promoted to Chief Mate to boot. As soon as I had handed over to Les Barnes I was to take a week off in Hong Kong but during which time I would be required to attend the office, then get on a flight that would take me to Sasebo in Japan where the new ship would be taken over after having been dry docked. The Marine Superintendent left my cabin soon afterwards and went in search of Les Barnes and 2nd Mate to break the news and offer them their new jobs. My head was spinning at the speed at which events had unfurled; it was less than 4 months since I had been promoted!

The Marine Superintendent left the vessel before lunch, having first instructed me officially to commence handing over to Les Barnes, he obviously having received formal acceptances to the job offers from both the Chief Mate and 2nd Mate.

At lunch in the Dining Saloon there was much conversation concerning the events of earlier in the morning. Les Barnes seemed to take it all in his stride and the younger 2nd Mate had a twinkle in his eye. We had a busy few days ahead of us to implement all the changes but my job was made easier due to my relief being familiar with the ship, and so was the 2nd Mate for that matter. A new Hong Kong Chinese 2nd Mate joined the ship and quickly settled in to his work. Four days later I said my goodbyes having handed over to Captain Barnes and headed off towards Queens Pier, once again, in the company launch. That night I went home, had a few drinks with my folks and made a phone call to Tasanee. I was quite relaxed about it all now!

Ports of Thailand

This is a scene of absolute peace and serenity from the **"Land of Smiles"**. The photo was taken up one of the many Klongs that branch off the Chao Phraya River, which winds its way from the Gulf of Thailand up to Bangkok. At certain times of the year Klongs can become choked by rafts of Lotus Weed similar to what is shown in the picture. The colorful Long tail Boat in the photo is typical of those used as "Water Taxis" to ferry passengers between the remote villages or Temples that are scattered about the banks of the various Klongs to more commercial locations on the main waterway. In part, the elevated bow of the craft is designed so it can skim above and push aside floating vegetation, such as Lotus Weed or river grasses.

During my so called week off I had visited the office almost daily during which I learned much about my new command. She was only 5 years old, 8,500 gross tons, a Multi-Purpose type but still retaining narrower tweendecks. Built in West Germany she had until recently been engaged in the Orient-South Africa Service by her previous owners. She had the capability to carry a certain number of containers above and below decks, general cargo and even Logs. Seemingly all four of these ships had out lived their use being proven too small for their liner route which called for larger replacements to enhance their Liner Service..

My company had purchased all four sister vessels en-bloc. My ship was to be renamed "Hoi Yun" (loosely translated Sea Gift) and placed under Hong Kong flag. I inspected the general arrangements plans together with other associated documentation and was at once impressed by the beautiful sleek and practical design, which featured engines and accommodation all situated aft. She had 3 large cargo holds segregated into 5 separate hatches, which were serviced by 5 swinging derricks each of 25 tons safe working load mounted on Mast Tables and served by electric winches. The various derricks and cargo gear was rigged from 3 stout masts. The streamlined Funnel was atop a substantial accommodation area, all cabins having several large windows each and most importantly she was air-conditioned throughout.

My flight was to Fukuoka and I had to go by road to Sasebo, the drive took under 2 hours. Sasebo was a large American Naval Base and renowned for its dry docks and ship repair facilities and later became a major ship building center. Sasebo is in the prefecture of Nagasaki.

Since it had taken me all day to get as far as Sasebo from Hong Kong the Agent checked me into a hotel for the night. I was to be taken to the vessel next day as she was still in dry dock. My Officers and crew were expected to arrive in Sasebo several days later so take over was still a while away.

Early next morning our Japanese Agent collected me from the hotel at which I would stay until the vessel was physically delivered and we moved on board. I arrived at the dock yard and after registering with the shipyard security walked with the agent towards the dry dock in which my new ship was situated. On the way I stopped at the dock office to change into my clean new boiler suite, work boots and hard hat before carrying on to the vessel.

She was a very handsome ship, with prominent bulbous bow, a typical German design of the era. The general arrangement plans I had looked at in Hong Kong did not do the ship justice. Not only was she sleek in design but also, outwardly at least, in immaculate condition. As I walked across the long gangway that connected the ship to the dry dock walls I was greeted by the outgoing Captain. I later discovered he was from a small town between Hamburg and Lubek. Although he was not a young man, he looked very much the part, wearing matching khaki shirt and shorts, a battered Captain's cap with Khaki cover that had seen many years of service and he smoked a pipe, which he lit upon entering his quarters. At first glance he did not look unlike General McArthur from pictures I had seen, even though he was nowhere as tall. He spoke immaculate English, but heavily laced with a German accent. We proceeded to the Captain's office and after removing my boots I entered and sat down. Steaming hot Coffee was served along with some small pastries cooked on board, all in typical German fashion.

The Master and I chatted for a while then the Chief Officer arrived. Following introductions he proceeded to give me a comprehensive tour of the ship. She appeared a fine vessel. The interior bulkheads were real timber veneer, slightly dark in color, yet not too dark. It gave an air of comfort and was not too drab considering all the complementing fittings. This was typified throughout the entire officer's and crew's accommodation but the Captain's cabin had many additional features including an artificial fire place, comfortable lounge suites, in built book shelves and furniture plus a number of very nice oil paintings of a nautical theme situated on various bulkheads. In one corner of the Master's dayroom stood a small bar counter made from solid timber with brass fixtures. There was a nicely furnished conference room and small private dining saloon (with adjoining pantry) that could comfortably sit 8, which I assumed was for passengers if and when carried. It was all together delightful and it had obviously been designed for entertaining charterers and shippers as well as the odd passenger or two. The Captain's office was located next to the private dining saloon, (which I was informed was seldom used) and featured an impressive desk, chairs and filling cabinets as well as the usual office fittings. The Captain's quarters took up the entire deck below the Bridge level.

The wheelhouse was large and spacious with excellent all round visibility and the ship was equipped with two powerful Radars and the very latest in navigation technology. The vessel was highly automated for the period and Engine controls could be operated directly from the Bridge by the Chief Engineer when entering or leaving Port. As her main propulsion she was fitted with a 8000 BHP (Brake Horse Power) MAN Diesel of German manufacture which developed a service speed of 15 knots.

Officer and crew accommodation was also very nicely appointed and she even had cabins for 6 passengers. It goes without saying there was a comfortable Officers Bar and smoke room. The Dining Saloon was simple but very elegant with several round dining tables apart from the Master's table situated in the center. Having viewed the interior, I spent the remainder of the day on deck and in the Engine Room which was immaculate, all of which did not disappoint. I departed the vessel about 5pm and headed back to my hotel together with our Japanese Agent.

As the vessel was changing flag there were numerous surveys and inspection by surveyors appointed by Hong Kong flag state. We progressively worked through all the formalities. I had been informed that my Deck, Radio and Engineering Officers would arrive within a week. The Chief Steward/Purser was to arrive imminently and the remaining catering staff would arrive two days before other crew so the ship could be made ready to accommodate all officers and men upon arrival. The Bosun, deck and engine ratings would arrive along with the officers. The sellers had kindly agreed to retain their Chief Officer and 2nd Engineer on board for two days following the handover to ensure a smooth transition.

I was kept busy ordering charts and admiralty publications at the same time attending to the various Class and Flag State surveyors. Meantime, the Chief Steward had arrived and placed a provision order that would be sufficient for 2 weeks along with other essential items. The plan was that we would take delivery of the vessel in Sasebo then sail direct to Hong Kong where the ship would be fully fitted out and stored, rather in the same way as I had done with "Hoi Hing". The "Hoi Yun" had sufficient fuel, fresh water and reserves on board for us to safely make Hong Kong without the need for further replenishment before departure.

The day arrived when we eventually took formal delivery of the ship. By this time all the new certificates were in order and the names and Port of Registry changed. The Chief Steward, with whom I had not sailed previously, was a highly organized fellow and he did a sterling job preparing and ordering all the basic items necessary so our crew could move aboard with minimal fuss.

My Chief Officer was a Filipino, quite an experienced fellow who had been serving with our company for two years on various ships. He held a Chief Mates Certificate (issued in Hong Kong) and was anticipating sitting for Masters at the conclusion of this assignment, his name was Silvio Ronaldo Del Pelardo but he went by the nickname of "Bolo". I did not presume to enquire as to the origins of the nickname which did not seem even remotely connected to his real name. Our 2nd and 3rd Mates were both Hong Kong Chinese and had each been with the company approaching a year. Radio Officer was Portuguese Chinese from Macau, quite young, only about 23 years of age. The Chief Engineer was a Scot, Alistair James who lived permanently in Hong Kong and had worked for various Hong Kong outfits over the years. He was widely experienced and came highly recommended. His hobby of painting pictures in his spare time whilst at sea was well known and by all accounts he was quite an accomplished artist. He lived in Kowloon and was married to a Chinese lady who had a shop somewhere in Tsim Tsa Tsui that specialized in selling his art work. Occasionally she would join her husband on board for a short trip. The ship's 2nd, 3rd and 4th Engineers were all Hong Kong Chinese and all had been with our company a while. We also carried 2 junior engineers as well as a Fitter and

Electrical Officer on this vessel. Our Deck and Engine Room ratings were a mixed bunch all from Hong Kong but seemed willing enough.

Upon receiving the formal notification from my Office in Hong Kong that the sale transaction had been concluded, we all moved aboard the ship. We soon shifted to an anchorage where we lay for 2 days whilst we organized ourselves and gained some kind of familiarity with our new toy. The 2nd Mate plotted our passage plan to Hong Kong which was only some 1500 nautical miles distant and which I approved following my review. With outward clearance in hand and the previous owners' two officers safely back on dry land, we weighed anchor and departed the anchorage bound for Hong Kong. From the outset the handling characteristics of the vessel appeared good and she performed and responded well. Hong Kong was only about 5 day's steaming away given fair weather conditions, the Chief Engineer not wishing to push the vessel until all his staff had become settled, requested we proceed at a reduced power setting for our voyage to Hong Kong so I agreed to a reduced sea speed of 13 knots for this initial voyage.

Before leaving Sasebo our Japanese agents had mentioned to me unofficially he had heard rumors that after Hong Kong my ship was bound for Australia. I decided not to mention this to anyone but to wait and see knowing that I would receive all the details formally from my management in due course. I was stoked at the prospect of a trip to Australia it being a good few years since I was last there.

Hong Kong was as expected, a number of visitors from our office coming aboard soon after we arrived to look at the
latest addition to the fleet. It was true, we were going to

go to Australia but first the company wished to overhaul all the cargo gear, life saving appliances and Radio Station to avoid any possible conflict with authorities "Down Under" who had a reputation for being extremely thorough and zealous in their safety inspections of ships, especially if foreign flag on a first call at an Australian Port.

Undeservedly, Hong Kong was viewed by some as being a dubious Flag, only registering clapped out old buckets on their last legs, poorly manned and maintained; used mainly to tramp around the China Seas and Asia out of the sight of regulatory authorities. Whilst Hong Kong did have its share of ageing tonnage (so did many other registries) in fact the concept of it being a second rate Flag was far from being true since the Hong Kong Registry was very strict and demanding in its requirements and cloned to closely followed the United Kingdom in the implementation of most shipping rules and regulations. Based on my previous experience with our company, as far as I was concerned, our operations and maintenance standards were excellent and in some cases far superior to those of many other major seafaring nations; so any doubts about the Hong Kong Flag in my view was a pure myth. Much of the criticism came from those who were limited in their knowledge of the worldwide shipping industry or had conflicting commercial interests; true, Hong Kong did have its share of shady ship owners out to make a fast buck any which way, at the expense of their ships, but then Hong Kong was not alone in that regard. In my view Hong Kong ranked towards the top of Flag States.

Rightly or wrongly, the Maritime and Stevedore Unions in Australia were also flagged as being very vigilant and known to be militant on occasions, but in fairness to them, suffice it to say there is seldom smoke without fire. Hence our owners' wished to make certain that everything was in absolute tip top order before we headed south, safety being the absolute priority. Maintenance work at Hong Kong was expected to take 7-10 days but whilst in progress it afforded us the opportunity to fully settle in on board, conduct some emergency drills – including lowering lifeboats to the water, and take on stores, provisions, bunkers and Fresh Water. We would soon be ready.

I was summoned to the office for a briefing and whilst sipping my iced coffee it was confirmed that owners were serious in their intention to establish a regular liner service between the Far East and the East Coast of Australia. The final rotation would always be subject to cargo inducement but our main marketing Hub in Australia would be Brisbane. To this end, our company had established an office in Brisbane some months earlier to pave the way for this new enterprise.

35 Inaugurating a New Trade

In the overall scheme of things, "Hoi Yun" was to
depart Hong Kong on the inaugural trip with assorted
general cargo and containers and proceed via
Melbourne, Sydney and Brisbane, in that rotation. The
ship would then revert with whatever break bulk or
containerized cargo that could be secured for Singapore,
Bangkok and Hong Kong. Calls at any intermediate
ports en-route, in either direction, were always
dependent on cargo bookings..

Apparently market research conducted by our chartering
and marketing departments demonstrated clearly,
although the route was currently serviced by others,
there was generally a carryover of cargo due to a
shortfall in multi-purpose shipping capacity. This
shortfall was our target. The secret was that our ships
were fully self-sustaining for both containerized and
general cargo so therefore were not required to rely on
specialized container berths. In addition we had 16
reefer points for "Freezer Containers" which enabled us
to carry frozen products in containers on deck. We were
advantaged by being more flexible than some of our
competitors and being a ship of some 15 knots, and
hopefully soon to be supplemented by one or two sister
vessels, a regular express service could be provided for
prospective shippers at competitive rates. I was excited
by the prospects of this new trade. Our ship would be
considered a feeder vessel in some ways particularly in
terms of containers, offering transshipment at either
Singapore or Hong Kong for onward Ports, East or
West, outside the scope of our operations.

Over ensuing days we loaded a good many containers in
mid-stream ex barge as well as 1700 tons of assorted
General Cargo mostly manufactured goods, much of it

originating in China and transshipped in Hong Kong. Once completed, we wasted no time in getting under way. We sailed in the evening, slowly and majestically towards Green Island and the Sulphur Channel, amongst a magnificent array of lights that typified Hong Kong at night. Our Pilot disembarked off Green Island and we worked up to full sea speed as we sped off down the Lamma Channel, Singapore bound. The ship was very solid in the water and rolled and pitched majestically to fresh winds and moderate seas which we encountered once clear of the off lying Islands to the South of Hong Kong.

Morning brought overcast skies and high following seas which helped us on our way. The Walker's Log which we always streamed, indicated we were doing a speed of almost 16 knots. The constant whining of our diesel engine turbochargers was reassuring. At this rate of progress our old friend Horsburgh Light House would be on our beam in only 4 days time.

The favorable weather remained with us as we navigated our way between the Paracel Islands and Maclesfield Banks. There were few fishing boats about due to the freshening conditions, which was good because they could be difficult to spot when there were many white caps about and being small they often dropped out of sight momentarily, when in the deeper sea troughs. Additionally, being of wooden construction they did not make strong echoes or targets on the Radar screen. This trip was a turn up for the books because contrary to many previous voyages the weather around the southern part of Vietnam was surprisingly placid, which remained until we passed our old friend, the Horsburgh Light House, and entered the Singapore Straits.

At Singapore, additional containers and break bulk cargo was loaded for our 3 main ports of call in Australia; Melbourne, Sydney and lastly Brisbane. This was also when I learned that on our return trip from Australia we would call at Port Moresby in Papua New Guinea where we were to load 1500 tons of bagged Coffee for part discharge at both Singapore and Bangkok. A northbound call at Surabaya in Indonesia was also flagged as a possibility but would only be confirmed later and closer to the time. This early information gave me the opportunity to order the necessary additional Admiralty Charts for both destinations.

Our sea route from Singapore to Melbourne was to be through the Karimata Straits, Java Sea, Lombok Straight and then across the Indian Ocean; finally paralleling the west coast of Australia as far south as Cape Leeuwin, at which point we would then alter course more south easterly to cross the Great Australian Bight towards Melbourne. The sea distance was about 4550 nautical miles and provided we averaged our anticipated sea speed of 15 knots, the passage would take about 13 days, but in the final analysis it was really all dependent on the weather. I reveled in the challenge.

It was a humid and miserably rainy afternoon when we sailed from Singapore and the visibility was only moderate at the best. Nevertheless, once underway matters started to resolve themselves; the visibility improved and the sun came out and soon dried off the decks. By 6 pm we were passing our familiar beacon the Horsburgh Lighthouse and not long thereafter the duty officer set our course for the Karimata Straits.

The next morning we were behold with a beautiful sight of the mountainous terrain as we approached the Karimata strait. The mountains appeared to be dancing in the heavens in the early morning mist. Obviously a mirage caused by refraction. Traffic was unusually scarce but as we edged more towards the Java Sea the numbers of ships began to build. The weather was perfect, with the sea being as flat as a pancake and with just the slightest of light airs. The sea was so calm and flat that it was difficult to distinguish the horizon from the sea as they merged into one. The only disturbance to the shimmering sea was the Dolphins that played about the vessel for an hour or so, leaping continuously yet easily keeping pace with us as we forged ahead at a steady 15 knots. By late afternoon we were making fine progress when we came upon a fleet of about 6 beautifully painted Arab Dhows heading across our bows in the direction of Borneo, but becalmed because of the lack of wind. We passed relatively close astern of them attracting waves from their crews as we rushed by, soon leaving them in our wake. It was not long before they had disappeared over the horizon astern

By this time, being well away from any visible land except for the odd volcanic peaks on remote horizons, we reverted to celestial navigation, taking sights morning, noon and night of the Sun, Stars and planets. From time to time I joined the Mates in these daily activities in order to keep my mind sharp. Our 2nd Mate who was the ship's principal navigator was very keen and diligent regarding his duties all of which he performed admirably. His work was exquisitely neat and well presented. Another aspect of his work was to draw up Cargo Plans and the ones he produced were excellent, beautifully scaled and color coded. I was entirely satisfied with his performance. However, in fairness, I should say that all officers and crew were functioning well which went a long way towards making the "Hoi Yun" a very happy ship.

The Java Sea, Laut Jawa to Indonesians, more or less runs East-West and is approximately 1000 miles long. To the north it is bordered by the Island of Borneo and to the north east by Makassar Island; whilst to the east lie the Celebes, Flores and Bali Seas. The large Island of Java lies to the South, from which the sea derives its name, naturally. The Lombok Strait (through which we would later pass) is one of the main arterial links between the Java Sea and Indian Ocean.

The Java Sea is a relatively shallow sea by comparison to some other waters in the Indonesian archipelago and is scattered with numerous coral reefs and atolls in some sections, many concealing their own stories going by the number of wrecks sitting askew high and dry on some of them.

Java Island itself is strewn with both active and extinct volcanoes and volcanic cones with their tell tale smoke plumes which can be seen with the naked eye from a considerable distance.

Our charted course would take us between the famous Madura Island and Kangean Island prior to entering the northern approaches of Lombok Strait which is flanked by the Island of Bali to the west, the Island of Lombok to the east with Nusa Peneda Island in the center of the strait's southern sector. It is quite a wide passage being about 25 miles in the north and 12-13 miles in the south. The length of the strait north to south is about 37 miles overall. The depth varies between 1000 meters in the north and progressively reduces to about 300 meters in the southern part; because it is much deeper than the Malacca Straits it is often the preferred route for the largest tankers and bulk carriers with deeper drafts plying east to west, it being considered a safer option. The currents within the straits are very fast flowing most of the time, the predominant direction being from north to south.

On the day before we were scheduled to arrive at the top end of the Lombok Strait I invited the Chief Engineer to my cabin for a pre-lunch drink. The Chief arrived with a gift – the most splendid water color painting of the "Hoi Yun" as she ploughed through the seas; it was superb and correct in every detail. I was absolutely delighted and intended to have it framed at the first opportunity and mounted on the bulkhead in my office where it would be in full view for everyone to see and admire. I offered to buy it because of its exquisite quality and artistic workmanship but the Chief refused to accept any offer whatsoever – I felt very privileged. Alistair claimed he had two others on the go which, when completed he intended to place in the officer's Bar. According to the Chief Engineer it only took him about 6 or 8 hours to produce such a work of art. He was very gifted indeed and claimed to be an artist out of love and a Marine Engineer out of necessity.

Our daylight transit through the Straits of Lombok was interesting. We attracted a large flock of seabirds that followed us in our wake all waiting to pounce on surface fish which had been disturbed by our wake and to take the food scraps that were discarded by the ship's cook. The picturesque scenery was stunning and all the waters appeared absolutely pristine except for the odd log floating by. By nightfall we were well clear and starting to feel the long ocean swells for which the Indian Ocean is renowned. The movement of the ship increased marginally but it was still quite comfortable for us on board. The Indian Ocean is the third largest of the world's five oceans.

With the mountainous terrain of Indonesia now disappearing astern we adjusted our course South South

Easterly towards the coast of Western Australia, intending to make a landfall about 20 miles to seaward of the Coral Coast and the Shark Bay area, from that point onwards we would parallel the coast down towards Cape Leeuwin, maintaining our distance off the land. This was quite a monotonous part of the voyage and the days passed slowly, nevertheless our Chief Mate "Bolo" kept our crew meaningfully employed carrying out a multitude of jobs to finally prepare ourselves for arrival at Melbourne. During our passage we had conducted our mandatory Boat and Emergency Drills and exercised the crew in various aspects of Fire Fighting and shipboard training. Meantime our main engine continued to run faultlessly under the watchful eye and guidance of Alistair James and his team.

Eventually, some days later we made our landfall off Cape Leeuwin. It was during the night and the piecing light house situated on the Cape was easy to sight. The lighthouse light, which has an intensity of one million candle power, has a range of about 26 miles so its welcoming loom was easily detected after our boring days at sea since passing Lombok. Surprisingly, the weather was not so boisterous as we rounded the Cape but some hours later we encountered the traditional building seas which were the signature of the "Great Australian Bight", progressively adjusted our course towards the Bass Straits and Port Philip Heads which is the entry point into Port Philip Bay in which the Port of Melbourne lies, at the mouth of the Yarra River.

The weather was now turning colder as we transited the more southerly latitudes. The following seas were quite steep and rough but they did not retard our sea speed by any significant amount as we rolled and pitched endlessly. We encountered strong winds and frequently solid green seas would cascade over our forecastle as our bows dipped into the deep ocean troughs causing showers of sea spray to engulf the decks. Nevertheless, "Hoi Yun" held her own riding out the weather comfortable and without causing us any kind of concern. By the time we passed the Port of Portland, the lights of which were crystal clear to Port in the cold environment, the seas had lost most of their vengeance for our arrival off the Pilot Station at Port Philip Heads.

I was surprised to see that the Pilot was a British fellow but whom had lived in Australia for some years. We entered Port Philip Heads with Point Lonsdale to port we transited the tidal race for which the "Heads" are well known and were soon within the expanses of Port Philip Bay, which is quite large. The bay is relatively shallow so navigation is restricted to a buoyed channel. To our port side was Queenscliff, Portarlington and the larger Port of Geelong. Melbourne still lay some distance away located off our starboard bow. As we progressed towards the mouth of the River Yarra and the Port of Melbourne the outer suburbs of Sorento, Frankston and St. Kilda glided past to starboard. Slowly the various seaside towns merged into the large city of Melbourne. Our berth was to be at Victoria Dock and within a couple of hours we were safely secured alongside – we had arrived.

Since our arrival was late on a Saturday afternoon our Agents informed us that offloading would commence at 07.30 am on Monday morning. This was greeted with enthusiasm since it meant we would have Sunday off in which to enjoy the hospitality of Melbourne for which it was famous amongst sailors.

Sunday in Melbourne greeted us with rain and windy conditions, rather typical for a city renowned for having all four seasons in a single day! Nevertheless, the weather did not dampen our spirits and our intention to make the most of what Melbourne could offer. About

10am the rain eased so I decided it was about time to set off on my trip ashore. Once outside the dock gate the first thing that struck me was how quiet it was being devoid of both people and traffic. Following a short walk, I hopped on a city bound tram (for which Melbourne was celebrated) and after a short but interesting journey I alighted near the junction of Collins and Elizabeth Streets. This was indeed the heart of the city. Unfortunately many of the shops were closed, it being Sunday, but all the same I was pleased to have the opportunity for a break from shipboard life and also stretch my legs for a while.

I meandered for a time just window shopping and then at lunch time I decided to visit China Town for "Yum Cha". China Town in Melbourne was great; located in an area bounded by Lonsdale, Bourke, Swanston and Spring Streets it covers quite an area and is ideally situated in the City Center. I headed for the recently established "Flower Drum" Chinese restaurant which had already become known as one of the top "Cantonese Style" restaurants in Melbourne. It was a very elegant restaurant that served excellent cuisine but what impressed me most was how well it was organized; unlike most "Yum Cha" restaurants I visited in Hong Kong which were bordering on chaotic with the number of people scrambling for a table and in some cases literally standing next to your table whilst you ate, waiting for you to depart. Weekends were the worst time for crowding.

My next stop was "The Mitre Tavern", by now it was after 6pm and the pubs were open. The "Mitre" was an interesting Pub with a friendly atmosphere. Being situated in Bank Place, just off Little Collins Street, it was out of sight for most passersby but I knew of its existence from previous visits to the city. Nevertheless, it was an architectural gem, very popular with a loyal clientele and was always well patronized. I only downed two beers then decided it was time for dinner and very conveniently, only yards away, was an Indian Restaurant.

Having enjoyed a good curry it was time to return to my ship so I decided to walk back, which turned out to be a mistake as it was little further than I had anticipated and it had started to rain again. In any event I was back on board by 10.00pm. As I entered the Victoria Dock gate I saw many of my Chinese crew heading off ashore; I suspect to China Town or perhaps towards the St. Kilda area which was the place for a sailor's night time entertainment. So ended my visit to Melbourne but next time I would make sure the shops were open.

At 07.30am on Monday morning the Australian "Wharfies" trooped on board and without any ado started rigging the derricks and hatchways ready for discharge. There was an air of anticipation on our part as Australian "Wharfies" were universally known for their reputation for militancy and difficult ways at times. However, there is never smoke without fire and from my experience in dealing with them if all ship operations were safe and the regulations complied with, there was generally no issue. In our case all went well and we kicked off our discharging without any industrial disputes (the efforts made by our Owners in Hong Kong in properly preparing the vessel paid off). We also received a visit from the Maritime Union V.O (Vigilance Officer) which was conducted without incident. We worked continuously from 07.30 through to 21.30 Hours daily. In the warehouse adjacent to our jetty was a large shed in which cargo was continually being received and stored in readiness for our back loading when the time arose.

We spent 5 enjoyable days in Melbourne during which
we successfully discharged our cargo and back loaded a
combination of containerized and break bulk cargo for
our Asian Ports of call. Our next Port was indeed
Sydney in the State of New South Wales, a distance of a
tad under 600 miles so about 2.5 days steaming for us,
all going well. Once clear of the Bass Straits our first
landmark of note was Gabo Island with its towering
lighthouse. Situated on Malacoota Inlet it more or less
marks the territorial boundary between the Australian
States of Victoria and New South Wales but importantly
for the mariner is the divide between the Indian and
Pacific Oceans. We sailed on by enjoying unusually fine
weather and pristine surroundings, leaving Cape Howe
astern in our wake as we progressed.

Just a little further up the coast is the aptly named
Disaster Bay and Two Fold Bay. Disaster Bay is
historically linked to the numerous shipwrecks that have
occurred in the area since the time of Captain Cooke and
later the First Fleet.

The prominent whaling port of Eden lies quite close,
only a short distance northward situated on Two Fold
Bay, so located due to its proximity to the routes taken
by Whales on their annual southerly migration to
Antarctica. In its hay day Eden was very busy and the
focal point to the then significant whaling industry in
south east Australia. However, since the decline of the
whaling industry this charming town has become a
favorite tourist destination not only because of its
historic connections to early Australian European
settlers but also as a spectacular location for modern day
Whale watchers. The Eden of today is still a working
Port and is supposedly the third deepest in the southern

hemisphere but it is now more reliant on its Timber related exports. This region of the coastline is appropriately named the Sapphire Coast, its rugged coastline making it easily visible to us from seaward as we continued our northerly course, passing the delightfully named towns of Pambula, Merimbula, Bermagui, Jervis Bay, Illawarra and Wollongong, to name but a few, as we edged closer to our destination of Sydney.

Port Kembla and Wollongong, which both almost merge with each other, lies only about 50 or so miles south of Sydney. Port Kembla is an industrial town being a major coal exporting port and also with a large Steel Works. It had been many years since I last visited Port Kembla, actually when as a first trip Apprentice, at which time we loaded a cargo of coal for Japan. On the other end of the spectrum the adjoin city of Wollongong has more of a seaside atmosphere and is nowadays considered almost an outer suburb of Greater Sydney.

Few places in the world can match the Australian Coast for pristine surroundings. Both the seas and skys are brilliant blue, spectacular beaches and picturesque coastline, not to mention the abundance of sunshine (well for most of the time) so it is quite easy to understand the passion all Australians hold for their native land. Australia always has been a favorite amongst seafarers who appreciate the countries unique beauty and friendly atmosphere. Our arrival in Sydney encompassed all of this.

There can be few places in the world that can rival the magnificence of Sydney Harbor. As one approaches from seaward one is awed by stunning panoramas aptly highlighted by now well known icons. The Sydney Opera House which was formally opened in 1973, not long before our visit, is dominantly situated on

Bennelong Point adjacent to the Sydney Harbor Bridge and close to the Botanic Gardens, all of which are within walking distance of down town Sydney. The development of the working Port and ongoing expansion of the city skyline is truly indicative of a city on the move.

It is easy therefore, to understand why Captain Arthur Phillip decided this would be an ideal location for a penal colony and the first European settlement when he arrived with the First Fleet at Sydney Cove in 1788.

On this occasion our destination was a wharf close to what is now Darling Harbor and therefore adjacent to the city itself, but unfortunately for me, Sydney was to be a non-event. I was suddenly struck with a severe case of influenza and following a visit to the local Doctor I was dosed up with medication and ordered to be confined to bed rest for 3 days. I have to say that I did not argue as I was feeling so unwell and very weak indeed.

The chief Mate looked after the running the ship very efficiently during my incapacitation and our young 2nd Mate, acting in his capacity as ship's medic, was very attentive to his duties visiting me 3 times per day to check me out and to ensure I was taking my medication. Luckily I recovered just in time for our departure from Sydney but I was very fatigued and tired quickly for some time afterwards. This bout struck me extremely harshly because I am the type that seldom if ever, suffers a sick day.

Whilst in Sydney I had been informed by our agents that when in Brisbane we would be loading cargo for calls at Bougainville Island in Papua New Guinea, The ports of Kieta and Anew Bay, prior to returning to Asia. We would be back loading cargo at Kieta for Singapore and Hong Kong. I had been to Bougainville on previous voyages, loading logs and bagged Sago, so I had a good idea of what to expect.

By comparison to Melbourne and Sydney, Brisbane appeared to be very relaxed and lay-back. It was quite picturesque and obviously somewhat warmer but nevertheless gave the impression of being less sophisticated than the other two cities. It was a friendly place, the residents being very welcoming, like in most other ports throughout Australia. It by no means fits with the notion held by some of it being backward or a "Cowboy" town. In fact it was very pleasant as a port of call with quite a distinctive charm

Situated in southern quadrant of Morton and Bramble Bays, at the lower reaches of the Brisbane River, towards Fisherman's Island, Brisbane is quite a sprawling city and from seaward the coastal plain seems quite low lying with only a few mountain peaks visible some distance inland. The Port itself, whilst not being the largest was undergoing a period of transformation at this time; basically preparing for the transition from bulk and break bulk to containerization. This is why a ship such as ours, being virtually multipurpose and self sustaining was such a valuable asset during this period of transition and was ideally suited. Our Chief Steward took the opportunity to stock up with some prime seafood and meat for our voyage north, much to the delight of officers and crew. I too took the opportunity to replenish the Captains Bond and supplement it with some very fine Australian wines for our ship's bar. I also purchased several cases of Bundaberg Rum, which proved very popular.

I did not venture ashore in Brisbane as I was still feeling quite weak following my recent bout of flu, I had been warned by the Doctor not to overdo things. It was a real effort to descend the several decks to the Dining Saloon and Officers Bar. We discharged our Brisbane cargo without incident and loaded a good number of assorted containers for Asian Ports. Additionally, we back loaded quite a large number of palletized provisions and general goods for Kieta, plus 25 containers of industrial machinery to be discharged at Anewa Bay for the Panguna Copper Mine. Although both Ports were only a stone's throw apart, it did require a two port call because the roads and infrastructure between Kieta and Anewa Bay was poor and not suited for the transportation of heavy container trucks. We were also booked to load 600 tons of New Guinea Coffee and Cocoa at Kieta for Singapore as well as 140 bundles of sawn prime Ebony for Hong Kong.

During our stay in Brisbane we replenished bunker fuel and fresh water as well as about 15 units of 200 liter drums of various lubricating oils. Our Chief Engineer Alistair James had kept his staff fully occupied whilst in Australian Ports pulling several Main Engine Pistons, overhauling Generators and other critical machinery. He was a man that led from the front and was down the Engine Room supervising his engineers most of the time. He operated very efficiently and was the type of man that exuded confidence.

37 The Solomons and Paradise Islands

We departed Brisbane on a sunny Wednesday afternoon
and it was not long before we were clear of Morton Bay
and heading northerly towards the Coral and Solomon
Seas towards the Island of Bougainville. Our initial
passage took us past the Township of Noosa Heads and
Fraser Island. This was the area in which the Singapore
registered ship "Cherry Venture" had been driven
aground at Teewah Beach due to very heavy storm
whilst on passage from Auckland to Brisbane. Due to a
combination of being in ballast and very high seas she
became stranded well up the sandy beach where she
remained until mid 2000s before her rusting remains
were finally removed. During this period she became
quite a tourist attraction for beachgoers and
photographers.

The Coral Sea is characterized by a warm and stable
climate, with frequent rains and tropical Cyclones at
certain times of the year. Within the bounds of the Coral
Sea are strewn numerous islands and reefs, It merges
with the Solomon Sea in the north as one approaches the
Solomon Islands Archipelago. It is pristine and is
renowned for its high concentration of different species
of fish, Turtles and birds which are abundant on the
scattered reefs and islets.

Our passage across the Coral Sea was quite good, for
most part we experienced South Easterly Trade winds,
from just abaft out starboard beam. We rolled a little but
otherwise we enjoyed a good transit. Our charted course
to Kieta took us through the passage between the
Shortland and Choiseul Islands at the far northwest end
of New Georgia Sound, then we adjusted course more to
the north and paralleled the coast of Bougainville
towards Kieta.

Bougainville Island is the easternmost island of Papua New Guinea, located in the Solomon Sea. Geographically, Bougainville Island forms part of the North Solomon Islands archipelago and is the largest of the Solomon Islands located near the northern end of that chain. Bougainville is about 90 miles long and 50 miles wide at the widest point, however for the most part it is elongated. It is very mountainous in the North and South regions. The shores are fringed with palm trees, mangroves, magnificent silver sand beaches and coral reefs. Occasionally one would pass a small village or Coconut plantation on the coastline nestled amongst the palms. It is highly tropical in every way imaginable, extremely beautiful with turquoise blue seas. It was every person's idyllic notion of paradise. In fact, Papua New Guinea including some of its satellite Islands, is the home of the Bird of Paradise which live in the dense tropical rain forests of the islands. The Bird of Paradise is of significant importance in local culture, especially their beautifully colored plumage; it also features prominently in their national flag, following their granting of independence.

Bougainville is also the location where the Japanese Fleet Admiral Yamamoto, the architect of "Pearl Harbor" was killed when the plane in which he was travelling crashed into the jungle. On April 8th, 1943 his aircraft was intercepted and shot down by American fighter bombers near Buin in the southern part of Bougainville Island, after allied code breakers were able to decipher signals and details of his flight plan and organize aircraft to wait in ambush.

Originally, Bougainville Island was under German administration but was occupied by Australian forces in 1914 and included in an Australian mandate in 1920. The Japanese occupied the Island during the Second World War but were ousted by the Americans and Australians in 1944. Papua New Guinea, including Bougainville, was administered by Australia from 1945 to 1975 when Independence was granted. At the time of our visit however, most of the Island administration, Port Officials, Senior Customs and Police Officers were still Australian or New Zealand expatriates.

Kieta is a beautiful little port located in an inlet surrounded by heavily forested mountainous terrain. The Port is quite small and only provides a single deepwater berth which is generally used by ocean going vessels and therefore in constant demand, although it does have a small coastal jetty close to hand. Upon our arrival it was occupied by a very handsome looking Bank Line vessel, so we spent a peaceful day at anchor in the calm crystal clear waters soaking up the picturesque tropical scenery and atmosphere. The small white buildings encroaching the hillside behind Kieta Port made for an idyllic setting and very conducive to sitting on deck in the evening drinking Gin and Tonics as the sun dipped below the horizon, lighting up the sky in a brilliant variety of colors, and casting a shadow over the surrounding mountains. Sunrise or sunset always enhanced the sweet tropical odors drifting seaward on the light airs, originating from the lush jungle.

Alistair, our Chief Engineer, took to painting during the time at the anchorage and brought out his paints and easel to capture the land and seascapes and transform them to canvas. What amazed me was the ease and speed at which all of Alistair's paintings came to life.

Even pictures of shipboard activities and portraits of crew grew from a single stroke of his brush and became a beautiful canvas in what seemed like no time at all. They were all excellent; he was indeed a very gifted artist and it all seemed effortless and come so naturally to him.

The Pilot cum Harbor Master was a New Zealander, ex Union Steamship Company, who had been resident in Kieta for some years. Both he and his wife were local celebrities amongst the expatriate community. The Harbor Master was a great conversationalist always ready to convey a litany of sea tales of the South Pacific, where he had been and how he had done everything, he claimed to be the most experienced mariner in the Pacific Islands (??).

Not wishing to be outdone and sensing the opportunity to promote our ship's participation into the new trade, I arranged a Curry lunch on board for all the Port dignitaries, officials and shippers, who were mostly Australian expats at this time, along with their wives. Fortunately, our ship was blessed with good accommodation and facilities for entertaining, so it seemed appropriate it should be utilized. As our stay in Kieta was estimated to be two-three days the party was organized for the day after we got alongside the main wharf.

Once alongside the single wharf, which our ship alone occupied, we set about discharging the cargo we had loaded in Brisbane. Pallet upon Pallet of food stuffs, most destined for the local "Steamships" supermarket and smaller trade stores; simultaneously we commenced back loading our bagged Coffee and Cocoa in separate cargo holds. The bundles of sawn Timber would be loaded in N0 1 lower hold which had been prepared and reserved for the purpose.

Our Chief Steward and his team had been busy preparing for the Curry Lunch I had sprung on them at the last moment. Party day arrived and even I was surprised by the variety of curries and complimentary dishes, deserts, fruits and other delights. I had given the Chief Steward AU$400 from ship's funds to spend on local produce – he was a very astute shopper because I even received back change of $75.

All of our invited guests arrived at 12 noon (every single person invited turned up). Pre-lunch drinks in the Ship's Bar followed by a magnificent curry buffet lunch, consisting Fish Head, Mutton, Beef, Chicken and Prawn curries with a wide selection of excellent Asian deserts. Everyone tucked in heartily and obviously enjoyed it going by the numbers that went for a second (and in some cases third) round.

Eventually, at about 4pm, the last guests departed very contented, and the catering staff set about cleaning up ready for normal evening meals. I was very pleased with the outcome and made a point to thank the Chief Steward and his catering staff for such an excellent turnout. No doubt our ship, and Company, would be remembered for some time to come.

Below is a snap of the delightfully picturesque Kieta Bay showing the main wharf, at Bougainville Island, in mid 1970's. It was remote, undisturbed and idyllic, epitomizing the perfect escape.

PNG Ports Corporation Ltd – Port of Kieta

With all our cargo for Kieta discharged, which was likely already on display in the supermarket and trade store shelves, and our bagged Cocoa and Coffee Beans together with the bundled Timber nicely stowed on board, it was time for us to depart. The New Zealand Harbor Master came on board for the short Pilotage to Anewa Bay. At the time of our visit there was a small resort situated on "Arovo Island" that lies just off the main Island between which is a narrow but deep channel connecting Kieta Bay to Anewa Bay. It was very pretty and always a popular weekend getaway for expats working for Bougainville Copper (BCL). Sadly, I am told that the resort no longer exists because of the closure of the Copper Mine and all that now remains is a jetty and shipwrecked fishing vessel, which according to locals is home to a very large snake. The island has since become something of a bird sanctuary.

To avoid a long trip outside the outlying reefs to Anewa Bay we carefully negotiated the narrow "Arovo" passage much to the delight of the many holiday makers enjoying the resort beach. The beautiful "Pok Pok Island" also lies close to hand. "Pok Pok in Tok Pisin (Pidgin English) means Crocodile so if you wanted an adjustable spanner for example, you would request a "Pok Pok.Spanner" because of the open and closing jaws It is a very descriptive language and not too difficult to learn rather quickly. It was spoken by most expatriates with varying degrees of fluency.

Once clear our Kieta Pilot departed and the Anewa Bay Pilot embarked. Kieta was a Government Port whereas Anewa Bay was a Private Port, leased and built by Bougainvill Copper Ltd who operated the copper mine up the mountain at Panguna, hence the need for different Pilots. Anewa Bay operated a small tug of about 500 BHP and a small landing craft type vessel used mainly to service local navigation buoys and markers.

Anewa Bay is no less beautiful than Kieta although a little larger and more open. There are two jetties, one deepwater jetty for oceangoing vessels such as ours and the Large Bulk Carriers that transport the bulk Copper Concentrate exported to overseas destinations. The other was a small jetty for coastal shipping which lies a short distance away. A single buoy mooring was located across the other side of the bay, used by tankers to transfer fuel and oil to a small tank farm nestling amongst the Palms on the shoreline, which was known locally as "Shell Corner".

Coasters plying the New Guinea waters mainly consist of landing craft type vessels fitted with bow ramps so that they can just pull in to any of the numerous copra plantations dotted around the coast line. During this period in time it was often the case that the Master and Chief Engineer on such coasters were Australian expatriates who had resided in Papua New Guinea for decades, many having been "Coast Watchers" during

WW2 in some of the more remote outlaying Papua New Guinea Islands, and had opted to stay on. They were so familiar with various islands and surrounding waters in which they traded, they seldom if ever used nautical charts. A number of these expatriates had gone "Tropo" (local term for assuming a semi-native lifestyle) over the years but irrespective were very competent with a wide knowledge of the local waters and of course were fluent in "Pidgin" spoken widely by most of Bougainville's population as well as throughout PNG. Many had married PNG women and had "Pikininis", which in Tok Tok Pigin means Children. Many of these mixed race children had delightful personalities, the largest of large eyes and even blondish colored hair in many cases. Unfortunately, there were some "Tropo" types that relied on the Gin Bottle and local wives, mostly to support their derelict ways.

Many of the plantations scattered around the coastal regions were managed by large trading companies and supervised by resident expatriate planters so these small coastal landing craft were their lifeline to the outside world. It must have been a very lonely existence sailing on the coasters or living on the plantations with little opportunity for interaction with mainstream society. The only other regular visitors were missionaries, of which there seemed no shortage. The missionaries moved about in style, mostly in single engine light aircraft and used the jungle airstrips which most plantations had constructed and subsequently maintained in case of emergency.

At Anewa Bay the large wharf was free so we immediately berthed starboard side alongside. The Pilot cum Assistant Harbor Master was British, as were most of the supporting supervisory personnel. News travelled fast because the Pilot knew all about our curry extravaganza in Kieta and what a success it had been.

Anyway, I gave an undertaking that the next time we called at Anewa Bay it would be their turn.

Once alongside I noticed that the Port was beautifully manicured and landscaped. I was led to understand by the Pilot that the local stevedore labor who were enlisted by BCL where kept employed during periods when there was no scheduled shipping, to beautify the Port and gardens. This included the gardens of senior Expats' houses in Arawa, the main township and administrative center, which lies more or less mid-way between Anewa Bay and Kieta. It was indeed a botanical garden with numerous species of plants and trees all meticulously tended. Not far distant from the main wharf was a large single story building, nestled in amongst very ornate gardens, which was used for Port Administration. It was nick named the "Pink Palace" because the material from which it was fabricated turned a light shade of pink when it rained. We did experience a short period of rain during our stay and the nickname turned out to be quite apt.

A short drive away from the Port area was "Loloho". This was a superb little beach with "Dongas" (small self contained living quarters) that were available for rent for those BCL staff from Panguna or Arawa who wished to spend leisure time at the beach. Some single expats working on the Copper Concentrator at the Port also chose to reside at Loloho in a compound known as Camp 6.

The beach itself was not overly large but secluded and magnificent with ionic silver sand and lazy Palms swaying gracefully in the sea breezes. The water was absolutely clear and safe. About 200 meters off shore was a coral reef (Mango Reef) which prevented sharks and the like from venturing too close to the beach but once crossed there was a sheer drop into the dark blue depths of the Pacific Ocean. At night one could watch out door movies on the big screen or enjoy B-B-Q's and of course "South Pacific Beer" which was the local brew and readily available from several small beach bars close by. To be honest South Pacific Beer (locally referred to as "SP") was not bad at all and in my view did not warrant the local nickname of "Swamp Piss".

About 500 meters from the main wharf was another lovely beech, named "Baird's Beach" going by a brass plaque on one of the largest rocks (reportedly named after one of the Port Officials) also great for swimming but it was surrounded to deep water and not so well protected from the open ocean's nastier creatures, in particular high numbers of sea snakes which frequented the vicinity – hence swimming was not recommended because it had its risks. It was also only about 100m long so soon became crowded at weekends with sun worshipers looking for an improved bronzy or venue for a beachside B-B-Q.

Just off "Baird's Beach" was a buoy mooring used exclusively for the pleasure yacht belonging to the BCL Managing Director. It was a beautiful craft and named "Loloho" (I think) but it was more commonly known to all as the "Panguna Maru".

At that time the closest township of Arawa had no airstrip but was serviced by a very good airport facility built by BCL, not far beyond Kieta. It was called Aropa International Airport and catered for BCL corporate jets, Fokker F27 and DC 3 aircraft belonging to Air New Guinea. Daily services were available to Port Moresby and direct to Melbourne for BCL executive jets. It also catered for some of the smaller PNG regional air operators. It was quite a busy little airport as it was the only conduit for expatriate BCL staff and families moving on and off the island.

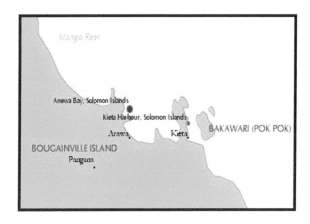

A sketch Map showing Kieta and Anewa Bay. The resort of "Arovo Island" was located just North of the Kieta Peninsula next to "Pok Pok"Island.

The beautifully placid Loloho Beach, the Dongas were scattered all about amongst the Palms.

Our stay was just one day, it only took us about 6 hours to offload the small consignment of containers but we were required to wait until they had all been deconsolidated and the empty modules back loaded. The reason for this was that Anewa Bay was a little off the normal shipping route as far as containers were concerned, rather like an "Outpost of the Empire" so in order to ensure we received our containers back quickly it was necessary to wait until they were emptied. This only took about half a day and it was around 6pm when the stevedores finally back loaded the last empty unit.

Departure from Anewa Bay necessitated us passing close between two Coral Reefs. They not being very well marked and without lighted beacons, I decided therefore, to delay our departure until first light the following morning for safety reasons. Anewa Bay can experience unannounced heavy rain squalls which reduce visibility to zero and seriously wipe out the effectiveness of our radars in such conditions.

Our crew took the opportunity spend the evening at Loloho to watch outdoor movies and enjoy a few Beers – transport to and from had been conveniently arranged by the Port Manager so it was an easy excursion for them all and a nice ending for a pleasant visit to Bougainville Island.

Bougainville is without doubt a really beautiful location, a true Island of Paradise and I am fortunate to have seen it at its best. Unfortunately, later there was what was termed the Bougainville Crisis which was a huge political upheaval when Bougainville unilaterally separated from Papua New Guinea. This in turn developed into a rebel uprising which became so serious and dangerous that the Bougainville Copper Mine closed down and the owners (CRT) repatriated all their expatriates, completely abandoning the mine and Arawa administrative township, the consequences of which curtailed the Island's only real source of income.

The demise of the copper mine and the associated funds over ensuing years caused all the equipment and supporting infrastructure to fall into disrepair and become derelict very quickly in the hot, damp tropical climate. Much of the local economy dried up including such wonderful spots as the Arovo Island Resort, amongst other businesses. I have never been back since, preferring to retain my memories of what it was like when I last visited this Island of paradise.

Showing derelict mining equipment after abandonment of the mine by Bougainville Copper Ltd (BCL)

BCL - Panguna

As at time of writing in 2018 there were muted political moves afoot to try to reactivate Panguna Mine but I fear such a project would take many years to regenerate, if indeed it is financially viable. Much good will and collaboration would be required between traditional land owners and developers, which going by past history is not always easy to acquire and foster

38 Transiting the Torres Strait and Spice Islands Route

Our Anewa Bay Pilot disembarked once we had cleared the outer reef, whereupon our trusty "Cherub" Log was cast from astern and I set course towards the South East following the coastline to pass south of Bougainville more or less a reciprocal route followed to come. Our 2nd Mate calculated our voyage to Singapore as approximately 3500 nautical miles so we expected a passage time of something in the region of about 9-10 days, all going well and dependent on weather. This time our passage would take us back into the Solomon and Coral Seas, passing the Torres Straits, then the Arafura Sea transiting north of Timor into the Java Sea; through the Karimata Straits and finally the Singapore Straits leading to our destination of Singapore.

Once into the Solomon Sea the South Easterly Trade Winds freshened and blew a constant Beaufort force 5. These winds were seasonal and were more or less on our port beam. Our decks were partially loaded with containers 3 units high, this acted rather like a sail causing the vessel to make significant leeway for which we compensated from time to time by adjusting our course to windward. We rolled gently all the way until we cleared the Bougainville Straits and southwestern peninsular of New Guinea and skirted the Gulf of Papua at which time the winds abated a little and shifted more Easterly, helping to push us along. By now the weather was fine on our port quarter. We headed on towards the Bligh Passage and the Torres Straits.

The Torres Strait is the main conduit between the Coral Sea to the east and the Arafura Sea to the west. The strait is an important international sea lane for shipping; lying to the north of Australia's Cape York and Papua

New Guinea. It is relatively shallow averaging about 13-15 meters, and the clustered coral reefs and islets can make it dangerous to navigate in some of the narrower channels. There are also very strong and unpredictable currents, heavy precipitation in the "Wet" season and sea mists during the period of South East Trade winds. It is therefore, highly recommended a Torres Straits Pilot be engaged for the transit. As we were approaching from the North East our Australian Agents had arranged a Pilot to guide us from Bligh Passage and Dalrymple Island via the Great North East Channel, through the Prince of Wales Channel as far as Booby Island where we entered the Arafura Sea. The highly prized job as a Straits Pilot was very well paid. Only the most experienced Master Mariners were engaged and I think it fair to say that around about this era it was a relatively "Closed Shop" and considered a very prestigious position within maritime circles.

Our transit through the captivating Torres Straits with its bright turquoise seas, silver sand Islets and Coral Cays was a magnificent spectacle. To add to the fascination we did sight a single Pearling Schooner forging a south easterly course. This was in the proximity of Prince of Wales Channel and it was a beautiful craft, painted white and under full sail. We passed at quite close quarters and could see only a single white man amongst the visible crew on deck which we estimated to be about twelve. Sailing on undaunted and making good speed it was a wonderful sight. According to our Pilot in the1970's, the Torres Straits Pearling Industry was in its twilight years, compared to the vibrant industry it had once been. Soon this wonderful vessel faded from our view becoming enveloped into a patch of sea mist some distance astern and was not seen by us again. The sailing skippers on these craft were expert seamen and knew the idiosyncrasies of the Torres Straits and adjacent waters, inside out, resulting from many years working the area. It must have been a wonderful life style for those so engaged but probably grew on the participants over the years as many had been doing it all their life from childhood days. The last pearling schooner I had seen was many years earlier, also in the Torres Straits, whilst serving my apprenticeship.

At last we approached Booby Island at the western end of the Torres Straits where we said our goodbyes to our friendly Pilot. Once clear of other shipping in the area we set our course towards the sea passage that I had selected to take us into the Banda Sea It was a relatively short and uneventful passage across the Arafura Sea and unexpectedly we did not observe a single ship during the crossing. Almost to the hour our Radars picked up distant echoes of the mountainous Pulau Leti group of islands off the northeast tip of modern East Timor, which marked the start of our entry into the Wetar Straits.

The Wetar Strait separates the eastern part of the island of East Timor from the island of Wetar. Hence, it lies between Indonesia to the north and East Timor to the south. To the west is Atauro, and beyond it the Ombai Strait, while to the east the southern part of the Banda Sea and the southernmost of the Maluka Islands. At its narrowest point, the strait is about 20 nautical miles across and deep with meandering strong currents that need to be closely monitored when navigating in these waters.

There was a lot of refraction in the prevailing humid conditions as we approached the narrows. Islands appeared to be floating above the horizons in the early morning sunlight. I had timed our arrival to be at sunrise for safety purposes since it was the first time I had used this route to the Java Sea. Once the sun started to gain amplitude in the sky visibility was outstanding and we could see great distances with the naked eye from the Bridge wings.

Soon we left the larger Island of Pulau Leti well to starboard as we forged ahead in the characteristically flat calm seas; Pulau Kisar was next which we passed on our port hand before navigating through the Pulau Wetar passage. Once clear of the islands further course adjustments towards the west were made to complete our entry into the Banda Sea. It had been a straight forward exercise in coastal navigation as good clear and recognizable land marks were plentiful. We were also aided with exceptionally clear imagery on our two Radar screens. We were once again in amongst the Spice Islands; the heady sweet and fragrant tropical aromas persisted as they drifted seaward on the light airs coming off the beautiful nearby coast lines, signaling to us that we were entering familiar waters as we commenced our passage through the Flores and Java Seas towards the Karimata Strait and onward to our destination of Singapore.

Once established in the Java Sea we more or less steered west paralleling the 7 Degree of latitude, until passing Sumbawa and Lombok to port. More northeasterly course adjustments were made once we cleared Pulau Kangean and Pulau Bowean to follow a more direct track towards the Selat Karimata. We passed numerous islands; some of the more distant ones featured the familiar belching volcanoes. This was not an uncommon sight in the Java Sea, one which we had observed numerous times. We also encountered a number of Arab Dhows or Indonesian two masted Pinisi sailing in convoy towards Borneo (now called Kalimantan) or the Makassar Straits.

Old tramp steamers were still in abundance, belching their thick black smoke which stained the pristine atmosphere. This area of Asia was the grave yard for such aging ladies. Most times far off vessels, which were hull down on the horizon, could only be detected by the far distant smudges of black smoke emitted from their funnels, lingering above the horizon and reaching skywards. In most cases ships that were hull down on the horizon could not be seen by the naked eye, only their smoke trails and occasionally their Masts indicated their presence. Ramshackle in most cases, it amazed me how such ships continued to operate in any kind of safe and economic manner - their rusty and run down appearance was completely out of place with the picturesque surroundings and in sharp contrast to our own presentation. Our Chief Mate "Bolo", did a splendid job of keeping the ship clean, tidy, well maintained and nicely painted; he managed his crew well and "Hoi Yun" always looked an absolute picture and was a credit to him personally.

One old ship flying the Indonesian flag tried crossing our bows from port to starboard relatively closely, ignoring the international anti-collision regulations and "Rules of the Road". These rules were designed for the guidance of wise men and the disregard of fools. The watch keeper on the dilapidated old tramp obviously fell into the latter category. Our 3rd Mate who was on duty at the time, quite correctly called me to the bridge as he felt uncomfortable with a developing close quartered situation. I was on the bridge in a flash and did not hesitate placing the helm 20 degrees to starboard in good time, once I had ascertained that the bearing of the old steamer was changing only marginally, and in any event she was far too close for comfort. I made a complete circle to starboard sheering away from the rogue vessel and passed astern of her. As we turned

sharply we heeled to port quite noticeably, mainly due
to the high deck cargo. By this time I had my binoculars
firmly focused on the wheel house of the culprit but saw
no sign of any activity so I assumed no one was keeping
watch or if they were then they must be asleep – it was
some moments later – after I had taken the evasive
action and eliminated the obvious risks, I saw someone
running from the boat deck up to the bridge - a few
seconds passed when I noted the same guy looking at us
through binoculars – he was given a very suggestive
gesture by our young 3rd Mate. I could just make out the
name of the ship amidst all the rusting paint work on her
stern "Splendid Glory" registered in Jakarta. I distinctly
remember thinking how inept the name was for such an
ancient rust bucket. I praised the 3rd Mate for his
initiative in calling me and impressed upon him he had
taken the correct action. All other traffic encountered
during the remainder of our passage complied with the
correct rules and regulations and we experienced no
further anxious moments.

Now was a period of the full moon and our nights spent
transiting the Java Sea were marvelous. We enjoyed the
calmest of calm conditions, cloudless skies and a crystal
clear atmosphere. The flat sea shimmered endlessly
under the moonlight and the light airs lingered the usual
heavy smells of our tropical presence, land being
seldom more than 80 miles distant, made for very balmy
evenings. I spent these hours sitting outside my cabin on
deck, in absolute solitude and deeply engrossed with my
own thoughts, reveling in gazing at the heavens above
and the millions of stars that appeared so close that one
felt one could almost reach out and touch them and
which extended right down to the distant horizons. I
would occasionally be joined by my Chief Engineer and
we would yarn for hours. These nights were my favorite
times at sea and I never tired of soaking up the tropical

ambience, it was a pleasure to behold and an absolute delight. Tasanee was also featuring prominently in my thoughts. I missed her charm and elegance.

Our tranquil days in the Java Sea were marred by an accident by one of our sailors. He tripped whilst on deck which resulted in him severely gashing his arm, a wound about 5cm long. Our 2nd mate did a good job of cleaning the wound and calling me to have a look at it. We placed the injured sailor in the ship's hospital. Following my consultation of the "Ship Master's Medical Guide" I decided that the wound should be stitched so I set about collecting all the instruments and sterilizing as appropriate. As Captain it fell upon my shoulders to undertake the procedure – I was not too concerned as I had done suturing before on a number of occasions. I closed the wound as neatly as I could and administered 10 surgical sutures. After the job was done it was dressed and the sailor's arm placed in a sling. As we were only about 4 days from Singapore, I considered the patient's condition was stable and he was comfortable enough until arrival Singapore whereupon he would be sent to Hospital immediately for any additional necessary treatment. As a precaution against infection he was administered the recommended course of broad spectrum anti-biotic and closely monitored.

To cut a long story short – when the injured sailor attended the medical center in Singapore the consulting doctor declared all was fine and the sutures could be removed aboard ship in another 3-4 days. By this time the wound had almost healed and looked reasonable without any excessive scaring likely to be sustained.

39 Pirates and Home Waters Again

Arrival in Singapore was fortuitous as it was a National
Holiday and the Port Labor was not working. The
officers and crew took advantage of the additional
leisure time myself included.

I decided to go ashore early and call Tasanee from the
Cable and Wireless office which was open even on
Public Holidays. It had been a few weeks since we last
spoke and it would be good to hear her cute voice again.
I would be back in Bangkok soon and we would meet of
course.

Since joining the Chief Engineer and I had become firm
friends and during the voyage so far we had spent
numerous hours yarning and enjoying the odd libation
when time allowed. It was Alistair who introduced me
to the world of painting and was instrumental in
stimulating my future interest in collecting maritime art.
Alistair had also promised to do a facial portrait of
Tasanee for me when next we arrived in Bangkok.

On this occasion the "Chief" accompanied me ashore.
As we stepped off the launch at Clifford's Pier the
heavens opened and we were caught in a heavy
downpour which lasted more than half an hour. We
were both drenched through. There seemed no
alternative but to dash across the road to one of the Shop
House Bars to wait for the rain to cease and so we could
dry off a little before moving to the C&W telephone
office, which was not too distant, before going
elsewhere. Needless to say one beer turned out to be a
good few.

Having completed a phone call to Tasanee we headed
off walking in the direction of Newton Circus, pleased
at the opportunity to stretch our legs. It was a longish

but stimulating walk but a little stressful in the humid conditions after the rain, which only served to parch the throat and the need to quench our growing thirst with a few more beers. We had an enjoyable evening, the highlight of which was a magnificent curry we enjoyed at the "Banana Leaf" café. After an enjoyable and relaxing evening, on our way back to the ship I noticed a haze was developing over the anchorage and there was a distinct smell of burning in the air. I didn't give it a second thought and went to bed very satisfied with my outing.

As it turned out, over earlier days the annual burn off had been taking place in Sumatra – this is a traditional practice that has taken place for centuries. It was the time of the year "slash and burn" was usually conducted and it was alarming to see the amount of smoke haze that was quickly accumulating over the Singapore Strait. Unpredictable and light winds during the pre –monsoon period did nothing to help matters and caused the smog to linger with a marked reduction in visibility. Not only was it a hazard to navigation but also a seriously harmful to health as the smoke haze was quite toxic making the eyes water and nostrils sting. This was a real annoyance because the Indonesian Government appeared impotent and did not seem to prevent the burn off.

The result was that due to the light airs and lack of strong winds around the equatorial latitudes the smoke haze remained for prolonged periods. Unfortunately many of the locals in Indonesia considered the prevailing situation as "normal". On board ship the stench of the smog got into the ventilation system and could be smelled inside the accommodation – the only solution was to close down the ventilating machinery that serviced the accommodation areas which did not make life on board very comfortable. On this occasion the haze was still very evident when we departed Singapore for Bangkok a few days later. Once clear of the Singapore Strait and well out into the Gulf of Thailand the smog cleared as quickly as it had developed. It was good to enjoy fresh air again and it did not take long for the odors to dissipate and the air-con to take effect.

Our trip to Bangkok was as usual just over 2 days and was uneventful. Entering the Chao Phraya River was its normal chaos with long tale boats darting in and out of the various Klongs, their passengers waving to us as they sped by, not to mention the overloaded barges full of bagged rice being towed downstream towards Ko Si Chang anchorage, where deeper drafted ships eagerly waited for them outside the river mouth. Occasionally we would see a long tail boat full of Buddhist Monks in their flowing ochre robes heading in the direction of one the various temples that lined the river bank or nestled serenely up some half hidden Klong.

During this period substantial amounts of bagged rice was exported to China as it was still suffering food shortages, hence it attracted some of the older ships many of which were rust buckets, mainly because Chinese importers were not that particular how cargo was shipped as long as it arrived. They were always on the lookout for the "cheapest of cheap", anyway, the excellent system of stowage for bagged rice with its ventilation ducts and rush mats loaded by expert Thai stevedores did much to prevent any damage to speak of. These old ladies could often be seen struggling upstream against the fast flowing river, propellers thrashing and belching grey black smoke from their long thin funnels. It was always an interesting river transit and a hive of activity.

As usual we secured alongside at Klong Toei, rather close to the Mosquito Bar and Seaman's Club to the satisfaction of the crew. As soon as I had completed all arrival formalities I went to the Agent's office to call my Tasanee. Intending to keep Alistair to his promise I asked Tasanee to come to the ship to have her portrait painted. Initially she was shy and reluctant to be the subject of a painting but I gently persisted and eventually convinced her. Our stay in Thailand was 5 days during which time Tasanee stayed onboard and sat a number of times for her portrait. Following 3 days Alistair produced his final work – it was stunning in every respect and bore a true likeness. I was enthralled with it and even Tasanee agreed it was of very high quality with a really remarkable likeness. Once it had time to properly dry I rushed ashore to have it professionally framed. I took it with me on every voyage thereafter and today it holds pride of place in my study. Despite my numerous requests Alistair point blank refused to accept any form of payment I offered. I am truly grateful for this stunning piece of art which is greatly admired by all who come into my "Man Cave" and cast eyes upon it. It raises many complementary comments.

Alas, far too soon it came time to say goodbye to Tasanee and to depart from Bangkok, but not before I had arranged with the Company for her to fly to Hong Kong to join the ship there and sail a few trips with me. I had previously suggested to her she obtain a passport which by now she had done so.

Having wound our way down river to the Gulf of Thailand we set course towards the south to round the southerly point of Vietnam and thence into the South China Sea. The weather was kind for a change with good visibility. As we approached the Vietnamese coast we were once again engulfed in huge fleets of fishing boats. We tried to keep clear but the fleet seemed never ending, navigating between these vessels during the hours of darkness was extremely hazardous but nevertheless we tried our best to avoid the mass of craft. It was just coming up to 8pm when the bridge look out reported he could see a vessel on fire about 5 miles distant to seaward. The 3rd Mate and I focused our binoculars on the vessel. The radio officer confirmed he had received no distress signal. Nevertheless under Maritime Law we were obligated to render assistance to any vessel visibly in distress if possible, so we altered course towards what we presumed was a vessel engulfed in flames and obviously in distress.

As we approached, it became obvious that the flames were contained to two drums on the foredeck of the fishing vessel. Despite all efforts to raise them by radio and VHF – silence prevailed. No crew members were visible but the craft did not look abandoned because she remained underway at a constant speed and was maintaining a steady course. The craft was ramshackle, very old and dilapidated quite typical of those fishing boats that frequent the Gulf of Thailand and Vietnamese waters. As we cautiously approached to closer quarters the fishing boat appeared to remain deserted. We trained one of our search lights on the wheel house area which seemed abandoned but this could have been simple ploy to entice us to come even closer or even alongside. I was aware of this strategy and prepared for a quick getaway if needed.

Quite suddenly a number of crew appeared and the craft abruptly altered course towards us at high speed. I had earlier smelled a rat and had already rigged fire hoses about our decks in case we were required to quell the flames on the fishing boat or to repel boarders in case of treachery. Assembled about our decks were also an assortment of long boathooks and similar implements that we could use to fend off unwanted boarders. I immediately increased to full speed and veered away towards clear water just as our fire hoses sprang into life with long jets of high pressure water, ably manned by our crew. The fishing boat had a good turn of speed and was slowly closing on us but I tried to keep them right astern so their advancement would be hindered by our increasing wake, as we built to our maximum speed. Eventually, after some minutes, the boat ceased giving chase and gradually faded into the distance. This was a relief; heaven knows what may have happened had they been able to board us.

Most Pirates are murderous thugs and not hesitate to cause injury or even death. Many do not believe that piracy is such a serious issue, in fact throughout the 1970-1980s and up to present days the number of incidents has increased alarmingly, causing many nations to position their own naval ships in international piracy prone waters. Highly organized criminal syndicates are behind most of these vagabonds. They obtain their own intelligence and know when and where to strike. Nowadays piracy has gone well beyond boarding ships to rob but also in many cases hijacking the entire ship and cargo as well and holding crews hostage for ransom.

There can be little doubt that in this case these were pirates, not only because of their attempt to get alongside us but also because as soon as it became obvious to them they could not catch us they quickly doused the fires in the drums on their foredeck. This was a good lesson for all of us and increased our awareness thereafter. I sent a radio broadcast to all ships and an urgent telegram to Singapore, Bangkok and Hong Kong Radio stations reporting the incident and providing the position and description of the fishing vessel so that other mariners transiting the area could be forewarned. Fortunately, the remainder of the trip to Hong Kong was uneventful. I later learned that one other freighter in the same area had been boarded by the Pirates only the day following our encounter.

As we approached the Pilot Station at Lai Ye Mun we gained an excellent view of Junk Bay where dozens of old ships were anchored in the relatively deep water waiting to be broken up by the various Iron and Steel works that abounded its shores. There were many more ships compared to our previous visit.

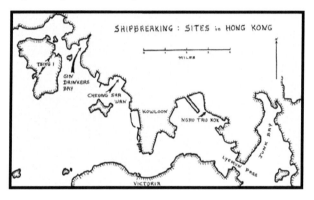

By early 1970's Hong Kong ship breaking was established as a major industry in the Colony, employing thousands of workers – in fact around that time it was the largest Ship Breaking center in the world. Old rusting wrecks, old war time liberty ships amongst them lying quietly at anchor with all their secrets remaining intact, awaiting their demise. Junk Bay eventually became so overcrowded and much of the overspill of derelict tonnage awaiting demolition was relocated to Gin Drinkers Bay to the West of Kowloon peninsula.

The original Gin Drinkers Bay was where the Container Terminals are now situated opposite Tsing Yi Island. As shown in the depicted sketch.

We were witnessing the last of an era because by the late 1970s and early1980s the demolition industry declined and had mostly shifted to Taiwan and China as valuable land surrounding both Junk and Gin Drinker Bays was reclaimed and developed as part of an ever growing appetite for suitable building land in Hong Kong.

On the western flank of Junk Bay, not far from Mount Davis, in the Sai Kung area was located Rennie's Mill. This was a small township established by a Canadian businessman who opened a Milling Company (which subsequently failed) on the site, hence the name. During the early 1950's the Hong Kong government opened up Rennie's Mill as a refugee haven to cope with the surge of Chinese Nationalists who had fled China after the takeover of the Communist Chinese. Many of the refugees were either ex Chinese Nationalist soldiers or followers and officials of the Kuomintang. There were always a number of Republic of China flags openly fluttering in the area so it could not be mistaken for what it was, a strictly anti-communist community. Today, Rennie's Mill no longer exists but is now a thriving new township with numerous high rise apartment blocks and private estates noticeably void of the ROC flags. It is now known as Tiu Keng Leng.

It was in overcast conditions as our Pilot boarded but matters quickly brightened once we passed the narrow Lye Ye Mun channel and were greeted by the awe inspiring views of Victoria Harbor, Kowloon Peninsula and Hong Kong Island. Typically at this time of year the Peak was capped in a shroud of mist. Like most arrivals at Hong Kong there was always something new to see, new and taller skyscrapers, more lights and of course increased activity about the harbor itself. Once we were cleared by the Port authorities and obtained pratique we weighed anchor from the Mon Kok immigration anchorage close to Kai Tak airport. Our experienced Pilot guided us through the almost chaotic harbor traffic to our designate mooring buoy, which was not too distant from Stonecutters Island. It took us about 30 minutes to moor and no sooner secured to the buoy container and cargo Barges together with some cargo Junks were alongside us, ready to break out the cargo and containers for offloading.

The following day Tasanee arrived in Hong Kong and I went to meet her at Kai Tak Airport. She looked radiant as she emerged from the Customs Hall and she was so obviously happy to be with me again. We hailed a cab from the airport taxi stand and drove direct to Kowloon Pier where we hired a "Walla Walla" to take us the short distance to the ship located in mid-stream. She was welcomed aboard by all and made to feel very welcome. The following morning she went ashore with the ship's agent to Port Immigration to sign on ship's articles as a supernumerary. Her ensuing days in Hong Kong were spent site seeing and shopping; when I was busy on board (mainly free only in the evenings) the Radio Officer accompanied her ashore for safety reasons. When in port the Radio Officer has more free time than most so he was the logical choice for escort duties. Going by what I was told by the Radio Officer, Tasanee was absolutely awe struck by the crowds in the Malls and sheer number of busy shoppers. She returned onboard every afternoon laden with all sorts of things which soon started to fill my cabin and dayroom. Labels from the best of shops such as Dai Maru, Wing On and of course Lane Crawford's featuring prominently amongst her purchases. She was obviously reveling in her shopping spree. Nevertheless she was the same Tasanee, always appreciative of her new acquisitions and thanked me profusely.

Since our voyage had been hectic with little time spent in the various Ports, our outer Hull plating was starting to become somewhat rust streaked and untidy. Not heavily encrusted but rather discolored due to small areas of corrosion bleeding rust stains. Hence the Chief Officer had arranged for the company to provide a "Side Party" to come to the vessel and undertake Hull maintenance. In this case it was the Mary Soo Side Party, whom we had engaged previously.

A side party consists of a number Sampans each manned by about 6 workers, usually elderly ladies. Their job is to chip and scrape rust patches and paint the Hull (usually all round) whilst the ship is at anchor, or in our case secured to the Typhoon Buoy. They are jovial old ladies who work rapidly doing a good job. Unless otherwise specified by her, the leader is generally referred to as "Aunty Mary" – as was this case. Depending on the draft, size of the vessel and job scope it usually takes two or three days working from their Sampans or rigging numerous painting stages over the ship's side from the working decks but once completed the Hull looks like new. They also paint ships names and visible draft marks and Plimsol line. The ship provides the paint, tools, brushes and rollers and most importantly the ladies receive free meals provided by the Chinese cook. They are always very popular with the crew when in attendance. The charge for an average side party is reasonable and very cost effective.

On this occasion the job was finished in just over two days and was nicely completed by their talented team. Other types of "chipping gangs" are also regularly used in Hong Kong – each gang usually has a contingent of about 50 laborers (male and female) all equipped with chipping hammers. The noise is deafening but the amount of work completed in only a short time is really quite remarkable.

These chipping gangs give the ship's crew the opportunity to really get on top of the job, especially the steel decks.

The next morning I went ashore in the early boat with Tasanee. Whilst she continued her shopping I walked to the office to show my face, report on the voyage and vessel performance and of course to find out what was in store for us and our next trip.

It was a miserable wet morning with consistent light drizzle as I said my goodbyes to Tasanee at Blake's Pier; she went off in search of a new shopping extravaganza whilst I headed towards Central on foot towards the office. I wondered what lay ahead.

After the usual greetings, formalities and a traditional coffee pot I eventually discovered my future destiny. I was to take my ship "Hoi Yun" northbound as far as Japan. I would disembark at Yokohama and hand over to a new Captain, as yet un-named. Following a couple of weeks leave I would stand by the fitting out and take command of a new building container ship at a Japanese shipyard. I did not miss the opportunity to request Alistair to join as Chief Engineer if he was agreeable. More details of the new vessel would be forthcoming over ensuing weeks so I was informed. However, I did glean that she was the first of a breed of new fuel efficient multi-purpose cellular container vessels planned by our company and would be engaged on a regular express run within S.E. Asia, with scheduled calls at Port Klang (ex Port Swettenham), Singapore, Pasir Gudang, Bangkok, Hong Kong, Keelung and Yokohama; a sort of high end feeder service for the major players trading between Asia, Europe and North America Pacific northwest. Hong Kong was to be our container transshipment hub. Obviously our company was in top gear when it came to expansion mode.

This factored into my future plans perfectly as the leave time could be well used in Hong Kong to decide upon a residential base for Tasanee and myself, whilst my dear "Hoi Yun" would continue on here now established service between Asia and Australia, together with her remaining sister vessels that had been recently acquired for the purpose.

I had prearranged to meet Tasanee for lunch at Maxim's in Central, adjacent to Telephone House, just directly across the road from the building in which our Office was located. It was a little early so I took the opportunity to go to the Gloucester Hotel Arcade and Lane Crawford to do a bit of shopping for myself. Shoes and shirts were on my list. I bought a new pair of dark brown leather Brogues and a pair of suede Desert Boots along with three cream colored raw silk shirts and one pair each of light grey flannels and cavalry twills. That will do me for a while I thought to myself.

Over a light lunch I explained everything to Tasanee and we discussed our future excitedly – we both agreed we were closely bonded and promised each other that "we would start and finish together". It suddenly dawned upon me the new responsibilities I had taken on. Tasanee talked often about visiting Japan and voiced her plans for our stay there – as she chatted away I found myself looking at her in awe and enjoying every moment of her Asian beauty and charm.

We departed Hong Kong a few days later. Our trip north was uneventful but as we were coming towards the end of the year the weather was turning much colder. The North East Monsoon had been blowing at full strength during our trip north. By the time we had reached Yokohama the ground was covered in snow. This was a novel experience for Tasanee since it was her first time experiencing snowy conditions. She played about like a youngster throwing snowballs and the like. After two days in Yokohama the new Captain arrived. He was new to the company and I did not know him. He was about 40 years of age and Anglo-Indian. His name was Ian Fernandez and he originated from Goa (Fernandez being a common name for Goanese) but he resided in Singapore. He was a charming fellow and very suave. He came highly recommended based on company reports.

By this time the company had confirmed that Alistair would join the newbuilding ship with me as Chief Engineer. The plan was that he would remain on board his ship until the ship arrived in Nagoya then hand over to the 2nd Engineer who was to be promoted. Alistair would then return to Hong Kong for a short leave before joining the new ship in Japan, along with Tasanee and I.

I handed over command of the "Hoi Yun" to Captain Fernandez on the designated date then Tasanee and I moved to the pleasant Rokkosan Hotel in Kobe for a week before catching a Bullet Train from Kobe to Fukuoka then by road onward to Nagasaki where the new ship was being built. At that time Fukuoka was the main arterial point of entry for the island of Kyushu. Nagasaki is also on Kyushu Island and approximately 150 kilometers more or less south of Fukuoka. The City Port faces the East China Sea and is one of the principal shipbuilding locations in Japan. It is a pleasant drive from Fukuoka to Nagasaki and takes approximately 2 hours by limousine.

Nagasaki is famous for being the second city to be devastated by the atomic bomb towards the end of World War 2. Hence at the time my new ship was being built Nagasaki was a relatively modern city by Japanese standards. The city is overshadowed by Mount Inasayama which is not too distant from the city. Mount Inasayama offers superlative views of the city, especially at night and was quite a tourist attraction at the time.

Having arrived at Nagasaki Tasanee and I were driven to a traditional little hotel quite close to the city center.

It was designated a "Honeymoon Hotel" due to it being very popular with Japanese newlyweds. It was a truly delightful spot with grand views and designed in a traditional Japanese style.

41 A Beauty is Born

The construction of a new ship is an intensely complicated and detailed affair. It is highly regulated with the building process being closely monitored and certified by one of the internationally recognized Classification Societies, such as Lloyds Register, Det Norske Veritas, Germanischer Lloyd, Bureau Veritas, etc., as the building progresses it provides assurances to Owners and Insurers that the vessel is built in compliance with the design specifications and international standards and regulations.

The building of any new ship commences with the laying of the Keel. The Keel is the central fore and aft structural member at the bottom of the hull and extends the full length of the vessel from stem to sternpost. Basically it is the backbone of the vessel. The modern technique used in ship construction is for various sections to be pre-fabricated then lifted and welded into position. This enables a number of sections to be constructed simultaneously then lifted and attached in the required sequence. It makes for a more rapid construction period and enables easier inspection and testing by the Classification Societies. Once the Hull construction is completed the Hull is usually launched with the attachment of accommodation, machinery and upper works carried out whilst afloat, right up until completion and sail away.

Obviously, any new ship once completed is subject to the most comprehensive of sea trials to verify the vessel's handling capabilities and characteristics and to satisfy Owners and Insurers of the vessel's performance and safe operation as well as suitability of purpose.

Captioned below is the majestic **"Emma Jebsen"**, she was a typical multi-purpose cum early generation container feeder vessel of the 1970's commonly seen trading around the Asia region. Due to the fact that many major ports in this part of the world were still developing their container terminals, most ships of this type remained self sustaining in order to provide greater flexibility in handling containers at various secondary ports that did not have dedicated container terminals available at that time. She lasted with Jebsen's until late 1970s when she was sold and eventually went to the breakers in India sometime in 1998.

The **"Heinrich Jessen"** looked similar in many aspects to **"Universal Venture"** save for the fact that the **"Universal Venture"** was fitted with container cranes rather than slewing derricks.

Photo KP ©

"Heinrich Jessen" pictured whilst alongside an early container wharf in Keelung during 1974. At that time many container wharves were little more than open spaces used as lay down areas, hence the need to use ship's gear during the early days of containerization.

The day following my arrival in Nagasaki the company agent drove me to the Dock Yard to meet those involved with the building and fitting out. Construction was at an advanced stage when I arrived at the Ship Yard and it was expected that sea trials would take place approximately one month later. I was taken to the vessel riding high at the fitting out jetty. She was handsome in every way and I immediately noted her name painted prominently on her bow and stern, "Universal Venture", Port of Registry Hong Kong. This was the first I became aware of the name because hitherto I had known the vessel only by the Yard number (a specific number designated to each new build for identification purposes).

The **"Universal Venture"** was very sleek and featured a large accommodation block situated aft. She had 5 cellular container holds which were serviced by 3 special 360^0 slewing heavy lift container cranes that had sufficient span to reach the various container compartments which made her fully self sustaining, if and when required. A total of 600 TEUs (twenty foot equivalent units including 4 high stowed above deck) was her container carrying capacity. She was also equipped to carry 20 Freezer Containers (known as Reefers). At the time of her construction, being a first generation fully cellular container ship, she was considered quite a good sized regional carrier, most being somewhat smaller around 4-500 TEU carrying capacity at that time. However suffice it to say that with the massive growth in containerization over ensuing years she was soon overtaken by the economies of scale and considered just an average size container feeder.

The vessel was nearing completion so I had the opportunity to look through the accommodation, bridge and engine room. She was nicely fitted out and equipped with the latest technology in everything, whether it be electronic, machinery or otherwise. My quarters were very smart and spacious offering the latest in comfort and design, for which Japanese shipbuilders are renowned. I had several large windows in each of my rooms and the bulkheads were lined with faux veneer made of fire retardant material which nevertheless looked like the real thing. My Dayroom and Office were separate and my Bedroom and ensuite were also very comfortable. Not unlike my previous ship there was an Owners suite and small pantry adjacent to it. My quarters occupied an entire deck. There was also nice outside deck space covered by purpose built awnings. Of course the officers and crews quarters were equally as pleasing and the officer's dining room was large.

Adjoining the dining saloon was a very pleasant lounge and bar area which was separated by means of frosted glass folding doors sporting the company House Flag etched into the glass. I was very pleased with the ship. My only wish being she would handle and perform as well as she looked but I was quietly impressed and inwardly confident.

Tasanee and I enjoyed our time in Nagasaki. During the day I spent most of my time at the shipyard familiarizing myself with the new vessel, plans, specifications, technical details, etc., whilst Tasanee used the time for sightseeing or going on short city tours and visiting points of historical interest. We were together in the evenings for dinner and we enjoyed much quality time together. I think Tasanee was as excited as I was about the new ship and sailing with me on her.

At that point in time Japan was still relatively inexpensive and our money went a long way, since I was paid in USD. During the weekends I hired a car or we went on bus tours to the outlaying areas. Sometimes we took a high speed train to other cities such as Fukuoka or Kagoshima.

Modern Fukuoka has developed from what was previously known as Hakata until the merging of both cities in the 1970's. The main feature is the ancient Fukuoka Castle atop Fukusaki Hill more or less in the city center. The castle is very interesting and is sometimes referred to as Maizuru Castle which dates back to the early Edo Period in Japanese history. Like most things in Japan modernization is central to the development of the city and today the old castle grounds now sport a large Baseball Stadium.

Nowadays Hakata is a district or ward of Fukuoka and considered more or less a suburb within the prefecture of Fukuoka. The original Port of Hakata (which still exists and I had visited by ship on many previous occasions) lies to the East of the Naka River and has developed into a commercial center, whilst to the West of the river lies Fukuoka. Hakata was one of the original Japanese "Open Ports" which permitted trade between Japan, the United Kingdom and the United States, during the period when Japan was more or less closed to the rest of the world. Due to the traditional trades between Japan, Korea and China originating in the middle ages, attributable mainly to its location facing the Korea Straits with ease of access, Hakata was the first city in Japan to permit a "China Town". Consequently, the old town is steeped in history and tradition despite the modernization in more recent times.

By Contrast Kagoshima is located on the western shores at the head of Kinko Bay in the southern sector of the Island of Kyushu. Interestingly, this was the birth place of Admiral Togo who was the Grand Admiral of the Imperial Japanese Navy's Grand Fleet in the early 1900s. There was always plenty to see and do and relaxing in the numerous beautifully manicured and ornate gardens is an absolute pleasure. The serenity and peaceful ambiance becomes immediately evident to any visitor. Japan still remains steeped in culture and is a land of stunning beauty.

No matter where we went in Japan we never went hungry because of the never ending array of restaurants from which to choose. Tasanee and I became quite adventurous and were willing participants when it came to trying most types of Japanese dishes. Very few delicacies were barred from our table – one exception was Puffer Fish which is supposedly very toxic but we were assured it was not poisonous if properly prepared and cooked by a specialist Chef – nevertheless, neither of us could ever conjure up the courage or nerve to try it.

About 3 weeks prior to completion and sea trials of the "Universal Venture", our Chief Engineer and 2nd Engineer arrived to stand by the ship. It was good to see my friend Alistair again and we had much to talk about – the new 2nd Engineer was unknown to me and went by the name of Cameron Newstub. He was a Kiwi (New Zealander), rather quiet and reserved but reportedly very good at his job. Being Hong Kong Flag it was necessary for all officers to hold Certificates of Competency with "Commonwealth Validity" that were fully and jointly recognized by the UK and Hong Kong Marine Authorities – this was in the days prior to STCW Convention (Standards of Training, Watch Keeping and Certification for Seafarers) first adopted by the IMO in 1978 and progressively introduced and updated thereafter.

Time passed quickly at Nagasaki and it soon became time for the remainder of the ship's crew to join. The Chief Officer and 2nd Mate arrived some days before the bulk of the crew who were all billeted in another Hotel within the township. They worked on the ship each day familiarizing themselves with the layout and compiling store and provision lists. Like other company acquisitions we would load minimal stores and equipment in Nagasaki, only sufficient to take the vessel to Hong Kong where, in accordance with company policy, the ship would be comprehensively stored and provisioned.

Eventually the time arrived for sea trials which were conducted over a 3 day period. Only the Captain, Chief Officer along with Chief Engineer and 2nd Engineer accompanied the vessel on its daily trial voyages outside the harbor. We departed at 7am each morning and had usually returned back to the dockyard and were tied up by 4pm. During these daily excursions a wide range of tests were conducted to prove the vessel's capability and performance.

After 3 days the vessel was accepted by the Owners and crew moved on board. We remained in port a further 4 days whilst we provisioned, stored and prepared for our initial voyage to Hong Kong. Tasanee was kept busy settling in and unpacking our cases whilst I was busy with ship's business along with all the other officers and crew in preparation for our departure and maiden voyage to Hong Kong.

Our 2nd Mate had prepared the route for my perusal which was relatively straightforward; Nagasaki, East China Sea, Taiwan Straits then more or less direct to Hong Kong. The distance was approximately 1100 nautical miles so at 14 knots it should take us some 3.5 days. Alistair and I had discussed the passage and both agreed that the first voyage should be executed at 13.5-14 knots until the Main Engine had settled and was given something of a shakedown. Besides, our departure day being a Wednesday there was little point in burning fuel unnecessarily only to arrive on a weekend, a Saturday when the office would most likely be closed. Hence, I planned the voyage to arrive on Sunday, just after lunch, so we would be ready for when the masses from the office came on board. I informed the office accordingly who concurred with my rational.

About 2pm, some 3 hours after clearing the zones of dense traffic our Chief Engineer Alistair came to see me. He reported that there was a badly leaking oil seal on one of the main engine cylinder heads and he would need to stop the engine for repairs which he reckoned would take about one hour. Whilst stopped he would also check other vital seals which were also showing signs of bleeding oil. These were basically teething problems common on most new ships. I went to the bridge to ascertain our position and to check for traffic congestion. Fortunately we were well positioned with few ships about so I authorized the vessel be stopped as requested by Alistair. I opted to remain on the bridge throughout, whilst repairs were carried out.

True to Alistair's word, some 45 minutes after stopping I was startled by the shrill ringing of the Engine Room telephone. It was the duty engineer advising me that all was well and we could proceed on passage. The buzzing of the electric engine telegraphs signaled we were building up to our nominated full speed as the duty bridge officer slowly brought the ship back on course towards the Northern entrance to the Taiwan Straits. An hour or so later Alistair dropped into my cabin to let me know all was functioning correctly and the temporary delay was nothing serious just down to teething problems.

We sped down through the Taiwan Straits and Sunday afternoon saw us approaching Lye Mun Pilot Station. A lovely sunny afternoon with light airs made entering Hong Kong Harbor an absolute pleasure. Once our Harbor Pilot was on board we moved slowly inwards, leaving the white beacon situated on the cluster of rocks that act as a sentinel to the narrow passage, well to starboard. At that point in time squatter huts encroached down the hillside almost to the water's edge where dozens of young kids delighted in swimming fearlessly close to the shore line and passing ships.

Having passed the water playground we were immediately confronted with the magnificent contrasting panorama of the Harbor and in particular the skyscrapers of Hong Kong Island. Motorized junks, ferries, cargo lighters and launches of every type all darting every which way confronted us, but our experienced Pilot knew his business and guided us quietly to our designated Mooring Buoy. The sun was just dipping as we completed mooring to the Buoy and already the neon advertisements and lights of Hong Kong Island and Kowloon Peninsula were ablaze on the tall buildings and displayed a welcome to the soul. Our timing for arrival had been perfect.

Once Port formalities were completed and the Agent had departed following his brief visit it was leisure time. Some of the crew went ashore in walla wallas to see their families but I was content to sit outside on my deck with Tasanee and Alistair quietly chatting, savoring our Gin and Tonics and soaking up the serenity and sweet harbor fragrances of the moment. This was the Orient at its best I thought to myself. It must have been 2am before we called it a night with the harbor being so still and quiet.

42   A Prosperous International Hub

During this period of the mid -1970s Hong Kong, whilst still maintaining all its alluring and unique qualities, was nevertheless, still undergoing a transformation from old to new. One could still find the odd Traffic Pagoda with traffic cop in white sleeved uniform, ladies wearing Cheungsams (although progressively becoming less popular unless on auspicious occasions) as well as the occasional Rickshaw. The iconic Kowloon Canton Railway Station complete with clock tower located in Tsim Sha Tsui close to the Star Ferry remained only temporarily, the station was eventually demolished in 1978 (although the Clock Tower alone was retained and still stands). There was an abundance of new five star hotels, skyscraper office buildings, tall apartment blocks, thriving businesses, heavily congested road traffic all denoting the prosperity and affluence of Hong Kong. Not to mention the vast number of high end Rolls Royce and Mercedes cars cruising the streets.

In my personal opinion 1975 to 1988 were the golden years for Hong Kong which did much to enhance its claim as being the top financial and shipping hub in Asia at that time. It became more expensive for everything like most other places in the world, however residential and commercial property was top of the list and was listed as one of the most costly places in the world to buy or rent residential or commercial real estate.

In August 1972 the first of three Cross Harbor Tunnels was opened. This consisted of duel tunnels each with two traffic lanes spanning an underwater distance of 1.8 km and linking Kowloon Peninsula from Hung Hom to the reclaimed area adjacent to Kellet Island in Causeway Bay, on Hong Kong Island. This development had a major impact on the colony at that time. The original tunnel was further supplemented by an additional two tunnels, namely, the Eastern Harbor Crossing opened in 1989 and the Western Harbor Crossing opened in 1997.

A land based tunnel was also constructed under Lion Rock offering a rapid road link between Kowloon Tong with the New Territories. At the time of writing it understood that a 4th cross harbor tunnel is under consideration and a bridge motorway linking Hong Kong with Macau.

The fast growing economy of Hong Kong brought about another major development during the 1970s. This was the Mass Transit Railway (MTR). Construction commenced in 1975 and the first line was opened in 1979 but has since expanded to such a degree it now included East to West Hong Kong Island, Cross Harbor to Kowloon Peninsula, The New Territories as well as other out laying areas of Hong Kong – there is also an extension of this fast rail link to the International Airport at Chep Lap Kok to the north of Lantau Island. The MTR now claims to be one of the most profitable Metro Rail Systems in the World and has been used as a model for similar developments in Mainland China and Singapore.

By 1972 it could be clearly envisaged that the future for shipping lay in the utilization of Containers. To this end Kwai Chung Container Terminal commenced construction in 1972. Reclamation of the Rambler Channel between Kwai Chung and Tsing Yi Island on the western flanks of the Kowloon Peninsula provided the space for this development. It was well ahead of its time when constructed and rapidly expanded into a major export outlet and regional transshipping Hub for Mainland China container traffic. Eventually it became one of the busiest container ports in the world and certainly played its part in the prosperity of Hong Kong during this era.

This new Port facility stamped containerization on the map as far as Hong Kong was concerned and encouraged many Hong Kong entrepreneurs to diversify into shipping. Container transport and handling, as well as container storage facilities, utilized every spare plot of land. This caused the emergence of numerous new support services now being demanded and considered essential by the industry.

It became a boom time in Hong Kong and heralded in the start of a golden age for shipping. During the 1970s many ship owners made their move away from traditional shipping into full containerization. This resulted in an abundance of older but good tonnage flooding the market at very competitive prices which enabled many to establish themselves in the break-bulk or general cargo shipping business, especially in regional feeder services to and from the Hong Kong "Hub". By this time Kwai Chung Container Terminal had become a major international player in the league of the world's rampant shift towards containerization.

As indicated earlier, the increasing costs of marine fuel continued progressively throughout the 1970s and by the late 1970s had forced many of the world's oldest and most respected ship owners to rethink economic viability of some older less fuel efficient ships and trim their fleets and sell off uneconomical vessels to many Asian concerns for continued trading or demolition. The dynamics of the shipping industry consequently changed forever. The prevailing situation allowed the "Accountants" to take control during this era the outcome being many of the world's leading shipping concerns disappeared into oblivion or diversified into other business ventures.

Another huge development was the planned new Airport at Chep Lap Kok. An entire island required to be manmade to facilitate this endeavor, just to the north of Lantau Island. Saturation of the original airport at Kai Tak brought about this scheme. Chep Lap Kok commenced construction in 1991 following exhaustive feasibility studies and a number of delays (mostly political). It was finally completed in 1997 and formally opened in 1998. Chep Lap Kok is one of the regional transit centers within Asia and remains an important destination for many world airlines that feature Hong Kong as a major tourist destination. Relatively recent statistics show it has 65,000 employees, handles 68.5 million passengers per year and is the World's top cargo handling airport.

As a consequence of all these developments new townships and mini-cities evolved laying the foundation for new expressways and transport schemes being borne all over Hong Kong – especially on the Kowloon peninsula and New Territories, including Lantau Island. In fact the Discovery Bay housing development at Moi Wo on Lantau was just being advertised. This featured rather nice houses right on the beach front with unimpaired view over the Western Anchorages looking towards Hong Kong Island with a. magnificent view and an ideal living environment. Tasanee and I had decided to go and look at one of the beach front villas which were available, as soon as the opportunity arose. It was a very convenient place in which to reside, frequent fast ferries to and from Blake's Pier operated daily from 6am to 12pm (later upgraded to a round the clock Hovercraft service). The transit time was about 20 minutes each way. As a matter of interest, for a while we did in fact reside in one of the beachfront houses and I recall some years later hearing of an ocean going freighter becoming stranded high and dry on the beachfront, during a typhoon, not more that 200m from where my front garden had once been. This was one of twenty two ships grounded or wrecked on the occasion of Typhoon Ellen which was the strongest to hit Hong Kong since Typhoon Hope in 1979.

The possibility of being isolated during a Typhoon was one of the factors that influenced us to relocate our residence back to Hong Kong Island. We eventually dropped our anchor at our new apartment at 101, Pok Fu Lam Road.

43   My New Ship is Invaded

The Chief Officer had the crew on deck early the following morning to give the ship a quick hose down with fresh water after our arrival. Everything was immaculate for the office visitors. There must have been about 20 that came up the accommodation ladder at 8am. Company Directors, senior Managers, Superintendents, Operations and Marketing staff not to forget a couple of accounting Managers (likely to make sure they had received value for money with the new vessel). My Cabin was invaded by the seniors whom I offered coffee and then a conducted tour of the main features of the ship. Alistair was similarly occupied in conducting visitors around the Engine Room.

By 11 am most of the more junior staff had left and returned to the Office, only my direct bosses remained on board for lunch. They all seemed very satisfied with their new acquisition and my favorable report thus far. We were expecting to be in Hong Kong about one week during which time it was planned to give a large cocktail party on board for shippers, marine department and other Government officials. Tasanee was requested by the Managing Director to act as the official hostess along with myself. This made her very happy and being Asian gave her much "Big" face. She took the task very seriously.

The ensuing days saw us kept busy doing all the necessary things to prepare a new ship for its shakedown voyage. I was kept so busy I had no time to for myself and reluctantly sent Tasanee ashore by launch for visits and outings with Alistair's wife. Of an evening we would sit on my deck just engrossed in the splendor of the harbor lights whilst sipping our drinks. Tasanee and I often talked and tried to plan our future. It was clear to me that Tasanee was extremely attached to me and relied on me for everything – hence I could not envisage her staying alone for any prolonged period whilst I was away at sea.

It was intended that the vessel would commence its operation by loading in Hong Kong for Port Klang (previously called Port Swettenham), Singapore, Pasir Gudang and Bangkok as an introduction to the service and then start back loading full containers for the main cargo Hub in Hong Kong where containers would be loaded for the northern ports of Keelung and Yokohama on other designated feeders – the southbound trip would then be repeated to Hong Kong, Port Klang, Singapore, etc. The round trip Hong Kong to Hong Kong was scheduled to take about one month.

However, I did glean that during our stay we were to load a full cargo of empty containers, a mix of both 20 and 40 footers. These were brand new from the container manufacturer and would be loaded ex Barge using ship's cranes – a good shakedown for the ship. Approximately 50 percent of these units were for Labuan in Eastern Malaysia and the 50 percent for Kota Kinabalu in Sabah, which formed part of the company's container inventory for the feeder service to be inaugurated to include both locations to and from the hub in Hong Kong. It was a relatively short round trip. We would sail back to Hong Kong in ballast ready to load and enter our Liner Service. It would be pleasant visiting Labuan and Kota Kinabalu again as it had been some time since my last visits.

During our stay in Hong Kong we sporadically loaded the empty containers, we had our cocktail party which was a great success, mainly because of Tasanee's organization. We also bunkered the ship. Vitals, deck, engine and cabin stores were taken on board in abundance. I did manage a couple of evenings ashore with Tasanee who was now starting to consider Hong Kong her second home. Alistair brought his wife on board to stay whilst we were in Hong Kong. All said and done it was a busy week for us but the time came when we were all secured ready for sea. Once clear of the Port we more or less followed a southerly track across the South China Sea taking us towards the Port of Kota Kinabalu.

Our arrival in "KK" was timed for sunrise. The heavens were ablaze with pink and gold hues which provided a magnificent backdrop for Mount Kinabalu as the sun gained amplitude in the eastern sky. This was a truly unforgettable sight. Needless to say, this subject featured as one of Alistair's true to life works of art.

There was no compulsory pilotage at "KK" only upon request. I personally never used a Pilot at any of the ports around Borneo if I could avoid doing so, besides I preferred to rely on my own ship handling skills rather than the locals. There were few serious snags at the ports of Labuan, Kota Kinabalu, Sandakan or Tawau in any event. Besides, the "Universal Venture" was fitted with a powerful Bow Thruster which made life easier and mainly avoided the use of Tugs except in cases of very strong winds or currents prevailing off the berth.

Pictured is the original Kota Kinabalu wharf – formally known as Port of Jesselton, as it was in erarly 1970s. The last of the good days – with not a container in sight!

New container wharf and facilities were eventually constructed including container cranes, early to mid 2000s. The narrow causeway out to the main jetty tended to restrict access to and from the main berth slowing operations due to congestion caused by the need for a large fleet of container trucks. Often, operations came to a standstill due to lack of trucks to handle the containers from shipside to lay down area and vice versa. I recall, even up to early 2000s, it taking 3-4 days to discharge and backload only a couple of hundred units due to lack of transport infrastructure. This was very slow when compared to other fully containerized Ports where the vessel's stay was counted in hours, not days. In "KK" it was often the case that empty containers were discharged, consolidated with cargo and then the same units once full, back loaded on board the vessel. This is the reason why we delivered empty containers so they could be stockpiled for use by shippers and expedite future feeder vessel dispatch.

Hence Kota Kinabalu was always a favorite with ship's crews because of the longer stay. They took full advantage of the good seafood, night life and cheap prices the town offered.

Since it was a straight forward case of off loading empty units it took less than one day to land the required number of TEUs for Kota Kinabalu and once completed we quickly got underway to Labuan so we could still arrive in day light.

Approximately 4 or 5 hours steaming southward one arrived at the Island Port of Labuan which was also an enchanting old town. It featured only a single finger deepwater cargo jetty which could accommodate a number of smaller coastal trading ships. No wharf cranes were available so it was always necessary to use ship's gear. One of the problems with Labuan was the approaches to the Port. There was a buoyed channel but frequently the buoys were unlit or out of position. There was an anchorage which was always crowded with smaller ships (many with no lights) which made anchoring a larger vessel during darkness somewhat hazardous. The safest way was to restrict Port arrivals and departures to daylight hours only. When a harbor pilot was engaged he only boarded about 500m from the main jetty, the rest was up to the vessel's Master so it made good sense to arrive early morning and proceed directly alongside the wharf or depart before sunset and proceed directly to sea clearing the port before the onset of darkness. As was my normal practice, I avoided using a pilot whenever possible. Labuan was also notorious for its Pirates so it was never the best idea to stay at the local anchorage at night if I could prevent doing so. This became my modus operandi over the years.

The Port at Labuan Island had become a focal point for the British Military during the 1964-5 uprising and the insurgency of Indonesian Forces into Borneo and West Malaya in opposition of the formation of the Malaysian Federation. Labuan was the supply point for many of the UK military in Borneo. Most equipment was transported from Singapore by the large Ministry of Defense LCT's, such as "Empire Gannet" and "Empire Kittiwake" which became regular visitors. This legacy prompted the opening of numerous Bars and girly hot spots to meet the demand of armed forces personnel. There were also good restaurants and decent hotels, a popular venue was the Waterside Hotel which was a comfortable 20 minute walk from the Jetty and set in pleasant surrounds. It can just be seen to the right in the image below, the smaller white building adjacent to the yacht Marina.

Labuan Port Authority

Labuan Port as it was in the 1970s prior to slow progressive transformation to containerization. The container or cargo carrying vehicles can be seen on the wharf

The "Universal Venture" required almost the full length of this deepwater jetty in order to berth and conduct Container Operations. Once again container operations were slow, only self sustaining container vessels could be used and there was very limited container storage areas, one area of which can be seen at the landward end of the jetty. The single narrow pier created bottlenecks for container trucks causing loading operations to be slow and arduous, particularly if both sides of the finger jetty was occupied by cargo or container vessels.

Between 1950-1990s the entire region of what was then British North Borneo Island including Kuching (Sarawak), Jesselton (Kota Kinabalu), Miri, Bintulu, Tawau, Sandakan, down as far as the Indonesian Port of Samarinda, was a haven for Pirates, especially on the East coast where Filipino Pirates based in Jolo Island (Tawi Tawi Group) which was very close to hand, joined ranks and roved about plundering the coastal waters more or less at will and unhindered.

During the migratory season the east coast of North Borneo (Kalimantan), close to the Sibutu Passage and Reef in the Celebes Sea is a great place for Whale watching. This is a world Class Scuba Diving venue but fraught with danger with a high risk of kidnapping by Pirates roaming around the Tawi Tawi Group of Islands.

We arrived in Labuan without incident and immediately set about discharging the balance of empty containers. It was a quick operation as far as the ship's cranes was concerned. However, progress did slow a little due to the shortage of container trucks. We stayed one night at Labuan as we were unable to complete and depart the port in daylight

Tasanee and I went ashore for dinner and a stroll around. At my request we were joined by Alistair who knew his way about the town much better than me and guided us to a very fine Indian restaurant, which much to the delight of Tasanee, served excellent spicy hot Vindaloo and Madras varieties. The next morning at

7am we let go our moorings and headed back towards Hong Kong, some 1100 nautical miles distance and almost due North. We estimated a passage of 3 days at 15 knots.

It was heavily overcast and we were about mid way between the Paracel and Spratly Islands when I was suddenly alarmed by the marked change in Engine tone and the ringing of ships electric telegraph. I was on the bridge in a flash to be greeted by the ringing of the bridge phone. It was Alistair calling from the engine room. A problem had arisen with the main engine turbo chargers which meant we would need to stop for a few hours but once temporarily rectified we would be required to proceed at a much reduced speed for the remainder of the voyage to Hong Kong where full repairs would need to be carried out. Alistair explained the technical details and the need to strictly observe the builders instructions for such an event as the ship was still under builder's warranty. I immediately sent a cable to the Owners in Hong Kong to appraise them of the situation, stating I would revert once underway again with revised ETA at Lye Ye Mun.

For the next 6 hours we wallowed in the swell and thankfully we were in good waters well clear of any danger. Meantime the ship's routine continued normally, save for that of the Engine Room department. Tasanee became a little concerned and worried but I soon put her mind to rest with assurances that we were in no imminent danger and would soon have the problem sorted and be underway again. I further explained that such temporary breakdowns in mid ocean were not uncommon. This seemed to satisfy her anxiety. About 10am Alistair came to the Bridge to brief and update me on progress of the need to isolate the turbocharger. He hoped to be able to resume the passage at reduced speed around 2pm all going well.

By mid afternoon we were able to resume our passage but at only half speed. I updated the Owners of our resumption of passage and revised ETA. Alistair asked if he could send a full technical report to the Engineering Department at Head Office, to which I readily agreed. Preparations needed to be made in Hong Kong for the necessary repairs.

It was late evening when I received a response from Owners to inform me that a Builders Representative from Japan would arrive in Hong Kong the day following our arrival to inspect the engine, so a berth had been arranged for us at a Dockyard for the carrying out of repairs. Dockyards were always busy and it was therefore necessary to make early arrangements for wharf space.

Once we had arrived in Hong Kong and secured to the shipyard jetty we had the Engineer Superintendent come aboard together with a Mr. Iino who was representing the Japanese Shipbuilder. They were also accompanied by the Shipyard's Repair Manager

They all went into huddled conversation with Alistair and spend a good few hours in the Engine Room before coming to brief me with the latest heads up. In short repairs were required, I had assumed this naturally, which were expected to take in the region of three weeks because some critical spare parts were essential and could only be sourced from the Turbo Charger manufacturers in Japan and Europe. Much depended on the availability of these spare items and their timely arrival in Hong Kong. Normally ships are required to carry a certain number of critical spares but in this case it was outside the usual scope, because in an emergency the Engines could still be engaged in limited operation without the assistance of Turbo Chargers.

The next day I paid a courtesy visit to the company office where I learned that it was intended to transfer some of the officers to other vessels within our fleet, namely the 3rd Mate, Radio Officer, Electrician and 3rd Engineer. These crew members were to be replaced by new recruits from the UK on two year contracts. It would mean that we would not have a full complement whilst in the shipyard but this did not matter as the ship was classified as nonoperational whilst in the dockyard. As long as we were at full strength again prior to our departure that would be in order. In any event the crew change was only estimated to take about a week until we would be back to full strength. According to the personnel department we required more certified officers for future fleet expansion and the UK was the best source, it should be remembered during that period there was no such thing as STCW so Officers were required to posses Certificates that were recognized those being of Commonwealth validity in order to serve on Hong Kong registered ships. We were also going to carry an additional 2nd Mate, Chief Mate and 2nd Engineer, in readiness for the next new building. It would be a sister vessel so experienced gained on our ship would be invaluable for them. So it was to be.

By this time Tasanee had been sailing with me for a while so I suggested she may like to take the opportunity to fly to Bangkok for two weeks whilst we were in the shipyard, so she could see her family. The plan was she would rejoin me in Hong Kong about a week before we sailed. Having given assurances I would call her daily, she went along with the plan because she obviously missed her family but nevertheless she was a little reluctant in leaving me alone. Anyway, a day later I booked her on a flight to Bangkok with a return ticket in her hand. Tears and hugs and then she went on her way. Sitting in the taxi on the way back to the ship I was suddenly overcome by a feeling of intense loneliness, obviously I had underestimated how closely attached to Tasanee I had become.

It was about 3pm by the time I arrived back on board the "Universal Venture". I popped into the Engine Room and from the top plates could see below all the shipyard repair crew busy working on the Turbo Chargers. Alistair was there in his supervisory capacity as was the builder's representative. I did not disturb them and departed leaving them to their work. By this time the outgoing officers had signed off and transferred to other ships. The new arrivals were due in 2 days time so we were only shorthanded for a total of about 7 days.

Time dragged a little in the shipyard but I kept my promise and every morning after breakfast walked across to the Yard Office to telephone Tasanee. She was always so excited to hear my voice. The same questions, was I OK, eating enough, etc., I got the strong impression she was counting the days until her return.

Like clockwork the new Officers arrived on queue – a fancy looking coach parked at the wharf side and they all piled out. I was watching from my dayroom window. Having come on board and been directed to their allocated cabins by the Chief Steward they all streamed up to see me and hand over their papers. The new 3rd Mate was tall and blond from Cardiff and an ex Reardon Smiths cadet – he had only recently obtained his 2nd Mates Certificate and this was his first job. Our new Radio Officer was from Hull and was reasonably well experienced, he looked like a sharp dresser and I therefore immediately assumed to be a bit of a lady's man. The replacement 3rd Engineer was ex Elders and Fyffes and had been made redundant when they had sold off some of their older tonnage but he came well recommended nevertheless. Finally our Electrician was a very distinguished looking fellow with jet black hair, well trimmed moustache and longer sideburns. Very suave indeed which I put down to his time spent with the B and I. He told me he was looking for new horizons in the Far East and he had enough trading to India. I wasn't quite sure what that remark meant!

As far as the supernumerary officers were concerned, the Chief Mate was from Liverpool and had recently married a Chinese lady from Singapore so he was looking to be based in Asia for obvious reasons. This was his first assignment after having past his Masters examinations but he had a solid background with Ellerman Lines and some experience of the Far East trade as a consequence. Finally the 2nd Engineer and 2nd Mate were jovial Geordies and ex shipmates in the Ropner shipping company. They seemed hard workers and down to earth types so they would do well. Not a bad looking lot I thought to myself. That evening following dinner we all met up in the ship's Bar when fuller introductions were made.

By now the new spare parts for the Turbo Charger had arrived on board but it would still take another week to complete the job. Tasanee would arrive back on board in good time and I was looking forward to meeting her at Kai Tak in a couple of days. Finally the day arrived when Tasanee returned. I met her at the airport as planned and was immediately captivated by her usual beautiful smile and elegance. My life was now complete once again and back to normal.

The remaining days flew by and we were soon to leave the shipyard and proceed on sea trials. We slipped our lines early morning and proceeded cautiously through the Lye Ye Mun passage and worked our way towards the Llama Channel where the trials were designated to take place. Our sea speed was progressively increased under the watchful eye of Alistair together with dockyard and builder's officials as well as our company Engineering Superintendent. The sea trials lasted approximately six hours at which time it was agreed by all that the repairs had been successful. At this point I set course to pick up the Pilot off Green Island as we had been instructed to secure to a Typhoon Buoy, the mate having prepared the anchor chain on our way back up the Llama Channel. By 5pm we were all secured at the Buoy to await orders. The repair crews and officials wasted no time in getting into the company launch and heading ashore.

Coincidentally, the majestic Danish Far East trader "Jacob Jebsen" was on the adjacent buoy to us. She was absolutely surrounded by large sailing junks all rafted along her sides. She looked a bit like a mother Hen with all her chicks….in fact she was probably discharging parcels of rice from Bangkok under the watchful eye of Tally Clerks.

Photo KP ©

"Jacob Jebsen" – seen working cargo at Typhoon Buoy in Hong Kong. She was a stylish little ship in her day.

45 Life on a Container Feeder

We lay idle at the Typhoon Buoy for two days before we commenced loading containers from the Barges. The owners did not wish to arrange and coordinate cargo operations until they had been certain the Turbo Charger episode was well and truly concluded.

The "Universal Venture" was considered quite a large container feeder for the time but nevertheless we soon discovered we spent very little time in Port except at Kota Kinabalu and occasionally Labuan which of course stemmed mainly from wharf congestion and lacking Port infrastructure during that period. Other Ports were generally a one day affair (or often less). We generally timed our arrival for daylight and first Pilot in Ports where Pilots were compulsory for foreign flag ships. Of course many ships tried to do the same thing so the anchorages of the Pilot Boarding Grounds were frequently congested and widespread. To overcome the congestion at the Port Klang outer anchorage following 4 consecutive trips I underwent examination for Pilot exemption.

The exam was conducted by the Port Manager and was relatively thorough, most focusing on Tides, Buoyage and Port Regulations. Once obtained it meant I was permitted to proceed upstream without a Pilot and go to enter the inner anchorage. This arrangement turned out to be good because rather than wait overnight outside the Port limits we could go in and the crew would enjoy the benefit of a bit extra shore leave. However, no matter what the circumstances, Pilotage remained compulsory from inner anchorage to wharf. When sailing, there was no benefit to the ship so I engaged a Pilot from wharf side the full distance to outer Boarding Ground. This kept the local Pilots contented because they were not losing all their bread and butter, only a tad.

Of all our Ports of Call the best organized were Hong Kong and Singapore, and to a slightly lesser extent Port Klang (by now no longer named Port Swettenham). This trio, were making the greatest and fastest inroads towards a full suite of container facilities with various designated container terminals and berths under construction, progress was rapid. That is where we spent the longest Port time loading or discharging which suited most of those on board, obviously. With luck we would generally get a night in Hong Kong and Singapore but not anywhere else, unless I took the vessel upstream to Port Klang inner anchorage. Naturally, Port time was directly linked to container numbers at each destination as well as berth availability.

The Malaysian Port of Pasir Gudang in the Johor Straits was also undergoing a more measured degree of expansion. Seldom did we spend more than 12 hours alongside. PG was not one of my favorite Ports because it necessitated crossing very dense conflicting traffic in the Singapore Straits, which could be quite chaotic and even hazardous because some ships failed to obey International rules of navigation. The Traffic Separation Scheme (TSS) for East and Westbound traffic in the Singapore Straits was not introduced until about 1981. Once established this did much to enhance vessel control and safety of navigation and eliminate the "Cowboy" element.

The "Cowboy or Rogue" element was a problem which came about due to the significant growth in global shipping, rapid expansion in numbers of vessels under Flags of Convenience and the serious shortage of experienced and qualified seafarers. This was enhanced by the low standards of training and certification accepted by some maritime administrations, fledgling ship-owners, not to mention corruption and reported availability of "Certificates" being issued in return for payment was rampant amongst some Asian administrations of the era. All this reflected on the quality, safety and reliability of crews. Consequently, this situation in turn lead to the introduction in the mid 1970s by the International Maritime Organization (IMO) of the STCW (Standards for Certification and Watch keeping) regulations, which, has developed into the mainstay of worldwide Maritime code of practice for qualification and certification.

It was long hours and hard work on board – not so much in terms of manual labor but rather in the constant need for officers and crew to maintain sea watches. With Port time being so limited one never got a break from the daily routine, day in – day out. If anyone went down sick it placed a definite burden on others and everyone became affected having to share the extra workload.

The workload was also hard on the Master in trying to maintain the shipping schedule. If the ship missed a specific berth allocation time at a Port for whatever reason, the ramifications could cause costly delays. Obviously many delays were entirely beyond the control of the ships, for example, adverse weather, fog, and the like. Nevertheless, delays frequently amalgamated and compounded creating and provoking ongoing hold-ups through the entire schedule cycle. One of the biggest features of containerization was the speeding up and rapid handling of the cargo transit process – obviously any delays encountered went against the scheme of things.

The feeder service soon became second nature to us and we accepted that to a degree we were becoming somewhat robotic in various ways. It was like running on "Tram Tracks". Over many consecutive trips we became quite familiar with the Ports of call, their quirks and benefits alike. Our crew achieved "squatter's rights" in many of the Pubs, our arrival being anticipated to the day from the shipping List in local newspapers. On the occasions when we were in Port some Pubs displayed miniature company House Flags on small wooden flag poles indicating the table or space was reserved for them, such was the value placed on their continued patronage. However, we were not the only ones that used this method of reservation, Maersk, East Asiatic, Ben Line, Manners, Blue Funnel, all did the same.

I remained as Master on the "Universal Venture" engaged in the same service for another two years. Life was becoming somewhat boring to say the least, only disrupted on one occasion when we were hit by a huge freak wave in the South China Sea. The wave severely damaged about 5 containers on the starboard side which were stowed on deck. Fortunately they remained secure and we were able to reach Hong Kong and have them discharged safely. No damage was sustained to the ship but the containers were badly deformed.

During this time Tasanee had remained ashore for a few trips to set up the apartment we had purchased. A woman's touch was needed. She did a wonderful job with the decoration and furnishings and every time my ship was in Hong Kong I was always delighted to go home and see the ongoing project evolving. I also discovered what an accomplished cook she had become.

From time to time Tasanee and I had spoken about me working ashore rather than remain sailing resulted in us being apart for several months at a time. Being so involved in home building it was not that easy for her to uproot and come sailing again quite so freely. Eventually, we decided that I find an opportunity to mention this to my employer. Hence, about a month later I was visited on board my ship by the General Manager whilst in Singapore. This seemed like an ideal moment so I dropped the hint that I was looking for a somewhat more challenging shore post within our company if a suitable vacancy ever presented. I thought no more of it because I speculated my comments would not be taken too seriously. He obviously took on board what I had said because about 3 months later whilst we were undergoing regular dry-docking in Hong Kong, I was summoned to attend the office because the General Manager wished to see me.

Our General Manager, Kip Wei, was a Eurasian, being of half Chinese and British origin. His father was Chinese and had been owner of a large Anglo-Chinese shipping company based in Shanghai. Following WW11 and the onset of communism in China the entire family relocated to Hong Kong where his father re-established his shipping interests, eventually becoming one of the major shareholders in our company. Kip was sent to Australia for his education, where he also attended University. In fact, Kip was more Australian than

Australian with a typical Aussie sense of humor and mateship, a very smooth operator who possessed an acute business brain. He dressed very tastefully and was about 5 years older than me and a true Anglophile. He was married to a very elegant and well educated Portuguese Chinese lady who originated from the upper echelons of Macau's elite and was named Lucrecia.

Tasanee and Lucrecia being in a similar age bracket had become friends over the months whilst she had been setting up our home. With me being away Tasanee had often been invited to female functions and gossip parties that Lucrecia had been hosting , which had forged the basis of their flourishing friendship. This was a source of some relief to me because I did have concerns about leaving Tasanee in Hong Kong whilst I was away, simply because she had made few friends in Hong Kong at the time.

The famous "Horsburgh Lighthouse" located on the small granite outcrop of Pedro Branca. The lighthouse guards the Eastern approaches to the Singapore Straits, like a solitary sentinel.

Originally built with funds raised from both public subscription and the East India Company it commenced operations in 1851. This is a relatively recent photograph as the VTIS tower is very conspicuous.

The islet of Pedro Branca lies some 29 nautical miles from the Eastern extremities of Singapore and falls under the sovereignty of Singapore; the lighthouse is operated by the Port of Singapore Marine Authority.

Singapore – MPA

46 Preparing to Swallow the Anchor

At 11am precisely I was ushered in to Kip Wei's plush office by his secretary and offered the customary coffee.

Kip's timing was perfect because I had just finished my coffee just as he strolled in and greeted me as if a long lost friend – this unsettled me a bit because I did not know what to expect as I had previously only met him once or twice. Initially I had thought I had made some kind of blunder whilst sailing but after a lot of thought dismissed this as a nonsensical notion. Nevertheless, I had no idea why I had been summoned to meet with the GM.

We sat chatting about ships in general and what my opinion was of the "Universal Venture" and if I could recommend any improvements in the vessel's layout, fitting out, handling capability and overall suitability of purpose as a container feeder This conversation lasted about 10 minutes until the Operations Manager entered the office and joined in the meeting.

Eventually, they both came to the point of the forum. It seemed that the Marine Superintendent was required to return to the UK for family reasons and would be leaving our Company in about 2 month's time. The replacement position was offered to me if I was interested! I was a little awestruck but tried to gather my thoughts best I could without appearing to dither. I agreed in principle but requested more information concerning the terms and conditions, lead time, etc., also 24 hours grace period in which to discuss this development with Tasanee, upon the satisfactory conclusion of which together with receipt of formal contract I would confirm my acceptance. The Operations Manager outlined the job scope which was of no real issue and which I personally considered to be well within my capabilities.

The position was based in Hong Kong but with some travel throughout Asia, as and when required in order to vessels within our fleet. I would be required to complete one more round trip on the "Universal Venture", during which I would familiarize the future Master on all aspects of the service. At this point I did not know who the designated Master would be but he would sail with me on the voyage. Once having handed over command I would take a short local leave prior to assuming my new duties.

After about 2 hours the meeting concluded in broad agreement and confirmation the contract and other necessary paperwork would be drawn up. We all went to lunch at a nearby restaurant before parting company for the day. I Jumped into a Taxi and went home to see Tasanee and convey the news.

It was about 3.30pm when I arrived home. Tasanee was busy arranging some fresh flowers she had bought from the flower market and was engrossed in her floral endeavors, also as to the placement of her new indoor pot plants. As usual I was greeted warmly but I detected a look of concern on her face, I assume because she knew I had been to the office and I had come home earlier than expected, instead of going back to the ship for a few hours beforehand. I quickly put her mind at rest that all was well. That evening over dinner I told Tasanee the good news about me coming to work ashore. Tasanee was ecstatic with the prospect of me being at home continuously which would allow for us to lead a more normal life together. I went on to explain that my rational in accepting was that since I was still not yet 40 years of age, if in the unlikely event working in the office was not to my liking I was still be young enough to return to seagoing as Master. I wondered what it would be like going to work in a suite, collar and tie.

Hence, the next morning after having visited the "Universal Venture" in Dry Dock, I dropped into the office to confirm my acceptance of the new position. The Operations Manager was pleased and then told me that the new designated Master would be my old pal Les Barnes, from my "Hoi Hing" days. That news pleased me because I knew from experience that Les Barnes was a top notch operator.

Having completed my tasks at the office I returned to the vessel in order to bring Alastair and others up to speed with the events of the previous 24 hours. Obviously, Alistair James, my valued friend and trusted Chief Engineer was the first to be informed. He was very happy for me and also due to the fact that upon arrival next call at Hong Kong Les Barnes would be assuming command. It transpired that Alastair and Les were old buddies and shipmates from years ago.

A day or so later we were refloated from the Dry Dock and proceeded to the typhoon buoy so that we could commence loading containers. Les Barnes arrived on board just as I was in the process of shifting all my gear into the adjacent Owners cabin, so that Les could occupy the Captain's Cabin and get the feel of things from the outset. It was good to see Les again and we had many stories to exchange over ensuing days. Les had not changed and was still the astute little guy with a pronounced Liverpool accent and sharp intelligent wit.

Since we were loading, the Chief Officer was on duty so that evening I invited Les home for dinner and to say hello to Tasanee after so long a time.

Two days later, at 8am sharp, I said goodbye to Tasanee and jumped in a cab to take me to Blake's Pier where I would catch the company launch out to the "Universal Venture" which was now at the buoys. The Chief Officer had informed me that loading would be completed by 1200 Hrs and Les Barnes had booked the outward sea Pilot for 1400 Hrs. Although technically still in command, I had arranged with Les Barnes for him to assume the role as the "Acting Master" in all matters except in case of emergencies, adverse weather, fog or when approaching navigation hazards which I had marked with pencil on the Chart in BOLD letters "Call Master". All this was covered comprehensively in my Night Order Book and New Standing Orders written to cover this particular voyage and which had been signed by all officers. Therefore, there was no ambiguity as to who did what, when and where. However, I would be closely monitoring proceedings at all times but this seemed to me the best way for Les to gain first hand operating knowledge of the vessel and the container service.

Exactly at 1400 Hrs, having received our outward Port Clearance we slipped the buoy and headed slowly eastwards through the busy Hong Kong harbor towards Lai Ye Mun passage. Our next Port was Kota Kinabalu in Sabah, after which we would proceed direct to Port Klang, Singapore, Pasir Gudang and Bangkok before returning to Hong Kong in approximately 3 weeks time. This was intended to be a slightly trimmed round voyage until we had amassed additional container cargo for all the scheduled Ports.

Our trip across the South China Sea was uneventful and we eventually arrived at "KK" about 6pm on a wonderful clear evening just on sun set. We had been informed the wharf was congested and we were not expected to berth until the next morning, so we anchored for the night in the Bay. This was not a bad thing because berthing would now be in daylight and best for Les since he would be handling the vessel for the first time. We did not use Pilots in Kota Kinabalu because it was not compulsory and frankly quite a simple Port in which to navigate.

About 10 am next morning we were asked by the Port Controller to proceed inward for berthing. It was a tight fit at the wharf with there being only just enough space for us to fit safely between two other vessels. Some two hours later the ships ahead and astern sailed leaving us alone on the jetty. Early afternoon saw the arrival of one of the cruise Liners tie up astern, but they seemed to be struggling getting their passenger gangway landed to the jetty because of the amount of overhang by their stern. I saw their predicament so called them on VHF suggesting I shift 10m ahead if it would be of assistance. This was greatly appreciated so we quickly warped the 10-15m ahead down the wharf.

No sooner had they secured their gangways when there was a knock on my door, upon opening I saw an Australian gentleman (going by his Aussie twang) dressed in immaculate whites sporting full Captain's braid. He introduced himself as the Master of the

Cruise Liner and said he had come to thank me for making his life somewhat easier in respect of the gangway issues. I offered him coffee and we had a short chat, at the conclusion of which he invited the entire Officers and Crew aboard for dinner that evening at 6pm. I told him it was not necessary but nevertheless thanked him and said I would pass the word to all those not on duty.

By way of interest I can say that about 90% of the crew took up the offer, they were met at the gangway by one of the female pursers and conducted aboard. Next morning they raved on what a fantastic buffet dinner they had all enjoyed and the excellent hospitality received.

Captain Les Barnes was settling in very well and coming to grips with his soon to be new command. He being on board allowed me plenty of time in which to get all the ship's accounts, paperwork and files up to date ready for an efficient handover in a few weeks time. It being quite a short stay we soon departed and sped on our way towards our transit of the Singapore Straits and ultimately Port Klang.

Upon our arrival at Port Klang and since my Pilot's exemption remained valid for the Port I took the ship up the meandering channel to the inner anchorage where we waited for a vacant berth. Fortunately, we did not idle for long at the anchorage because only a few hours later our harbor Pilot boarded and we proceeded to our designated berth. I suggested to Les after he formally assumed command and once he had completed 3 consecutive calls at Port Klang he also apply for a Pilot exemption as it was very convenient and saved quite some time in the overall scheme of things, especially during times of Pilot shortages. I passed on details of the Port Information he should read and a number of hints as to the type of questions he would likely be asked at time of his application.

Contrary to our stay in "KK" we remained alongside in Port Klang for only 8 hours before sailing for Singapore where we expected increased loadings, but still only a port stay limited to hours. Singapore and Hong Kong were leaders in container handling productivity at this time it must be said.

After more than two years frequently plying this route I was by now very familiar with the tides and currents around the Malacca and Singapore Straits, nevertheless navigational aids were often unreliable, especially in the Indonesian sector. Risk of collision was always a reality due to the convergence of heavy traffic using the through routes. Conflicting and crossing traffic as well as local fishing craft with drift nets, posed the biggest hazard as they often demonstrated little regard for larger vessels navigating the Straits.

The most conspicuous navigation marker in the Malacca Straits was the "One Fathom Bank" lighthouse which lies approximately 10 miles West of the Port Klang Fairway Buoy and was used as a mid-way check point for all vessels traversing the seaway from both north and south. It consisted of a concrete pile structure. Built by the British in 1907 it was very conspicuous. The "Old" lighthouse was eventually deactivated in 1999 when it was replaced by the "New" lighthouse, some 500m distant from the original one.

The navigation aids improved as one progressed southward towards Singapore, with the introduction of "Racon" markers on some important buoys and beacons, "The Brothers" light house at Pulau Lyu Kecil and eventually Raffles Light and the well maintained buoy and light system provided by the Singapore marine authorities. Of course with the Traffic Separation Scheme (TSS) which was introduced for the Singapore Straits in 1981, navigation and safety improved remarkably. All the same one needed to remain very much alert when transiting these waters.

Port Authorities of Malaysia

Today's lighthouses, the "Old" black and white concrete Pile Lighthouse at **"One Fathom Bank"** in the Malacca Straits together with its "Newer" red and white replacement lighthouse commissioned in 1999.

Nonetheless, for my last departure from Port Klang the fishing fleets were in their usual element, from horizon to horizon, darting every which way and non compliance for rules of navigation and safety. It took us some 4 hours to rid ourselves of the fleet. Fortunately visibility was good with the sea like molten glass as normal, so not that difficult to weave our way through them. It suddenly dawned on me that I may not be seeing this sort of thing again in the near future. I always made it my practice to remain on the Bridge when transiting the Malacca or Singapore Straits. This was no reflection on the ability, or lack of confidence in my Mates, but rather being aware of, and trying to avoid, hazardous situations developing as the consequence of the idiotic and un-seamanlike actions of others. Believe me when I claim it could be a challenge at times. Soon we passed Pulau Lyu Kecil better known as "The Brothers", leaving the distinctive lighthouse to starboard as we sailed further towards Raffles Lighthouse and eventually the Pilot Boarding Ground, at Singapore Roads just off "The Sisters" Islands.

Singapore MPA – VTS

A lone and fearless fisherman pictured in the Singapore Straits. These fishermen often encroached into the restricted traffic lanes causing a real headache for larger vessels navigating within the confines of the VTS, especially at night or in poor visibility when the small wooden fishing canoes were poorly lit and could be easily overlooked on Radar screens being "lost" amongst the clutter of hundreds of other Radar echoes.

As mentioned earlier in this narrative, poor visibility is always a concern in the Singapore Straits. Especially in the period of very light winds that prevail during the inter-monsoon months. A sort of heat haze or mist hovers above quite often restricting visibility to about 1 mile. It generally develops just before dawn but in most cases dissipates by mid morning once the sun has gained some amplitude and heat.

This may not be considered too bad but when taking into account the volume of sea traffic in the area it can cause moments of anxiety even though nowadays mariners transiting the narrows are assisted by the VTS. High density traffic leaving and joining the VTS can be a bit daunting, in particular very large ships that take time to slow down or maneuver. The situation is made much worse during the "Burning Season" in Indonesian islands when "Smoke Haze" develops and lingers for days. The smell stings one's nostrils and triggers Asthma for those who suffer the infliction as well as other respiratory disorders. The "Burn Off" is a constant point of aggravation between Singapore and Indonesia and has been for years.

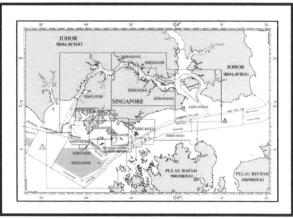

Above - Singapore Strait giving a chart overview of the Modern Day VTSS (Vessel Traffic Separation Scheme) which is strictly monitored and controlled by Singapore. **This snapshot should not be used for Navigation purposes under any circumstances**. It is purely intended to provide readers with a snapshot view of the Singapore Straits. Only approved and up to date electronic charts or Admiralty charts should be utilized.

As can be seen from the sketch, when transiting westward through the straits great care must be taken to remain within the TSS lane and not encroach into Singapore Port Limits.

Typically, our stay in Singapore was measured in hours and our short trip to Pasir Gudang only took us about 4 hours although it was necessary to drop anchor for a few hours at the Johor General Purpose Anchorage to wait for a pilot. This was first visit for Les so it was quite instructive for him.

In actual fact it was called "Johor Port" located at Pasir Gudang – now it is known as Pasir Gudang Port. It lies on the Malaysian side of the Johor Straits, close to

Sembawang ship yard and just opposite bank to the Punggol area of Singapore. During the 1960s the Malaysians concluded they relied too heavily on Singapore so a decision was made to establish their own Port at Pasir Gudang. The area chosen was blessed with deep water and an abundance of land that could easily be developed as the new port expanded. The construction of the port commenced about 1967 and progressed through to 1977 when the container port started to become operational. Up until that time it had been a multi-purpose and general cargo facility feeding southern regions of the Malaysia peninsula.

In retrospect, the history of JP/PG is deeply tied to Pasir Gudang town, which played a pivotal role in driving Pasir Gudang into becoming a thriving commercial Port for the Malaysian State of Johor. The dedicated Container Terminal commenced full operations in 1987 and is now a strong competitor to Singapore, albeit somewhat smaller. Our visits to PG were very much during the development phases but we could easily detect the speed at which the facilities were being advanced. Pasir Gudang is now the world's leading shipping outlet for the exportation of Palm Oil as well as being the principal focal point for exports from southern regions of the Malaysian Peninsula.

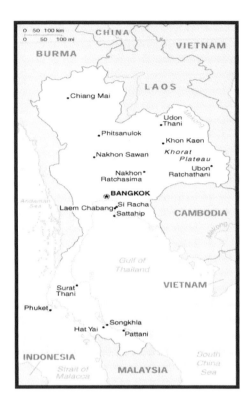

Map of the Gulf of Thailand showing principal Thai Ports.

We arrived in Bangkok on a Public Holiday. If memory serves it was His Majesty the King's Birthday. Thai people are very loyal monarchists and therefore the holiday was strictly observed with celebrations throughout the Kingdom. This necessitated us being held at Koh Si Chang anchorage for 2 days before proceeding upstream. It should be remembered that during the 1970s the Large Container Port of Laem Chabang had yet to be established so most traffic was directed to the river port of Bangkok (Thai name being Krunk Thrup – meaning City of Angels) which was

458

even then struggling to cope with the marine traffic as the Thai economy was growing rapidly.

Construction of the deep water Container Port at Laem Chabang commenced in 1987 and was completed in 1991. It is in an ideal location about 50 nautical miles south east of Bangkok and 32 nautical miles north of the Naval Port of Sattahip. The main township for Laem Chabang Port is Siracha but it is also within an easy drive to the "Playground" of Pattaya. Laem Chabang is now the largest Port in Thailand and is linked to Bangkok and other major cities by good roads and a rail network. Therefore the Port takes much of the pressure and cargo overspill from Bangkok Port.

Situated in the province of Chonburi, the townships of Siracha and Bang Saen areas are hot spots for many European retirees because of its idyllic climate, low cost living, location and close proximity to fine beaches and world class golf courses. The other major container Port developed over recent years in Thailand is Songkhla. Songkhla, located on the west coast caters as a focal for the southern regions of Thailand and the emerging Gulf of Thailand offshore industry.

The famous Thai tourist retreat of Koh Samui lies not far offshore from Surat Thani. I recall some years later spending a few days on the Island with Tasanee. We were stranded due to a bad Typhoon during which a Drill Ship close by capsized and sank. Some 2 weeks after our visit the aircraft in which we had travelled and the Pilot of which I knew, was involved in a fatal accident whilst attempting a landing at the Resort Island. It was a very sad episode.

My "Swan Song" voyage on the "Universal Venture" was almost over as I was scheduled to sign off and disembark upon arrival in Hong Kong in order to discover what working in a shipping office was like. It so happens all turned out fine and I remained working ashore within the industry for many years, only returning to seagoing for a 2 year "last fling" as Master on the "Kris Madura", re-entering the seagoing workforce from semi-retirement due to chronic shortages of qualified marine Offices.

So far Les Barnes had operated very well and upon arrival in Hong Kong, with the shake of the hand and good wishes farewells from all onboard I took the launch to Blake's Pier. I was touched to receive a beautiful rosewood cigar box as a farewell gift from the officers and crew, suitable inscribed with my name, etc. in a tasteful gilt presentation. However, it was not to be the end of my dealings with the "Universal Venture" and the many friends I had made on the years I had sailed on her.

My week's leave at home passed too quickly and soon it was time to get used to going to work every day in a collar, tie and suite; every morning before leaving home I was expected to pass muster by Tasanee.

Without a doubt I was privileged to serve in the Merchant Navy during the golden years and most certainly witnessed the end of an era. The changes within the industry were starting to become evident to me during the 1970s, especially with the demise of so many UK shipping goliaths due to economics of operating their ships that were no longer fuel efficient and the advent of containerization. It was therefore very apt and timely that the offer for me to work ashore posed itself at the onset of so many of these changes. I therefore consider myself as being very fortunate.

Having decided to cease working afloat and moving to forge and encompass a new career within the industry working ashore, I was not disappointed since there was no lack of new opportunities and challenges presented to me over the ensuing years.

Obviously, the main role of my position as Marine Superintendent was that involving day to day shipping operations, management and planning of our fleet and these functions alone did take up the majority of my working day. Occasionally, I was required to attend vessels at outlying Asian Ports but my duties were predominately at the Hong Kong head office. I soon started to settle in to a routine and found the work both interesting and challenging. In retrospect, I can say I did not regret my decision to work ashore and going home most evenings for dinner remained something of a novelty during the initial years.

I became involved in a number of new avenues such as Ship Broking, Sales and Purchase mainly and ship management for other owners which, for various reasons, we were requested to take under the guidance of our management team.

One interesting aspect of this during the early 1980s was the purchase of tonnage for the demolition market in Taiwan or Mainland China– in short we would purchase older tonnage that had a good weight of steel with a minimum of 6 or months classification remaining – we would retain that classification at most changing the name and registry to Panama or St. Vincent for the voyage to Asia. Most of these vessels were of European construction because they traditionally had a heavier steel content than those built elsewhere. Once we had taken delivery of the vessel we would seek a cargo(s) in the direction of the Far East, which basically paid the voyage costs.

This was a good earner for the company because we could negotiate a good demolition contract with delivery dates to suite. We also determined in advance the cost of vessel purchase, realistic voyage costs, cargo revenues and scrap sales price. It was easy therefore to get a very good handle on what could be expected by way of profit. We purchased about 8 vessels for this kind of exercise, over several years when buoyant demolition prices were being achieved.

Another way we made money was offering full operations, technical and commercial management of ships to stakeholders, mostly Banks and Financial Institutions. In the early 1980s with the increase of fuel costs and ageing oil hungry fleets, many ship owners found it very difficult to maintain mortgage payments on their vessels due to dwindling profits – the result was the financiers foreclosed, took possession and put the

462

vessel to anchor somewhere with a skeleton crew on board. Obviously this caused further losses to accrue for the Bankers because their asset was depreciating whilst lying idle.

Our solution was to approach the institutions and offer to provide full management, keep their assets working with cargoes until we could sell the ships on their behalf for further trading or demolition, enabling the Financiers to recover their losses (and in some cases even turn a reasonable profit). The institutions obviously receive all cargo and sales revenues to offset against their losses. As we already had a substantial ship management team within our company it was not difficult to manage a few additional vessels without the need to engage additional personnel. This meant we were able to secure a fair and reasonable fixed monthly management fee from the financiers. Apart from the management fee the only additional costs to which the stakeholders were subjected was fuel, Port Dues and Tariffs, Crew Wages, Insurances and the like. These costs they needed to settle in any event even if they opted to leave the ship in lay-up. We, also acting in the capacity of exclusive Cargo and Sales Brokers allowed us to legitimately claim commissions for such services recognized throughout the shipping industry. It was a win-win situation for both sides and the Financial Institutions found it a very attractive proposition. Over the worst 3 years of the fuel oil crisis we managed 14 ships on behalf of various financial stakeholders that suddenly found themselves with unwanted ships on their hands and not a clue how to avoid the asset being placed into a further loss making lay-up scenario. The word got about and we were soon being regularly contacted to undertake new ship-management contracts.

Like all ship owners and operators we experienced trends in the markets when fleet expansion or downsizing was prudent but on average we maintained a medium sized fleet throughout my years with the company. We had inaugurated a new building program with construction mostly in Japanese or Korean Shipyards and we sold several ships at a healthy profit margin whilst on the stocks prior to them even being launched. These were good years for all.

In conclusion, it is true to say that my working life ashore was one of personal achievement and satisfaction and I never regretted my decision to swallow the anchor. I remained with the company until just beyond 55 years of age when I retired as General Manager and Director. Tasanee and I sold up and relocated to Melbourne, Australia. However, contrary to my intentions, a few years after retirement, having always retained the validity of my Master's License, I was summoned back for one last fling as Master on a nice little ship called the **"Kris Madura"**. The intended single trip "Last Fling" lasted 2 years and was a great way in which to finally close the chapter on my seafaring life, operating around the Far East and my home stomping grounds since childhood.

During my retirement years I maintain close connections with Asia, particularly Hong Kong. I still conduct various marine assignments when requested to do so and to be honest I can never really see me entering into any kind traditional retirement or truly "Hanging up my Hat". I retain many cherished memories and much nostalgia.

....

Finis

49   Acknowledgements

My thanks to the following (and my apologies to the others whom I may have overlooked):-

Hong Kong Marine Department

Singapore MPA

Ports of Thailand

Sabah Ports Authority

Labuan Port Authority

Port Authorities of Malaysia

Calcutta Port Trust

Sri Lanka Ports Authority – Port of Colombo

P&O Lines – Post Card Collection

John Manners Group (Hong Kong based ship owners and managers) acknowledgement for images of their long past ships.

Fleetmon.com

Tony Westmore – internationally renowned Maritime Artist

Karsten Peterson – Global Mariner and superb Photographer

Hong Kong Tourist Association,

Port of Sydney

Port of Melbourne

Various East African Port Authorities

South African Port Authorities

Vietnam Ports Authority

Jebsen Shipping Company – Aabenraa (photographs of their fine ships, courtesy Karsten Petersen)

Various unknown sources Autonomous Region of Bougainville

John Beale for his photograph of the wrecked Kelvinbank

Various photographs from unknown or long forgotten origins acquired from numerous public databases many of which date back to early 1950s.

Bank Line Ltd, (ship owners) acknowledgement for images of their long past ships.

And last but not least, to Titus Maccius Plautus – Roman Playwright (254-184 BCE) for his very true quotation.

A Few of the Author's Favorites - selected at Random

Credit: Fleetmon.com submitted by mbbmikepsss

Ocean Zenith now Philippines Flag, ex **"Kris Madura"** – One of the better later generation fully cellular feeders, photographed at Manila in the Philippines.

Having re-entered the workforce from semi-retirement I served as Master on her for two productive years when under her previous name **"Kris Madura"** then operated by Singaporean interests. She was like a yacht, Gross Tonnage: 6100, Deadweight: 8530, LOA: 114m, BHP: 6000, 16.5 knots but when I was on her we maintained an economic service speed of about 14 knots. An ideal ship for working the Far East container feeder trades, especially due to her 2 x 36 ton SWL container cranes which made her fully self sustaining at some of the secondary Asian Ports. Japanese built, meant the ship was somewhat basic in terms of comfort but she never let me down and performed very well during my tenure on board.

Credit: Fleetmon.com submitted by arisrefug

A versatile Container Feeder at work. Ship's cranes were used in over half of the ports of call in the Far East feeder trade.

Photo KP ©

The **"Sangria"**. Now returned to German Registry and moored in Hamburg. Finally restored to her original splendor with her name **"Cap San Diego"** reinstated

The ex Hamburg Sud vessel is now displayed as a museum ship in Hamburg. The company I worked for bought this vessel in the mid 1980s. We took delivery in Europe, Changed flag, renamed her **"Sangria"** and then worked the ship with various cargoes towards the Far East where we intended to dispose of her for scrap. At the final moment, just prior to her demise, with the ship already in Asia, we were approached by Hamburg based ship conservationists who offered to purchase the vessel and have it returned to Germany so that it could become a Museum ship, since it was one of the last remaining iconic "White Swans of the Atlantic" and famous on the South American cargo passenger routes. We willingly accepted the offer as it gave us no satisfaction to see such a fine ship succumb to the breaker's "Torch". I had the honor of handing her back to the German buyers at Cuxhaven in 1985 – then with great ceremony she proceeded up the Elbe River to Hamburg - the rest is history. Without doubt this is one of the most beautiful

469

ships I had the pleasure of being associated with. A detailed scale model of this handsome vessel is displayed in my home study for the purposes of my own personal gratification and nostalgia.

A year earlier I had undertaken a similar exercise with the sister vessel **"Cap San Marco"**. She looked every bit as good as the day she was built when we accepted the vessel in Hamburg. We then reflagged and changed her name to **"Marco Polo"** which we thought appropriate for her voyage to the breakers in China. After carrying a combination of cargoes towards the Far East she finally arrived at her designated resting place and was handed over to Chinese buyers for demolition (if memory serves it was at the Port of Tsing Tao). On her final hours prior to arrival in Tsing Tao, and since she had more than adequate fuel remaining, she clocked 22.5 knots without any effort whatsoever for her final few hours of the passage.

.

Glossary of references made in Book - Phonetic Spelling for Cantonese Terms

Ayarh.	An exclamation – remark of alarm – non specific
BMH	British Military Hospital – Mount Kellet, Hong Kong
Chao Phraya River	Main Thai River flowing from Bangkok Bar through city of Bangkok and beyond
Chinese Junk	Traditional Chinese sailing vessel, commonly used for offshore fishing or coastal transportation of cargo
Chop	A Rubber or Ivory inked Stamp used to certify authenticity of documents
Chow	Common term for Food
Coolie	An old name given to laborers or stevedores that handle baggage, cargo or undertake other like tasks aboard ship, wharf side or Godown
Dai Pai Dong	Outdoor street food stall
Don Muang	Name of original Bangkok International Airport used at the time depicted in the book (now Suvanabhumi International Airport and Don Muang is mainly for domestic use)
Dor Jeir	Thank you – upon receiving an item or present
Falang	Thai term for Caucasian foreigner
Fide Fide	Quickly – Hurry Hurry
Fung Shui	Ancient science of receiving harmony by

balancing the surrounding elements

Gai doh cheen	How much money or cost of an item
Gwei Jit	Ghost Festival – 1st to 15th day of 7th month in Chinese calendar. Burning of fake paper money, Joss, food offerings
Godown	A large warehouse or storage shed
Gweilo	Derogatory (but common) term for pale skinned foreigners or Caucasian –literally means "White Ghost"
Ho Man Tin	Kowloon residential area and location KGV School, Kowloon
Hoogly River	Major Indian river flowing from Bay of Bengal to Calcutta and beyond
Ho Pang Yau	Close or good friend
Ho Sik	Good eating
Ho Yum	Good drink
Hung Hom Bay	Quarantine Anchorage close to old Kai Tak Airport seaward runway
Jo San	Good morning
Kai Tak	Name of Hong Kong Airport up until mid 1990's when it was relocated to another site at Lantau Island and renamed Chek Lap Kok
KGV	King George V School – Ho Man Tin
KJS	Kowloon Junior School - Kowloon
Koh Si Chang	Anchorage located at the mouth of Chao Phraya River used for lightening or final loading of vessels with drafts too deep to safely transit the Bangkok River Bar
Kumshaw	Common Chinese Term for hand outs

Lai See	A small red paper envelope (usually with ornate gold lettering) containing lucky money – Common at Chinese New Year, auspicious occasions, weddings, birthdays, etc
Lye Ye Mun	Eastern entrance channel to Hong Kong Harbor (Victoria Harbor)
Mai Dan	Bill for food or service
M'Ho	No good, or bad
M'Ho Cheen	No money
Milk Girls	Name given to girls who come aboard ship with small baskets selling soft drinks, often as a cover for other services – so called, mainly at Singapore anchorages
Mong Kok	Area close to Jordan Road, Kowloon
Nei Ho Ma	How are you – greeting
Nga Pin	Opium – illicit drug usually smoked with a bamboo pipe
Nullah	Open street storm water drain
Pok Fu Lam	Area where Reservoir is located – Close to Aberdeen on Hong Kong Island
Praya	Stone fronted dock or waterfront
Sarong	Malay or Tamil – cotton type wrap around garment like an ankle length skirt – used by both men and woman
Satays	Malay Dish-Usually Beef or Chicken cooked on wooden skewer. Usually served with tangy Peanut based sauce
Sew Sew Ladies	Name given to ladies who come aboard ship offering sewing, ironing or laundry.

Shum Shiu Po	Area in Kowloon close to old Cosmo Dry Dock
Side Party	Workers hired to chip or paint ship's Hull – generally from small boats
Small Chow	Finger food or small delicacies
Stonecutters	Island in Victoria Harbor – used mainly by British Military
Taipan	Wealthy Businessman – traditionally an expatriate and head of a large corporation
Tin Hau	Highly revered Chinese Goddess – Protector of seafarers (dedicated Temple in Wanchai, Hong Kong)
Tsim Sha Tsui	Popular shopping, Bar and Tourist area in Kowloon - close to southern end of Nathan Road
TSS	Traffic Separation Scheme
VTSS	Vessel Traffic Separation Scheme
Walla Walla	Small motor boat for hire used as water taxi to ferry passengers about Victoria Harbor to/from ships or when Star Ferry or HYT Ferry services are suspended
Yau Ma Tei	Area in Kowloon close to Star Ferry and Kowloon Godowns
Yum Cha	Drink Tea – a term used to signify morning tea and delicacies

Photo KP ©

Alas! Nostalgia – an old cargo Junk seen making good headway in a fair wind in Hong Kong Harbor circa late 1960s or early 1970s, the end of an era.